LONG SHA
TALE!
OF
SCOTLAND'S
NORTH EAST

DUNCAN HARLEY

Supported by The Doric Board

By the same author:
The A-Z of Curious Aberdeenshire
The Little History of Aberdeenshire

First published in 2021

Images and text © Duncan Harley 2021

The Legal Stuff

The right of Duncan Harley to be identified as the author of this work has been asserted in accordance with the Copyright Designs and Patents Act 1988 and all subsequent revisions of said Act and all subsequent Acts governing copyright of published work which supersede the Copyright Designs and Patents Act 1988 shall apply to the content herein.
A catalogue of this book is available from the British Library and a digital copy has been lodged with the Library of Congress and with various other worldwide library resources. All rights are reserved. No part of this publication whatsoever may be reprinted or reproduced or utilised in any form by any electronic, mechanical or other means, now known or hereafter invented, including photocopying or recording, or in any information storage or retrieval system, without the permission in writing from the author and or publishers except by reviewers who may quote brief extracts for the sole purposes of a review.

ISBN: 979-8533844628

Library of Congress Control Number: 2021916026

Cover image: Fraserburgh Harbour © Duncan Harley

CONTENTS

Introduction

Acknowledgements

1	Aberdeen	*Northern Lights and Furry Boots*	9
2	Aboyne	*A Historic Highland Village*	30
3	Alford	*Home of the Aberdeen Angus*	39
4	Ballater	*Capital of Royal Deeside*	45
5	Banchory	*Gateway to Royal Deeside*	52
6	Banff	*A Delightful Town on the Coast*	60
7	Braemar	*Highest Parish in Scotland*	67
8	Buckie	*Ask Not the Price of Fish*	76
9	Cove	*Home of the Last Fishwife*	84
10	Crovie	*Houses for Jellybeans*	88
11	Cullen	*Home of Skink*	96
12	Dufftown	*Malt Whisky Capital of the World*	102
13	Elgin	*Lantern of the North*	108
14	Ellon	*Pearl of Buchan*	116
15	Fochabers	*Soup, Jam and Zulus*	123
16	Fraserburgh	*The Broch*	128
17	Huntly	*Ancient Capital of Strathbogie*	136
18	Insch	*Close to which is Craigievar*	143
19	Inverurie	*Lang Toon o' the Garioch*	149
20	Keith	*The Friendly Town*	166
21	Kintore	*A Right Royal Burgh*	172
22	Lenabo	*The Buchan Brigadoon*	179
23	Lossiemouth	*Scotland's Bay of Naples*	186
24	Macduff	*Paraffin Sandwiches and Pondmasters*	193
25	Maggieknockater	*The Bees Knees*	199

26	Montrose	*Camels, Bears and Gable Endies*	202
27	Oldmeldrum	*Petrospheres and Cornkisters*	214
28	Peterhead	*Herring, Harbours and Jacobites*	220
29	Portsoy	*Village of the Drammed*	228
30	Stonehaven	*A Good Deal Romantic*	236
31	Tomintoul	*Where Not Much Happens*	247
32	Torphins	*A Pleasant Village in Royal Deeside*	256
33	Turriff	*Lendrum Tae Leeks*	262

About the Author

Bibliography

INTRODUCTION

In early 2014 I was commissioned by *Leopard Magazine* to research and write a series of articles featuring the towns, the people and the history of the North East of Scotland. The magazine was at the time owned by the University of Aberdeen and the brief was wide. The 'Our Town' series was the result and over the succeeding two years some twenty full length feature articles made the magazine's pages, alongside several other historical pieces which took shape along the way. The featured communities varied widely in nature, and included fisher towns, whisky towns and also places such as Braemar, Portsoy and Tomintoul which although small in size, are big in stature. This, my third book about the North East of Scotland comprises the bones of these original articles brought up to date and completely rewritten and with many important additions.

When choosing the original topics for the series I was acutely aware that many more towns and indeed villages deserved to be featured, but that various constraints made that impossible at that time. I have, I hope, made at least partial amends for these omissions and have included a chosen few within this volume. Fochabers, Cove, Maggieknockater and Lenabo are just some of those and, since Aberdeen was not part of the original brief, I have included a chapter featuring some of the lesser-known tales about the Granite City.

In my two previous books, I exposed readers to a mix of history and mythology. The intention of this new book is to expand on these themes in an entertaining and hopefully informative way. Please enjoy these wee snippets of Scottish history and smile gently at the past.

Duncan Harley – May 2021

"If something extraordinary happened in your town or village, it's probably in this book."
Mike Shepherd

"Harley has managed to pick up on some great stories, some with a real local human touch and others that have reverberated around the world."
Michael Stuart

"Relentless curiosity and wry humour."
Judy Mackie

"Entertaining but educating at the same time."
Patricia Healy

"A collection of strange tales from the North East"
The Scotsman

"The strange and the unusual from Aberdeenshire's past."
The History Press

"An alphabet soup for the curious. Highly recommended!"
Aberdeen Voice

"Readers will learn about the area's past."
Aberdeen Journals

"A primer for those who yearn to learn more about the people, the folklore and the events which shaped this exciting part of Scotland."
Aberdeen City Libraries

"An accessible tome ... there is a depth of information."
The Evening Express

"I enjoyed the read"
Paul Kohn

ACKNOWLEDGEMENTS

I am as always indebted to both the oral and the written recollections of the people of the North East of Scotland. There are many splendid publications out there, both in print and in digital form, which record the local history of Scotland from the perspective of the folk who talked the talk and lived the life. Often published in tiny editions by local printers, more used perhaps to turning out batches of weekly broadsheets and business cards, they were typically read by a very small audience. David Toulmin, Elizabeth Christie, Peter Anson, Inkson McConnochie and Robert Smith are just a few of the authors who have left us an unrivalled legacy. I have where possible referenced these local writers both in the text and in the bibliography and I am as always indebted to the staff at Aberdeenshire Library Service for their enthusiastic support throughout the writing process.

I am especially indebted to Paul Kohn who read the proofs and suggested many edits and corrections. Any remaining errors are mine and mine alone. Heartfelt thanks are also due to the likes of Charlie Abel, Mike Shepherd, Judy Montgomery, Shaunagh Kirby, Ronnie Watt, Aberdeen Lord Provost Barney Crockett and Aberdeen Voice Editor Fred Wilkinson for their encouragement in the making of this new collection of Scottish tales.

In addition, I would like to acknowledge the invaluable support of the Doric Board in the making of this book. Special thanks also go to broadcaster Frieda Morrison and Doric Board treasurer Gordon Hay. It takes a lot of fine folk to make a book.

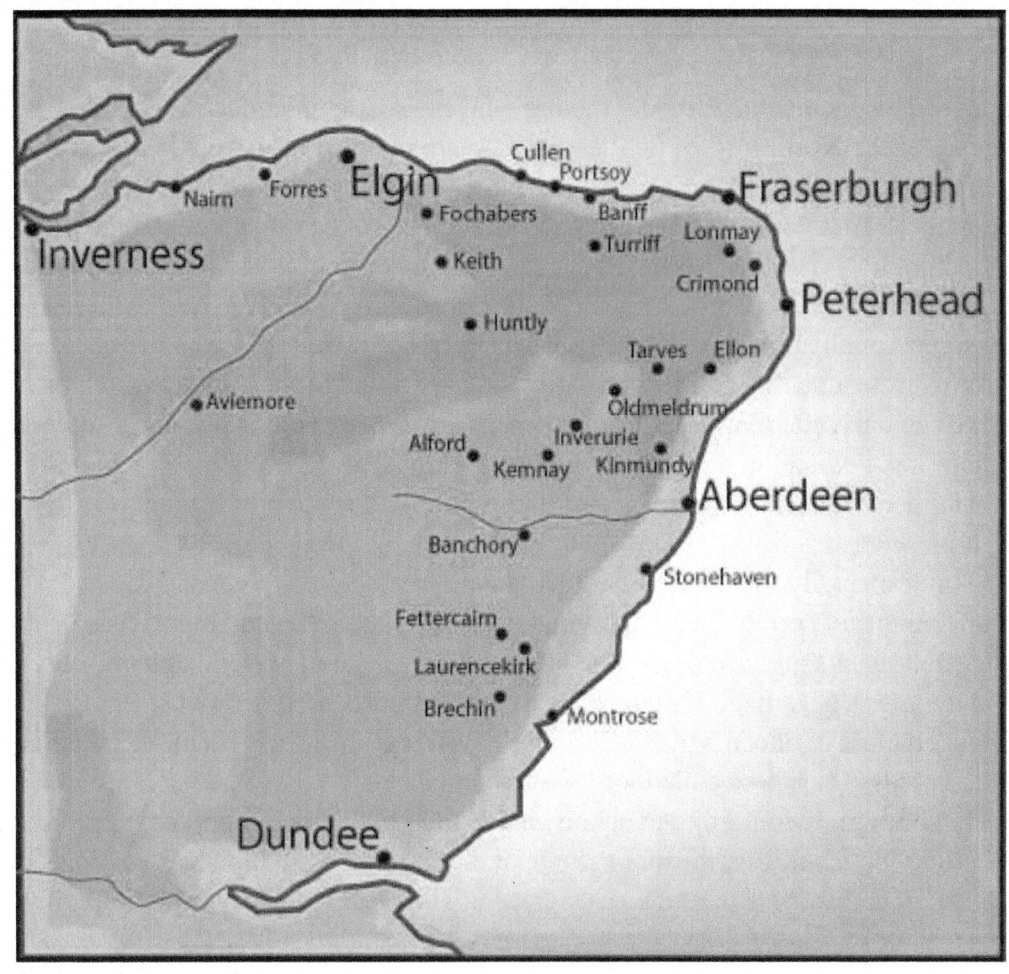

North East Scotland

1
ABERDEEN – NORTHERN LIGHTS AND FURRY BOOTS

What is there to say about the city of Aberdeen that has not been said before? The clichés and the folklore tell of an oil capital of Europe, a gateway to some mythologised castle country, a silvery city bounded by the rivers Dee and Don and an early home to an aspiring Byron. The loudest voice of the lot is the oil of course, and despite the ups and downs in the global energy market, the role of fossil fuel in the city's recent fortunes has dominated the local economy and propelled Scotland's third city from a sleepy penury to international stardom.

In April 1964 the UK government passed a piece of legislation called the Continental Shelf Act which enabled petroleum companies to prospect for oil and gas in the North Sea. Exploration licences were granted for a fee and the first gas was brought ashore in eastern England in 1965. Then, not much happened until the 1973 oil crisis. A nineteen-day all-out war between the State of Israel and several Arab neighbours had erupted and this led to a global oil embargo targeted at those nations perceived as supporting Israel.

The move, by OPEC (The Organisation of Petroleum Exporting Countries), shocked the global economy and in turn jump started undersea oil exploration in the North Sea and elsewhere. By the end of the embargo in March 1974 the price of oil had quadrupled. Crude oil prices leapt from three dollars per barrel to a giddy twelve dollars and North Sea oil and gas exploration was good to go. The first oil was brought ashore at Cruden Bay in 1975 and despite the ups and downs of the industry since then, it would be difficult to argue that Aberdeen and the surrounding Shire have had that bad a time of it over the succeeding years.

The city was badly bombed by the fascists in that Hitler war, although not as much as Peterhead which suffered twenty-eight raids compared to Aberdeen's twenty-four. There are still blast marks on buildings, although the first-hand accounts of these raids are fast passing into folk memory. In an earlier European war Aberdeen narrowly escaped bombing by a rogue German airship and vivid reminders of that conflict, in the form of shattered lives and rusting military hardware once littered the landscape. The Hollywood blockbuster *War Horse* featured a hugely expensive studio-built replica of a First War Mark 4 tank and the reproduction is now on display at the Tank Museum at Bovington alongside a very few genuine WWI armoured vehicles. Worth a king's ransom nowadays, these early castles on caterpillar tracks were at one time a common sight throughout the UK. Numerous examples were scattered around the land having been employed as mobile banks for the selling of War Bonds. After the 1918 Armistice, many more of these vehicles were surplus to requirements and were either sold for scrap by the Military Disposals Board, used as 'Gate Guardians' on military bases or in some cases donated to local councils for public display as memorial tanks to celebrate the European victory.

There's only one War Bond tank left in the UK and that is in Ashford in Kent where an original tank bank was converted into an electricity substation and survives to this day. The Aberdeen example, a Mark 4 listed as number 113, sat rusting for many years on Broad Hill at Aberdeen beach overlooking the Beach Ballroom. Just a few years later a second European conflict broke out and, in common with most of Scotland's park railings and manhole covers, the tank on top of Broad Hill was broken apart and melted down for scrap. The scrap value was maybe a few hundred pounds but in today's market the iconic vehicle would fetch perhaps £2.4 million. Aberdeen Lord Provost Barney Crockett has researched the history of this particular tank. Named Julian the Tank Bank, after General Julian Byng, an early proponent of mechanised warfare, it was seemingly one of perhaps five veterans of the Battle of Cambrai deployed around the country to raise money for the war effort. "The arrangement", says Barney "was whichever town or city raised the most per head in that tank's region would keep the tank. In Scotland, Aberdeen fought off a Glasgow challenge to win Julian, a matter of great local pride, the amount of money being stupendous, led by £50,000 from the council. By this stage in the war, the 'sell' from the Lord Provost was that he was not asking for money to 'continue the war but to end it'. In both wars Scotland was to the fore in making financial contributions with Aberdeen particularly prominent."

The Tank Bank Week in Aberdeen took place in late January 1918 just ten months before the Armistice and by all accounts it was quite a success. Crowds gathered on Union Terrace alongside the William Wallace monument to see first-hand the new weapon which would surely end the stalemate in the trenches by Christmas! A demonstration of the vehicle's agility was seemingly staged at the Castlegate where an admiring crowd watched as the metal monster crushed a makeshift enemy trench under its tracks. In reality this was a six-foot-high pile of granite rubble provided by a local quarry company especially for the newsreels. Miss Findlay, Secretary of the War Savings Committee, then clambered aboard a wooden platform atop the machine alongside various local dignitaries and addressed the crowd in patriotic terms "Bonds and Certificates are really weapons with which you can strike dismay into the heart of the Germans". Aberdeen's Tank Bank Week raised a total of £2.5 million from the patriotic pockets the of the allegedly mean folk of Aberdeen.

Nowadays firmly in the realm of the written word and perhaps a smidgeon of mythology is Aberdeen's link with Lord Byron (1788-1824). Although few would know it nowadays, or maybe even care, the romantic poet spent eight of his formative years in the city. Byron's time in Aberdeen was, some say, marked by poverty while others point to a domestic servant or maybe even two. A reminder of the Byron link stands outside the new Grammar School on Skene Street where a finely chiseled statue of the man gazes intently over the playground. It was however the old Grammar School at Schoolhill that Lord Byron actually attended and only for some four years. Yet rumours persist to this day that the new Grammar boasts his very desk complete with trademark signature carved deep in the lid next to the inkwell. Who knows? It may even be true. His granny famously lived a few miles north at Banff and folk are apt to claim he learned his swimming there. But that was before the advent of reinforced concrete. During the 1920s an Art Deco lido was built on the site and the Byron link slipped into folk memory.

Mind you, if you believe the swimming tale, he learned his lessons well and put the skills to use by swimming the Hellespont, a narrow strait in Turkey now called the Dardanelles. Legend says Greek hero Leander swam the same four-mile stretch a few centuries before, which may have sparked the poet's interest in such extreme water sports. Byron famously died young at just thirty-seven in April 1824. It was a fever that ended him although given the decades of flowery verse he might well have preferred heroic battle wounds. Despite the fact that the man left Aberdeen at the age of ten and never came back, the city still claimed him in death as one of their own. *The Aberdeen Journal* carried a lengthy obituary celebrating his life and over the next few months published several pieces detailing the landing of his body in England and his subsequent burial at Newstead Abbey. In June of that year, they began publishing verse penned in an unmistakably Byronesque style and submitted, or so they claimed, by an anonymous contributor:

"The scene is closed, the curtain's fall
Proclaims that life's poor play is oe'r
And seldom has the dusky pall
Diffus'd a deeper gloom before.

And fare-thee-well, repose in peace
Thou need'st not fame or eulogy
Thy funeral couch the shores of Greece

Now twice immortalised by thee."

The editors seemingly attributed the lines to an acquaintance of the poet but a few readers at least must have wondered if Byron himself had penned these lines from beyond the grave or if some budding hack had simply been inspired to flowery verse.

Alongside the romantic poet connection, there are some fine books about Aberdeen. Robert Smith (1923-2008) was journalist to trade and edited the Aberdeen *Evening Express* for many years. Alongside a host of titles describing the city and the surrounding land, he penned some tales about the local characters. About how Wattie the town drummer, a 'knocker-upper' who, dressed in lum-hat and big bow tie, was tasked with getting folk out their beds in time for work. About Mr Nisbet, a fast bowler who boiled soap for a living and put the fear of God into opposition batsmen with his infamous curve balls. About *The Bards of Bon Accord*, a vast book full of literary curiosities recording the work of otherwise completely forgotten wordsmiths who, aside from mention in that one set of pages, had had little chance of making it into print and whose only literary epitaph lay in the chapter titled 'Fugitive Verses and Verse Writers'.

Then there's Diane Morgan, a local historian whose detailed histories range forensically around the lost villages of Footdee, Spital and Mounthooly. She details, in her book *Lost Aberdeen*, the destruction of the city's architecture which if things had been different might have spiced up the tourism industry. There's even a book about the various other Aberdeens around the world. Seemingly there are thirty of them and who would have thought! Of course, Scottish place names travel the globe. Canada alone has an Arisaig, a Glendale, an Iona and even God forbid, a New Glasgow but without the razor gangs and the Billy Boy's bling. The Aberdeen book, written by Frederick Bull, records an Aberdeen in China and another in America's deep south. Seemingly, an Indian trader of Scottish descent called Robert Gordon had stumbled across a Dundee on the west bank of the Tombigee river at a place called Pontohoc. Now in case you don't know, Pontohoc is a Chickasaw word that means Land of the Hanging Grapes and the town is nowadays a county seat located not far from modern day Tupelo in the state of Mississippi. Tupelo is famous nowadays as the birthplace of Elvis Presley, but back in 1831 no-one apart from the locals had even heard of Tupelo never mind Dundee or Elvis Presley. I hope you're following this so far. Frederick Bull records that Robert Gordon was not at all pleased with the way the locals pronounced Dundee. So, writes Frederick - who spent 96,000 miles travelling the globe to research his book - "He simply changed it to Aberdeen." And of course, there's also a Booker White number titled 'Aberdeen Mississippi Blues', named after the place.

Lewis Grassic Gibbon's heroine Chris Guthrie famously inhabited a fictional house in the Granite City although Gibbon was later to claim otherwise saying loudly to anyone that who listen that Chris's Duncairn was "merely the city which the inhabitants of the Mearns (not foreseeing my requirements in completing my trilogy) have hitherto failed to build". Sceptics claim that Duncairn is probably Dundee but the jury remains out since it could have been any silvery city on the Scottish mainland although Topaz McGonagall's 'Silvery Tay' does seem a likely candidate. That kilted Glaswegian entertainer Andy Stewart (1933-1993) made fun of the Aberdonians and not at all to his credit. Homegrown music hall entertainer Harry Gordon (1893-1957) of Inversnecky Laird fame might have gotten away with it but Stewart's corny comment still resonates to this day: "Where in all of Scotland could five-hundred folk each get a slice of corned beef from just the one can?" he said. Mind you that was on stage at the Tivoli in Guild Street, a place where many a comic has died the death both before and since. His one-liner jibe came during an epidemic and maybe temporarily cheered an embattled audience fed up to the teeth with a local lockdown caused by the 1964 typhoid crisis, but I doubt if he would get away with it now.

Of course, worse had been said before about Aberdonians in the name of humour. Jibes like "how many Aberdonians does it take to change a lightbulb – Whit's a lightbulb? We prefer tae sit in the dark" and Chic Murray's infamous "My father was from Aberdeen, and a more generous man you couldn't wish to meet. I have still a gold watch that belonged to him and it's my most treasured possession. He sold it to me on his deathbed you know!" are still doing the rounds alongside fake headlines about deserted streets on flag days and "Titanic sinks, thousands die, man loses pound on Broad Street." The Harry Lauders with their 'wee Deoch-an-doris' have done their damage and that's a fact to be reckoned with even nowadays. Even writer Jack Webster got in on the act. In *A Final Grain of Truth,* he recalls visiting a well-known Aberdeen greasy spoon café which sported a sign by the door which read something like "Food, drink and a kind word one shilling and two pence". He ordered a pie and a cup of tea. As the waitress turned to go, he asked "And what about the kind word?" She cast an eye around to check if the boss was looking, then whispered "Dinna eat the pie!"

Although unproven, there is a suspicion that Shakespeare may have actually visited the North East of Scotland sometime in 1601. Seemingly a theatre company known as The King's Servants played in Aberdeen in that year and, albeit two years later, his name is said to appear on a Royal Licence granted by James VI which sent players from the Globe Theatre off on a Scottish tour. So, perhaps the bard who composed The Scottish Play had taken time out to gather some local knowledge of the murder of Macbeth. But without much shadow of a doubt, Charles Dickens spent a day or so in the city in the October of 1858. A newspaper of the time reported that he had given readings of 'Dombey and Son' and 'A Christmas Carol' at the County Rooms before heading off by train to deliver another talk further south the next night.

Eight years on, the man who invented Pumblechookery and dismissed the Sir Walter Scott Monument in Edinburgh as a complete failure was back in the Granite City. Older and perhaps wiser after a series of punishing foreign book tours, he returned in May 1866 and for a shilling or two you could witness him reading extracts from 'David Copperfield' followed by the trial scene from 'Pickwick'. Contracted by his agent, George Dolby, to a run of thirty readings, Dickens was paid a hefty fee for the evening. He was perhaps not on best form that night however and records in his diary that he had been "in a condition the reverse of flourishing, half strangled with my cold and dyspeptically gloomy and dull." Poor man. Mind you, you have to feel for those members of the audience who no doubt had great expectations.

Then there's the difficult story of Mary Webb (1901-1989), the woman who made the city famous as the home of the Northern Lights of Old Aberdeen. She herself only got some distant recognition and even that was only in later life. Her presence in Aberdeen was fleeting during her lifetime. But in death the city took her ashes when in the spring of 1989, they were scattered in the grounds of Kaimhill Crematorium. And many folks, even in Aberdeen, have never really heard of her. Some even confuse her with Mary Garden of opera fame or imagine that her song about those Northern Lights is some distant melody from Victorian times. It's something of a surprise to learn that she composed that world-famous anthem to Aberdonianism at a point in her life when she had never actually visited the place. In fact, the two visits were to come later, once whilst alive, at the Tivoli Theatre in 1958, and again following her demise at Easter in far off 1989. A straw poll insists that few under the age of twenty-five have heard of her at all and few over that age have any clear idea about her significance. There is no blue memorial plaque anywhere in the UK and no stone exists in that Garthdee Garden of Remembrance to record the scattering of her remains.

The lady in question was of course the Londoner who composed *The Northern Lights of Old Aberdeen* in about 1952 whilst working alongside a lonely Aberdonian lass by the name of Winnie Forgie in a hospital kitchen in the English capital. A well kent Scottish tenor by the name of Robert Wilson sang the song in the Albert Hall and later on in Aberdeen's Tivoli Theatre, where Mary was invited onstage to perform. It was a special moment for the lass from Leamington Spa. Robert Wilson died young and at the peak of his career after being dreadfully injured in a 1964 car crash. But before his death, he achieved fame and maybe a small degree of fortune hosting a pre-Andy Stewart White Heather Club on the black and white television. Mary for her part did not gain riches and nor did she achieve much in the way of fame during her lifetime. Her Canadian-born husband Mel died early and she continued throughout her long life to subsidise her concert career by working as a hospital kitchen prep-food operative. As for Winnie Forgie, well that is another story. After a spell abroad in Canada, she retired back to Aberdeen seemingly bitter at what she somehow supposed was Mary's financial success from that iconic tune.

Mary Webb eventually died in desperate poverty, aged 82, in April 1989 and in a London slum. And, apart from Maud-born journalist Jack Webster (1931-2020), few paid that much attention to her demise. In fact, Jack was to record that at her London funeral, which quite by chance he attended, "few had any idea whatsoever of her significance". And seemingly no one claimed her ashes following the sparsely attended ceremony. Mind you, he interviewed her at least once in London. And he writes that they shared a dram before that final stroke took her away. Early widowhood, a nervous breakdown and a lifetime blessed with poverty were to blight her career as a composer and concert pianist. But the spotlight of history surely shines on the memory of the Londoner who left Aberdeen a legacy to be proud of. In a final interview prior to Mary's demise, Jack Webster writes "It was another of these special moments. Turning from the piano stool she said 'I'm very proud of my song. I think it will be here long after I'm dead and gone'."

The song continues to enthral folk the world over. Her Broadwood piano, probably the very same one she used to compose the famous song, sat for a decade or so in the Mary Garden Room at the city's Music Hall. Nowadays, following the 2018 Music Hall renovation, it sits yet again within a council store awaiting a new home. There is talk of exhibiting the musical relic at Provost Skene's House and that will maybe happen soon. Meantime it seems that Aberdeen is happy to host a band of Dundonian cartoon 'Oor Wullies' on the beachfront for charity, but maybe struggles to celebrate a slice of its own history. Jack Webster presented the piano to the city many years ago following the scattering of Mary's ashes. It then "languished in a council shed for twenty years" he writes, before being re-discovered and displayed for twenty more.

Mary Webb's piano in Aberdeen Music Hall

Again, most probably, Mary's piano will need re-tuning on the way back from the museum store. It's not hard to imagine that poor Mary would be appalled at the absurdity of it all.

The city naturally has its own homegrown clutch of worthy musicians and artists. First off there's Annie Lennox of Eurythmics fame. Born on Christmas Day in 1954 and known globally for her androgyny, she had big hits including 'Sweet Dreams (Are Made of This)', 'There Must Be an Angel', 'Love Is A Stranger' and found time to engage in a little bit of political activism along the way. A supporter of Nelson Mandela and by definition a critic of Apartheid she spoke loudly about Pope Benedict XVI's approach to HIV/AIDS prevention in Africa. Not an Aberdonian to mince her words, she pronounced that the Pope's denunciation of condoms had caused "tremendous harm" and criticised the Roman Catholic Church for causing widespread confusion on the subject.

Then there's Mary Garden (1874-1967). Born in Charlotte Street she later lived in Dee Street, there is a plaque at number 41, and spent just seven years in the city before moving abroad. In some ways a forgotten diva in her home city, she got her big break in the Paris of 1900 when the regular soprano in Gustave Charpentier's opera *Louise* caught cold. As understudy, Mary took on the title role and she never really looked back. For many years Aberdeen Music Hall boasted the architecturally stunning Mary Garden Room although the winds of change in the form of a £9 million refurbishment of the concert venue re-birthed the shrine as 'The Rondo Restaurant'.

Like Lennox, Mary Garden was not one to avoid controversy. In a career spanning some thirty years she courted scandal and gained a degree of notoriety with her portrayal of an almost naked Salome at the Manhattan Opera House in 1908. In a well-timed review, a shocked *New York Times* reported that "Mary appears in a small piece of nearly transparent flesh-coloured silk. Her feet are bare, her arms are bare, and really it is impossible to describe this as a costume." An unrepentant Mary relished the role and would go on to shock Chicago audiences later in the run. This was Strauss as you'd never experienced it before! In a nod to the fate of Mary Webb, the once famous opera singer ended her days in some poverty and back in her native city. She died demented, aged 93, in a geriatric ward at the House of Daviot near Inverurie and journalist Jack Webster records that a mere fourteen folk attended her funeral. There is a story that her ashes ended up being scattered in the Garden of Remembrance at the Old Crematorium in Kaimhill. This may however simply be a confusion with the scattering of Mary Webb's ashes at the same location. A further oft-quoted Mary Garden confusion involves a gravestone bearing her name which sits in St Nicholas Kirkyard. But the dates are wrong since that particular Mary died in 1864.

Tombstones can be a pointer to both scandal and tragedy as a memorial in Aberdeen's Allenvale Cemetery poignantly records. Dundee poet William Topaz McGonagall certainly got it right when he penned his lines about the Tay Bridge Disaster:

> "Beautiful Railway Bridge of the Silv'ry Tay!
> Alas! I am very sorry to say
> That ninety lives have been taken away
> On the last Sabbath day of 1879,
> Which will be remember'd for a very long time."

And, love him or hate him, his words still resonate on each anniversary of the horrific event. But spare a thought for those lesser-known, but equally scandalous, bridge failures which haunted the early railways and endangered the travelling public. Over at Cullen for example, three arches of the town viaduct collapsed in December 1887 just months after the opening of the Tochieneal to Garmouth section of the Great North of Scotland Railway's Moray Firth coast line. It was pure luck that no trains were involved and that there were no casualties. The original triple arched railway bridge over the River Ythan at

Ellon also collapsed following a landslide in February 1861, delaying the opening of the line to Maud until it could be re-engineered with four arches. There were seemingly no injuries since work had already stopped for the day. There were however a large number of fatalities when, in September 1846, several spans of the rail bridge over the Dee at Aberdeen collapsed during construction. Seven construction workers were killed and a further four seriously injured. Their memorial stone in the grounds of Allenvale Cemetery sits just a few hundred yards from the place where they died.

Early canals fared no better and engineering solutions were often trial and error or subject to shoddy construction practices. The Aberdeenshire Canal for example, suffered so-called 'teething problems' in its early days. Alongside the costly failure of substandard lock-gates on the outskirts of Aberdeen, a section of the embankment at Kintore collapsed in 1805 flooding much of the town. Some residents only escaped drowning by climbing through the thatched roofs of their cottages.

Then there were the various scandals associated with Queen Victoria. It's well known or at least widely suspected that following the death of Prince Albert, Queen Victoria became close to first of all her Deeside-born gillie John Brown and later to her Indian manservant Hafiz Mohammed Abdul Karim. Her relationship with both men raised eyebrows at the very least and even today there are Chinese Whispers alleging impropriety. Karim came late into Victoria's life and their relationship was almost certainly platonic. Brown's status as her Highland Attendant has been subject of much wider debate and a recent history by Australian author Julia Baird suggests at least a mild degree of intimacy between the two. Referring to notes in the diary of Sir James Reid, Victoria's 'Royal Doctor in Ordinary', she quotes an entry from 1883 in which he recalls seeing the pair flirting at Windsor Castle. He observed the gillie lifting his kilt and saying "Oh, I thought it was here" and noted Victoria's reply in kind as she raised her skirt saying "No, it is here." Mild perhaps in nature, the supposed flirting was seen by the Royal Physician as a breach of protocol worthy of note.

Indeed, in later years when Victoria announced that she was considering a Knighthood for her Indian servant Abdul Karim, her son Bertie the Prince of Wales became apoplectic and urged Dr Reid to take direct action. Reid did not mince his words and promptly threatened to have his Royal patient declared insane. In a personal letter to Victoria, he wrote that "There are people in high places who know Your Majesty well who say to me that the only charitable explanation that can be given is that Your Majesty is not sane; and that the time will come when, to save Your Majesty's memory and reputation, it will be necessary for me to come forward and say so." Needless to say, Karim did not receive the promised knighthood and following his mistress's death in 1901 he was sent packing to his native Agra by an unforgiving Royal Family.

Another, perhaps lesser-known scandal, involved a Gordon Highlander officer by the name of Hector MacDonald (1853-1903) who was driven to suicide following accusations of sexual misconduct. Not much would have been made of it today in all honesty but the sexual politics of the military at the turn of the Twentieth century meant that men with men relationships were best confined to the shadows.

Raised by the Fourth Duke of Gordon, in the spring of 1794, and closely associated with Aberdeen for over two hundred years, the Gordon Highlanders Regiment was originally known as the 100th Regiment of Foot before becoming the Gordon Highlanders in 1881. Many early recruits were drawn from the Gordon estates. According to the Regimental Museum in Aberdeen, early recruitment was ably assisted by the Fourth Duke's wife, the Duchess Jean, an intimate friend of William Pitt the prime minister of the day, who is said to have proffered a kiss to each new recruit as an incentive to join her husband's regiment. A case of a selling a kiss for the King's Shilling perhaps.

The Gordons have it seems always been in the thick of it, seeing service in almost every conflict of the last two centuries including at Waterloo, in the various Nineteenth century colonial wars and in both of the Twentieth century's global conflicts. Now, dating back to 1886, Camp Coffee was a thick black syrupy substance originally manufactured in Glasgow by Paterson and Sons Ltd. The company marketed the product as a "secret blend of sugar, water, coffee and chicory essence", and it came in a tall glass bottle with a colourful label depicting a Gordon Highlander officer alongside his Sikh batman. The white military issue tent in the background was topped by a fluttering pennant emblazoned with the slogan 'Ready Aye Ready', while instructions on the reverse urged Camp drinkers to "Stir one teaspoonful of Camp into each cupful of boiling water, then add cream and sugar to taste. Made with heated milk but not boiled, it is delicious".

The officer portrayed on the label was, allegedly, Major General Sir Hector MacDonald. Son of a humble crofter, Hector had worked his way up through the ranks of the Gordon Highlanders regiment serving with distinction in the second Afghan War and in also in India. He was known variously as 'Fighting Mac' or 'Eachann nan Cath' in his native Gaelic, for his exploits at the battle of Omdurman in the Sudan, where the British Army under Kitchener had fielded some 6,000 men plus perhaps as many as forty field guns. The opposing army of around 60,000 Sudanese Ansar tribesmen (known to the British as Dervishes) and Egyptian troops were pretty much obliterated and a young war correspondent by the name of Winston Churchill reported that the Sudanese resembled nothing so much as a "twelfth-century Crusader army armed with spears, swords, and with hundreds of banners embroidered with Koranic texts." Indeed, it was perhaps not the most illustrious of the army's engagements. And to compound the industrialised slaughter, there were press reports implying that the enemy wounded were denied medical aid, slaughtered where they lay and left to die in the hundreds unaided and unattended on the battlefield. Churchill's own account of the battle was highly critical of Kitchener in this respect when it was first published although in a later book, he moderated the criticism mindful perhaps of the consequences for his emerging political career.

No one today really knows who the Camp Coffee servant was but over the years his humble status improved. In the 1980s for example, the silver tray disappeared and the Sikh servant was left standing with his left arm by his side, while his right arm remained in its original under tray position. In a recent marketing incarnation, he was finally granted a well-deserved seat alongside his master.

As for Hector MacDonald, he was wounded in the second Boer War and later given command of the regiment's troops in Ceylon where charges of homosexuality were brought against him. As far as I can work out, Hector shot himself in a Paris hotel, The Regina, in 1903. Rumours abound that he was encouraged to 'do the right thing' by a higher authority. However, more commonly his suicide is attributed to a newspaper headline exposing his unenviable situation. In June 1903 a Government Commission released a report on the tragedy which by and large exonerated poor Hector of any wrongdoing:

"In reference to the grave charges made against the late Sir Hector MacDonald, we, the appointed and undersigned Commissioners, individually and collectively declare on oath that, after the most careful, minute, and exhaustive inquiry and investigation of the whole circumstances and facts connected with the sudden and unexpected death of the late Sir Hector MacDonald, unanimously and unmistakably find absolutely no reason or crime whatsoever which would create feelings such as would determine suicide, in preference to conviction of any crime affecting the moral and irreproachable character of so brave, so fearless, so glorious and unparalleled a hero.

We firmly believe the cause which gave rise to the inhuman and cruel suggestions of crime were prompted through vulgar feelings of spite and

'Ready Aye Ready' - Hector the Hero.

jealousy in his rising to such a high rank of distinction in the British Army: and, while we have taken the most reliable and trustworthy evidence from every accessible and conceivable source, have without hesitation come to the conclusion that there is not visible the slightest particle of truth in foundation of any crime, and we find the late Sir Hector MacDonald has been cruelly assassinated by vile and slandering tongues.

While honourably acquitting the late Sir Hector MacDonald of any charge whatsoever, we cannot but deplore the sad circumstances of the case that have fallen so disastrously on one whom we have found innocent of any crime attributed to him."

There are two public memorials to Hector, one on the Black Isle, another at Dingwall and, in a nod to a much later Lord Lucan, conspiracy theories followed him well beyond the grave. He was seemingly spotted in Shanghai in 1909, six years after his suicide. Another sighting placed him in Manchuria having allegedly faked his death. Another even wilder rumour insisted that he had defected to Germany, taking on the identity of a Prussian Field Marshal. Banchory-born fiddler and composer Scott Skinner (1843-1927) composed a tribute to the man titled *Hector the Hero* and Aberdeen musician/composer Charlie Abel recently produced a cover version of Skinner's classic tribute for piano accordion.

Less scandalous but equally tragic is the tale of Aberdeen's three Victoria statues. There are literally hundreds of statues of Queen Victoria dotted around the UK and there are many foreign examples dotted around the former British Commonwealth. Most relate to her Golden or Diamond Jubilees in 1887 and 1897. Some celebrate Royal visits. Glasgow's George Square portrays her as a Boudica atop a charging horse in celebration of her 1849 visit to the city. This strange bronze made the national headlines as being the first in Britain to feature the monarch as a classical female warrior on horseback. Aberdeen's tribute to the head of the British Empire was also to make the headlines but for quite a different reason.

The best known of Aberdeen's three Queen Victoria statues is perhaps the one at Queens Cross. Dating from 1893 it was sculpted by an artist by the name of C. B. Birch. Birch was a second choice for the commission despite his international reputation. The initial plan had been to erect a new statue on St Nicholas Street to replace a frost damaged Alexander Brodie Italian marble sculpture erected to commemorate Victoria's Golden Jubilee. Inverurie-born James Pittendreigh Macgillivray was in the running for the new piece, but after deliberation by a local committee of worthies, Birch got the commission. It was not a bad choice for, in common with the likes of Rodin, who effectively ran a statue factory in Paris, Birch's output was also prolific and he favoured bronze as a medium, which of course allowed mass production and lowered unit costs considerably. He made perhaps as many as eight copies of the Queens Cross sculpture from the original mould and replicas can be found at Blackfriars Bridge in London, Scarborough Town Hall Gardens, Derby Royal Infirmary, Newcastle-Under-Lyme, Guernsey, Adelaide and at Udaipur in India.

So, the upshot was that the damaged Brodie statue was moved to the townhouse, where it still stands alongside the grand staircase, and the Birch bronze casting took over the Brodie plinth in the city centre; that is until 1964 when Marks and Spencer got permission to build on the site prompting Victoria to up sticks and move to the current Queens Cross location.

It was the earlier Brodie sculpture though which had raised eyebrows and indeed a few hackles. There were three Brodie brothers. Two, William and Alexander were artists of considerable ability. William, the eldest (1815-1881) was born in Banff, studied drawing under artist and photographer George Washington Wilson and in a long and varied career worked on what the *Times* newspaper was to describe as "More busts in portraiture than any other in the same line." His better-known works include the bronze of Greyfriars Bobby in Edinburgh and, again in Edinburgh, a set of free-stone carvings depicting characters from the *Waverley* novels for the canopy of the Scott Monument in Princes Street.

Alexander Brodie (1830-1867) was born in Aberdeen's Virginia Street. The family had moved from Banff to Aberdeen, the father was a merchant seaman and ship's master, and Alexander left school to take up an apprenticeship as a brass finisher in a local foundry. He then studied art for a bit and worked in Edinburgh before returning to Aberdeen in 1858 to specialise in graveyard monuments and bust portraiture.

As his reputation grew, larger commissions inevitably came his way and his public works include the Duke of Huntly statue in Huntly's main square and the William Copeland Monument in Aberdeen's St Nicholas Churchyard. In January 1864 a public meeting was held in Aberdeen chaired by William Leslie, then a councillor and later to become Lord Provost, at which it was decided to commission a marble statue of Queen Victoria. There was already a monument to Albert the Prince Consort which Victoria herself had unveiled three years before and it was considered appropriate to complete the set. Alexander was awarded the £1,000 commission and his initial design portraying the monarch in court robes was conveyed to Windsor for approval by the Queen. She was not amused however and, preferring a more blatantly Scottish theme to broadcast her Stuart heritage and status as High Chief of Scotland, she insisted on plaid in

The Royal toes in all of their naked glory (Brodie's plaster maquette - Aberdeen Music Hall)

the form of traditional highland dress plus a thistle brooch to hold it all together.

A sceptre was thrown in for good measure and Brodie began work on what by now had morphed into a latter-day mockery of the Queen of Scots bravely leading the nation to some heroic victory. The commission was initially worked up in plaster and the full-size plaster maquette was duly submitted for Royal approval. The new design met the Queen's requirements except for one small detail. The model showed her wearing sandals and if you peeked beneath the robes the Royal toes could be viewed in all of their naked glory. Officials and maybe even some councillors privately sniggered; the head of the British Empire could not be portrayed naked so a subtle alteration had to be made.

Brodie completed the commission in Sicilian marble in the summer of 1866. It was around eight feet in height and the monument was duly placed on a ten-foot plinth which dominated St Nicholas Street for the next twenty-seven years. On the thirteenth of September 1866 an official unveiling was held with the Prince of Wales, later Edward VII, in attendance to cut the ribbon and Brodie was widely congratulated for the quality of his work. There was however one small but quite significant difference between the plaster maquette and the finished marble version of the masterpiece. The skimpy sandals which had caused the sniggering had been quietly discarded and, in their place, Her Royal Highness was sporting a sturdy pair of outdoor shoes! A Royal Sandal Scandal had been averted but all did not go well for Alexander Brodie. The artist committed suicide at home in Aberdeen's Garvock Place on the thirtieth of May 1867 less than nine months after his Victorian triumph. His death was put down to a 'sudden mental collapse', although his death certificate records the cause of death more politely as 'Brain Fever'. He was only 37 years of age. Pressure of work was widely suspected and he had a three-year waiting list of commissions on his order book when he died. This was no whisky and revolver suicide and a piece in the *Huntly Express* dated the first of June 1867 provided lurid detail:

> "Mr Brodie's disposition was of a very genial cast and it is stated that his tendency to be over social was marked with some anxiety by those who looked to him to attain the high mark as a sculptor of which his genius and early success gave abundant promise. Of late too, his mind seemed to be giving way somewhat and on Wednesday morning he made a rash attempt to take his own life … Mr Brodie expired on Thursday morning. Thus, at the age of thirty-seven, has perished by his own hand [and] whose name now falls to be added to the sad list of human wrecks that strew the shores of time!"

An earlier unfinished bust of Victoria, commissioned privately by the Royal Household, was quietly completed in November 1867 by his brother William, and Alexander Brodie's completed and fully clothed marble Victoria currently stands inside the Town House in Aberdeen city centre. As for the scandalous sandal version? Slightly yellowed with age and patina, it remains on public display in the entrance hallway of Aberdeen's recently renovated Music Hall where visitors can still take a surreptitious peek at the monarch's naked toes.

Then there's the city's perhaps contentious links to Japan via the so-called Scottish Samurai, Thomas Blake Glover. Japan sent a great many students to the UK during the late Edo period (1603-1867) and the early Meiji period (1868-1912) in order to explore new ideas in science, share culture and import European technology. Cities such as Glasgow and Aberdeen provided rich pickings for the aspiring technologists and alongside acquisition of new skill sets the two nations exchanged cultural and artistic aesthetics which continue to create broad ripples to this day. Japan had participated in the second Glasgow International Exhibition in 1901. The Japan Pavilion was located near the main exhibition hall at Kelvingrove and there is a strong likelihood that Charles Rennie Mackintosh and many other influential Scottish designers of the day would have visited and been influenced by what they saw there. Some 11.5 million admissions were recorded during the eight-month span of the exhibition and contemporaries of Mackintosh certainly visited Japan at about this time. Kelvingrove Art Gallery and Museum holds a collection of so-called 'Industrial Art' collected by Glasgow-born designer Christopher Dresser who visited Japan in 1876 or thereabouts.

Aberdeen has its own very special claim to the forging of the burgeoning Scottish-Japanese relationship and one local man in particular played a pivotal role. Variously known as the Scottish Samurai or The Scot who shaped Japan, Thomas Blake Glover was probably born in Fraserburgh in 1838. His father worked as a coastguard officer and the family lived at various locations along the Aberdeenshire coastline including Sandend, Collieston and at Bridge of Don in Aberdeen. Young Thomas was educated first at the recently opened parish school in Fraserburgh, then in primary schools in Grimsby, Collieston and finally in Old Aberdeen at The Chanonry School. On leaving school, Glover began work with the trading company Jardine, Matheson & Co and quickly progressed to the Shanghai office before taking up a post in Japan.

His role in the Far East has often been glossed over in order to present a popular image of Glover as an enlightened trader intent on hauling an impoverished Japan into the industrial age. In truth however, Jardine Matheson & Co were happy to trade in everything from silks and tea to guns and opium.

Glover excelled in his role as trader and alongside making vast amounts of profit for his employer he soon started taking a substantial cut for himself. His move to Japan, in 1859 aged twenty-one, came at a time when various rival clans were warring for control of the country. For more than 200 years, foreign trade with Japan had been permitted to the Dutch and Chinese exclusively. However, following an episode of gunboat diplomacy in 1853, the United States Government had persuaded the Japanese to open trade up with the west. Glover arrived in good time to use his proven skills to exploit the situation. Soon he was supplying both sides in the civil war with guns and munitions. Before long he was taking orders for the building of warships, to be built in Scotland, to arm a fledgling Japanese Navy. The market for weaponry however soon became saturated and he turned to mining to maintain his by now dwindling fortune. Demand for coal had surged as steamships began to proliferate in Japanese waters. Glover, in partnership with a Japanese clan, invested in developing the Takashima coal mine on an island near Nagasaki in 1868. The mine was the first in the country to employ western methods. Mitsubishi acquired the Takashima mine in 1881 in the organization's first main diversification beyond shipping.
    Glover is often credited with importing the first steam engine into Japan and being instrumental in the formation of the Mitsubishi conglomerate. Japan also lacked modern facilities for repairing ships, so Glover imported the necessary equipment for a dry dock in Nagasaki in 1868. He later sold his shares in the company to the Japanese government, which leased the dock to Mitsubishi as part of a capital transfer deal in 1884. Just twenty years later, in 1905 Japan had, according to many accounts, become the fourth largest naval power in the world behind Britain, Imperial Germany and the US.
    There are many enduring myths surrounding the life and career of Thomas Blake Glover. One involves the popular notion that his Japanese wife Tsuru was somehow the inspiration for Puccini's opera *Madame Butterfly*. There appears to be little substance to this idea. A booklet produced by Aberdeen City Council to publicise the city's links with Glover and hence Japan relates that "the association of Glover Garden in Nagasaki and *Madame Butterfly* no doubt relates to the fact that American soldiers after the Second World War dubbed the house Madame Butterfly House." Thomas Glover eventually became famous in Japan and was the first non-Japanese to be awarded the Order of the Rising Sun. When he died in Tokyo in 1911 aged 73, his ashes were interred in Nagasaki's Sakamoto International Cemetery. Fraserburgh Heritage Centre hosts a permanent exhibition celebrating his North East links and his former house in Nagasaki attracts two million visitors each year.

A modern manifestation of the Glover legacy is the Order of the Scottish Samurai (OSS). Founded and overseen by Aberdonian and OBE Ronnie Watt, the 'Order of the Scottish Samurai' is inspired by the maverick entrepreneur. Alongside Lord Bruce and Joanna Lumley, recipients of the Scottish Samurai Awards include local businessman Sir Ian Wood, former Scotland First Minister Alex Salmond, composer Charlie Abel, politician Len Ironside (for services to wrestling) and film producer Compton Ross. There's even a tune, titled 'Ronnie Watt's 9th Dan', dedicated to OSS founder Ronnie Watt and composed by accordionist Charlie Abel, who says:

> "I wrote this tune for Ronnie on the occasion of him achieving his 9th Dan Black Belt after 50 years of karate training and teaching in December 2015. Ronnie is a living legend of karate in Aberdeen and has been awarded the OBE from the Queen, The Order of the Rising Sun from Japan, is a Burgess of the City of Aberdeen and has been inducted to the European Hall of Fame for Martial Arts. Ronnie has many other awards including an honorary degree from the University of Aberdeen".

Other famous folk from the city include Graeme Garden of Goodies fame, Annie Wallace of transgender soap opera fame, James Clerk Maxwell, the scientist who formulated the classical theory of electromagnetic radiation; and of course, Robert Gordon's College educated Michael Gove, the cabinet minister who famously suggested that being interviewed by BBC radio presenter John Humphrys was a bit like going into Harvey Weinstein's bedroom.

In more recent years the honours of Aberdeen have been extended to folk who might be termed everyday heroes and a civic project titled NUART commissioned a permanent memorial to the city's lesser-known heroes. Put together by London-based artist Carrie Reichardt and local school pupils, a mural consisting of several thousand mosaic tiles was installed at the Green just off Union Street in 2018. The artwork celebrated the contribution of football legend Dennis Law, Doric poet Sheena Blackhall, Paralympian Neil Fachie and public health pioneer Mary Esslemont as well as Toxik Ephex, an anarchist punk band fronted by *Aberdeen Voice* founding editor, arts activist and Burgess of Aberdeen Fred Wilkinson. Following a mixed reaction by a local property company, the NUART *Unsung Heroes* mural has now relocated to a more welcoming civic space at Marischal Square - on a wall at the junction of Flourmill Lane and Netherkirkgate - where it remains today on permanent display.

But there's much more to the Granite City than a smattering of Byron and a few tales of scandal and a bittie or two of famous folk. In fact, the place is positively heaving with history. With a population hovering above the two hundred thousand mark and a list of notable residents as long as your arm, Aberdeen is maybe best summed up as the Furry Boots Toon. Not, you understand due to the fact that even in summer it can be snowing down on Beach Boulevard or in Duthie Park. But down to Ian Rankin's Inspector Rebus who in his detective novels relates that when you first arrive in the silvery city by the River Dee and the River Don, the locals will maybe ask you questions like "So tell me, furry boots are you from quine?" Naturally there is no easy answer unless of course you spik the Doric.

2
ABOYNE - A HISTORIC HIGHLAND VILLAGE

Located on the very edge of the Cairngorms National Park, the largest National Park in the UK, and with the magnificent 25,000-acre Glen Tanar estate literally on the doorstep, the upper Deeside town of Aboyne is steeped in centuries of rich history and offers both visitors and locals alike a unique Royal Deeside experience. Just over three hundred years ago in the slow build-up to the 1715 Jacobite Rebellion, the town played what was to prove a seminal role in the resurrection of the Jacobite cause when John Erskine, the Earl of Mar, organised a Tinchal, or great hunt on Deeside.

Contemporary accounts suggest that upwards of eight hundred participants spent the early days of the September of that year engaged in feasting and hunting in the forests around Aboyne. Known in some circles as Bobbin John due to his tendency to transfer his allegiance to the highest bidder, Mar had been unceremoniously dismissed from his post as Secretary of State for Scotland in favour of the Duke of Montrose and had decided in consequence to transfer his loyalty from the Crown to what was rapidly becoming a popular Jacobite cause. Mar left London in August 1715 and in the disguise of a workman, some say he dressed in the black rags of a coalman for the evasion, embarked on a coal-sloop bound for the Fife coalfields. He landed at Elie after an eight-day voyage and made his way to Invercauld where a preliminary meeting of Jacobite sympathisers had been convened under the guise of preparing for the Tinchal. A final planning meeting was arranged for September the second at Aboyne Castle where, following consultation with the Marquis of Huntly, a deal was agreed involving the waging of full-scale war on the Crown with a view to installing a Stuart king on the throne. By the October of 1715, the Jacobites had gained control of much of Scotland north of the Firth of Forth. However, by the time the king in waiting landed at Peterhead, on the twenty-second of December the uprising was all but over. Faced with certain defeat and probable execution, the Earl of Mar and James Edward Stuart, the Old Pretender, boarded a tiny sailing vessel at Montrose harbour on the third of February 1716 and escaped over the sea to France.

The days of the Tinchal are long gone although hunting trophies adorn the walls of many Deeside buildings including the Victory Hall on Aboyne's Ballater Road. A 'C' listed granite building, designed by Aberdeen architect Alexander Mackenzie, the hall, locally known as the Aboyne and Glen Tanar Memorial Hall, commemorates the dead of the Great War and incorporates additions recording the names of those lost in both World War Two and the

Korean War. The entrance hall sports a stained glass panelled shrine commemorating those men who left Aboyne and neighbouring Glen Tanar during 1914-18, never to return. Completed in 1924 and refurbished using Millennium Funds the hall was officially re-opened in October 1999 by a modern-day monarch in waiting, HRH Prince Charles the Duke of Rothesay. The hall is nowadays host to the Formaston Stone, a Pictish stone fragment featuring three distinct decorative carvings, a mirror, interlaced Celtic knot work and a rare example of Ogham script. Described by archaeologists as "Pictish Cross-slab Ogham-inscribed" the Formaston Stone is sometimes referred to as the Aboyne Stone and sits just inside the hall doorway within a protective glass cabinet.

The Victory Hall, Aboyne

It took quite a while for the old stone to get there. Originally discovered at St Adamnan's Kirkyard by the Loch of Aboyne - local author Inkson McConnochie records in his Deeside History that it was found partially buried near the door-step of the old church - it was removed for safe keeping to the rose garden at Aboyne Castle at the end of the Nineteenth century. When the castle underwent extensive renovations in the 1970s the stone was displayed for a time in the, now closed, Andrew Carnegie Museum at Inverurie before travelling back to Aboyne in 2002 where, thanks to the generosity of the Marquis of Huntly plus financial support from the Heritage Lottery Scheme, it was put on public view.

Largely due to the efforts of Sir William Cunliffe-Brooks, an eccentric Victorian multi-millionaire banker and sometime MP for East Cheshire and later Altrincham, both Aboyne and neighbouring Glen Tanar, or Glen Tana as Sir William preferred to call it, feature architecture more often seen in the likes of rural Kent than Highland Aberdeenshire. Sir William enjoyed countryside pursuits including deer stalking, grouse shooting and salmon fishing and liked nothing better than to treat his many wealthy and important guests to what might be considered a modern-day version of the Tinchal. Deeside architect Mike Rassmussen describes the man as "a keen amateur architect who had a hand in designing all of the cottages, farms and school buildings on the estate as well as Glen Tanar House."

Sir William's architectural influence can be seen in many of Aboyne's buildings. The original early Victorian railway station for example was timber built as were many of the Great North of Scotland Railway station buildings. In 1896 the station was rebuilt in the form of the ornate granite pepper-pot turreted building we see today. This building and the bright red roofed and turreted former station garage, once used as a Royal Mail Sorting Office, bear the mark of Sir William's distinctive architectural style. All over the town and the nearby glen, farmhouses and estate workers dwellings were re-furbished and modernised at his expense and to his designs. Entire forests were planted, highways improved and a new town water supply was laid in from Glen Roy to provide around 45,000 gallons daily.

Sir William, a keen country sportsman, even commissioned estate kennels complete with electric light and central heating for his fifty or so hunting dogs. In 1887 in a fit of supreme extravagance he built the spectacular Tower of Ess at the Glen Tanar Estate entrance in a clear bid to impress visitors. In essence, the tower is a three-storey gatehouse designed to resemble a typical Scottish tower house. But for the estate staff who had to live in the structure, it must have been a challenging place to inhabit. The Deeside winters combined with the bubbling river below would have made for uncomfortable living conditions at the very least. In more modern times the tower has been upgraded to include central heating and a hot-tub and modern-day tourists can hire the place for a few hundred pounds a week and explore a riverside footpath romantically titled as the Fairy Riverside Walk. Perhaps though his most eccentric undertaking was the construction of a grand cowshed fit for that noblest of beasts, the Aberdeen Angus.

The Tower of Ess at Glen Tanar

Completed at a cost of some £6,000 by his architect George Truefitt in 1889 and designed to house the Marquis of Huntly's prize-winning beasts, the Coos' Cathedral accommodated around forty cows and several pedigree bulls in grey granite luxury. Replete with granary, grand turnip store and workers accommodation, the massive steading with its high beamed ceilings featured a miniature tramway for the carrying in of feed and the transporting out of dung. Nowadays the cathedral, set within the grounds of Aboyne Castle, the private family home of the Marquis of Huntly, has been refurbished and re-tasked as a wedding and corporate events venue and the interior space originally occupied by the Marquis's cows now accommodates some four-hundred delegates.

Alongside the improvements in both agriculture and housing, the Nineteenth century saw a transport revolution in Aberdeenshire which brought huge social and economic benefits to those communities fortunate enough to lie along the new and improved transport networks. For almost half a century, the township of Aboyne marked the end of the improved turnpike road from Aberdeen. In the 1850s however, pressure from Deeside coach operators and commercial carriers led to the extension of the improved road as far as Braemar. Earlier visionaries had considered the alternative of digging a grand canal linking Aboyne with Aberdeen and on to Insch and even as far as Monymusk, but this project failed to gain popular support due to major engineering issues including the need for several costly aqueducts along the proposed route. A much more modest canal, The Aberdeenshire Canal, was eventually cut linking Aberdeen docks to Inverurie's Port Elphinstone. A full account of this undertaking is to be found in my earlier book, *The Little History of Aberdeenshire*.

Alongside road improvements there was a need for improved river crossings. There were many ferries operating on the Dee, most were small craft operated by local Boaties who for a small fee would row folk across the river. The ferry at Aboyne was typical of the breed and crossed the Dee near the Old Boat Inn on Charleston Road. It operated until 1827 when a tragic accident, during the October St Michael Fair, occurred. Despite a sudden spate, the boatman left the north bank with his heavily overloaded boat crammed to the gunwales with late night revellers. Near the south side, the boat overturned and all on board were thrown into the water. Most managed to scramble ashore but a woman and her daughter drowned. Word of the disaster reached Aboyne some hours later when the boatman himself brought the news having hiked the twelve miles around the riverbank via the Potarch Bridge. The incident prompted the then Earl of Aboyne to fund a suspension bridge over the river. The present Aboyne bridge is the fourth to be built on the site.

For a brief period after the railway arrived in 1859, the town became the railhead of the Deeside Line. Aboyne suddenly found itself playing host to Queen Victoria, her entourage and her many distinguished visitors as they disembarked from Royal trains and stopped over at the likes of the Huntly Arms, perhaps Scotland's oldest coaching inn, before traveling on to the Balmoral Estate by road. The hotel nowadays sports a stained-glass window commemorating the world's strongest man, Birse-born Donald Dinnie. A sporting superstar, Dinnie achieved international fame when he carried two giant boulders, with a combined weight of 775 pounds, across the Potarch Bridge and back. Alongside a lucrative career touring the world's athletic circuits Dinnie reigned supreme as the Highland Scottish Sporting Champion between 1856 and 1876 as all-round athlete. Variously titled 'The World's Greatest Athlete' and 'All Round Champion of the World', Donald Dinnie entered into sponsorship deals and even lent his name to the Donald Dinnie heavy artillery shells being lobbed at the enemy at the Somme and at Passchendaele. In 1903 he famously endorsed Scotland's other national drink when his image was emblazoned on lemonade bottles alongside a caption proclaiming "I can recommend Barr's Iron Bru to all who wish to aspire to athletic fame." Aberdeen Art Gallery holds a collection of Dinnie memorabilia including many of his sporting medals and trophies.

With the building of the Deeside Railway along the Dee Valley, agricultural goods, foodstuffs and timber - which in pre-railway days had been floated down the Dee - now gravitated to the railways. Steam trains slashed journey times and as transport costs decreased tourism began to increase. The combination of Sir Walter Scott's romanticised tales of broadsword wielding tartan clad Highlanders plus the attraction of hunting, shooting and fishing proved irresistible and attracted hordes of tourists and summer visitors intent on sampling the Highland lifestyle. The Deeside resort towns including Aboyne benefited greatly. Queen Victoria's romance with the Highlands added value to the Deeside brand and by the time of her death in 1901 the town's population had more than doubled from a pre-railway 1841 figure of just 260 to 561. The 2011 Census recorded 2,602 residents. George Bradshaw's Railway Guide for 1863 records that Aboyne "offers an excellent starting point for the tourist to visit the picturesque scenery extending between Ballater, Braemar and Balmoral." Clearly George was intent on disturbing the monarch's peace and quiet.

Just a few miles west of the town on the A97 lies the parish of Logie Coldstone which at one time operated a set of natural springs thought by some to have curative qualities which could heal the sick and cure the lame. Robert Burns died in July 1796 at the early age of 37, and there are many theories as to the cause of his death ranging from venereal disease to rheumatic fever. The years of hard labour he spent as a tenant farmer must also have taken their toll and the severe winter of 1795 must have exacerbated his already poor health. In a final effort to regain good health, the bard was advised by his doctor, William Maxwell, to visit Brow Well near Dumfries, there to drink the spring water which contained the mineral chalybeate which was then widely believed to have good and curative properties. On July the fourth 1796, Burns duly drank the foul-tasting water from the iron cup attached to the well and waded chest deep into the freezing cold tidal waters of the Solway Firth. This event was infamously parodied many years later by Bill Brown of Glasgow School of Art who produced a series of ceramic plates depicting Burns taking the water on the Solway Firth with the now decommissioned Chapelcross Nuclear Power Station as a modern-day backdrop.

In a final letter to his friend Alexander Cunningham, Burns wrote "Alas! My friend, I fear the voice of the Bard will soon be heard among you no more! For these eight or ten months I have been ailing, sometimes bed-fast and sometimes not; but these last three months I have been tortured with an excruciating rheumatism which has reduced me to nearly the last stage. You actually would not know me if you saw me. Pale, emaciated, and so feeble as occasionally to need help from my chair … but I can no more on the subject … only the medical folks tell me that my last & only chance is bathing & country quarters & riding." It is perhaps little wonder really, that Burns died within days of his so called 'curative' water treatment experience and he was duly buried in Dumfries on twenty-fifth of July 1796.

Medical bathing, also called balneology, or even hydrotherapy, was an approach popular with physicians in Burns' time with various medical proponents claiming that exposure to mineral waters might well improve certain diseases and indeed effect cures where all other treatments had failed. In the sixteenth and seventeenth Centuries mineral springs became popular among royalty and the well-to-do. Many wealthy landowners constructed health spas on their estates and would invite the good and the great to take the waters for medicinal and recreational purposes. A sort of hot tub experience but without the heat perhaps. Ordinary people would also "take the waters" at local mineral springs for relaxation or to seek specific cures. Physicians began to set up shop beside the spas and would recommend specific water treatments such as baths, douches and the drinking of the spa waters. The book 'A Dissertation on the Use of Seawater in Diseases of the Glands' published in 1750 by Dr Richard Russell, remained a popular reference book on the subject for several decades and it may well have influenced Dr Maxwell, who famously recommended that Robert Burns try the springs at Dumfries's Brow Well as well as that final freezing dip in the Solway Firth.

Logie Coldstone in Aberdeenshire is home to the little known Poldhu Wells. The granite-lined mineral springs of Poldhu Wells were once believed to have curative properties and were, for a long period, a popular attraction for those seeking healing waters to cure them of most ills. The wells are mentioned in the *First Statistical Account of Scotland* (1791-99) and are described as "a mineral spring in the parish of Logie Coldstone, a little to the south of the church, called Poldow, which in Gaelic, signifies 'a Black Pool', the water of which some years ago was much and successfully used for scorbutic and gravelish disorders". By the Second Statistical Account (1834-1845) interest appears to have somewhat waned and the wells were said to be "occasionally resorted to by some for the benefit of their health, and by others for amusement". Gradually interest in the Poldhu Wells appears to have largely become confined to those living in the immediate locality. The Great Gale of 1953 caused widespread damage across Scotland and the woodland around Logie Coldstone and Poldhu Wells was devastated when the violent storms brought down the trees around the site and with time, a rhododendron thicket enveloped the wells and hid them from the sight of the casual observer. Over the next fifty-five years or so an accumulation of leaf mould and silt blocked the drainage outlets from the wells.

Poldhu Wells, Logie Coldstone

In recent years however, interest in the historic site has been revived following the chance discovery by members of the Cromar History Group of a 1912 postcard showing a vintage photograph of the Poldhu Wells. Following this discovery, the group decided they wanted to try and return the wells to their original condition. During 2008, and with the help of Cairngorm National Park, Craigmyle Estate plus funding from the Adopt a Monument Fund, they removed the overgrown vegetation, dug drains and refurbished the stonework. A new path was also laid between the two wells and a new bridge replaced the decayed Victorian structure. In this modern age, it may well be that these quite delightful, natural mineral springs no longer have curative properties attributed to them, but they are certainly well worth seeking out if only for a well-deserved foot bath at the end of a day's walking in the area.

Alongside the more traditional sporting pursuits, modern day visitors to Aboyne can engage in outdoor activities undreamt of by their forebears. Off road four-by-four experiences, Deeside Way walking tours and wildlife safaris vie with artistic and cultural activity for the tourist pound. Aboyne Highland Games, now into its 153rd year, the Aboyne and Deeside Festival and the Active Aboyne Festival complement the visitors experience of visiting what is in effect a Victorian country resort elevated to Twenty-first century status. When the

Deeside railway line finally closed in 1966 the old station buildings were retained and converted into shops and business units. Even the old rail tunnel running from the station under the town centre found an innovative new use as an underground rifle range. Although the rail link to Ballater has gone, probably for good, a nostalgic nod towards the steam age has been retained at Aboyne's Boat Inn where a scale model toy steam engine runs regular scheduled services between the lounge and the public bar. The experience is quite surreal, especially after a pie and a pint.

3
ALFORD - HOME OF THE ABERDEEN ANGUS

Boasting no less than three museums, a heritage railway plus Aberdeenshire's very own dry ski slope, the town of Alford, population 2180 and increasing, offers both locals and visitors a varied and unique range of attractions. A commuter town, with some sixty percent of the working population travelling to work elsewhere, Alford's economy, as is the case with many Aberdeenshire towns, depends heavily on the oil and gas industry closely followed by agriculture, forestry and tourism. With the imposing Kildrummy Castle plus a fairy-tale Craigievar Castle on the doorstep, Alford in high season is a tourist Mecca. Add to the mix the Grampian Museum of Transport, Alford Railway Museum and Alford Heritage Museum and it is easy to see why the town is popular both with visitors and folk intent on a bit of serious nostalgia.

Aberdeenshire Council's 2013 Marr Profile suggested a ten-year 7.1 percent population growth rate for Alford, some two percent lower than the then projected Aberdeenshire average. However, with developments such as the new Alford Community Campus, a Public-Private Partnership inhabiting the town's Greystone Road, that growth figure now seems conservative. The new £37 million campus was opened in 2015 and replaced the overstretched Alford Academy and Alford Primary Schools. Catering for 325 primary and 640 secondary students drawn from a 600 square mile catchment area stretching from the Lecht to the villages of Dunecht and Echt, the flagship "community hub" project features state of the art facilities including theatre, community café, library and swimming pool. A dance studio, sports hall and all-weather playing field complete the picture with substantial new-build housing development taking shape nearby. Alongside its three museums - farming, transport and railway - the town boasts a curling club and a heritage narrow gauge railway named the Alford Valley Railway. Nowadays, Alford Valley Railway operates as a narrow-gauge line running through Haughton Country Park. The line, maintained and operated by volunteers, was opened in 1980 utilising salvaged equipment from the New Pitsligo peat moss railway.

Vale of Alford Curling Club has played several local ponds during its long history including the now infilled Law's Dam, near the public hall and the Duke's Peel at Haughton Country Park. The present pond in Murray Park was purchased by the club in February 1930 and the *Aberdeen Journal* recorded that "Thanks to King Frost ... the pond at Haughton was officially opened with a hot lunch being served on the ice." The club nowadays sports a new custom-built clubhouse, the original having burned down in 2016, and features rare remnants of Aberdeen Corporation Tramways, in the form of ten cast iron tramline power-standards. Purchased in 1960 they are still in use today to floodlight mid-winter bonspiels.

Vale of Alford curling pond (showing the old clubhouse before the fire)

In the July of 1896 the folk of Alford witnessed the arrival, by train, of what was perhaps the first motor car to be driven down Alford's Main Street. A new Daimler Motor Horseless Carriage had arrived in town. The Locomotive Act of 1865 had recently been amended to permit motoring speeds of up to a giddy twelve miles per hour and the requirement for a man with a warning flag to accompany the new horseless carriages was removed. These changes spurred a dramatic increase in car ownership amongst those who saw the benefits of switching from horse drawn to liquid fuel powered transport. The four-seater Daimler had seemingly been purchased by a Strathdon doctor direct from the factory in Germany and was delivered to Alford by Daimler chief engineer Otto Meyer. The *Aberdeen Journal* the commented on the vehicle's "easy running and the control the driver had over it."

Grampian Transport Museum, the largest of Alford's three museums, opened in 1983. Exhibits include Billy Connolly's famous 'Boom Low Rider Motor-Trike', as used in the comedian's "World Tour of England, Ireland and Wales" plus an eye-watering collection of cars, motor cycles, steam transport, horse drawn vehicles and military vehicles. Past displays have included Pop Icons which showcased pop culture from the 1960s onwards. Besides the iconic blue painted Dr Who Tardis, which sits at the museum entrance, Pop Icons featured a genuine BBC Dalek, a Lambretta SX200 scooter plus one of the very first BMC Minis to roll off the Longbridge production line.

A Sinclair C5, one of only 12,000 produced at the Hoover assembly plant at Merthyr, completed the iconic line-up. Popularly thought to have been powered by a vacuum cleaner motor, the 'Hoover Hedgehog' as it came to be affectionally known was never a commercial success. With a top speed of only fifteen miles per hour Clive Sinclair's electric low-rider in some ways heralded a return to the days when a servant bearing a red warning flag was required by law to walk ahead of road vehicles; except of course the flag in the C5's case was a pole-mounted Hi Vis version.

The museum is also home to an early Twentieth century Automobile Association sentry box. Aside from museum examples, there are apparently just seven roadside AA boxes left in the entirety of Scotland with perhaps a further fourteen in the remainder of the UK. Wales has just the one. Once commonplace, these tiny buildings were originally constructed to shelter road patrols from the weather as they went about their business fixing early motor vehicles and saluting passing Automobile Association members. Eventually in the 1920s telephones were installed and for an annual fee, subscribers were issued keys and a shiny bumper badge to let people know that they belonged to an exclusive club. Early patrolmen drove motor-bike and sidecar combinations and wore jodhpurs and military style leather coats. And as any biker knows, there is no such thing as waterproof riding gear so goodness knows how they managed to do the job in all weathers never mind having to salute the members as they rode around the place. Mind you, a failure to salute was often a signal that a police speed patrol was in the area so at least they had a ready excuse in case of complaints by members who had forgotten that alongside fixing breakdowns, an early tenet of the organisation was to "Protect the interests of pioneer motorists against police persecution!" There were maybe around a thousand of these boxes in service originally, but by 2002 they had become redundant due mainly to the widespread use of mobile phones.

In 1645 Alford played host to what was perhaps the Marquis of Montrose's easiest victory of the Scottish Civil War. Following his defeat of Sir John Hurry's forces at Auldearn in early May 1645, Montrose had confronted a Covenanting army under Lieutenant-General William Baillie near Keith but had declined to engage due to what he judged to be an impregnable defensive position. At Alford, Montrose took up positions on Gallows Hill overlooking Boat of Forbes, a ford on the River Don. Placing most of his troops out of sight on the reverse slope of the hill, he exposed a small force on the crest in order to encourage Baillie's forces to advance. As expected, they took the bait and Montrose, who held the high ground sprang his trap. Accounts of casualties vary wildly with some sources suggesting improbably that some seven hundred Covenanters perished for the loss of a mere dozen of Montrose's force. In a curious twist of fate, Thomas Watt, great grandfather of steam engineer James Watt fought on the losing side. There is a small monument to the battle in the car park on Donside Road and a broadsword found on the battlefield was for many years on exhibition in Aberdeen's Marischal Museum.

In June 1878 the somewhat ponderously titled farming journal *The North British Agriculturist* published an article honouring Scotland's 'cattle king', a Mr William McCombie of Tillyfour who had, the previous Sunday, carried off top honours for livestock at the Paris Exposition Universelle; better known perhaps as the third Paris World's Fair.

> "This is indeed a proud week for Tillyfour and for the polled Angus or Aberdeen breed of cattle … Mr William McCombie having been adjudged the £100 prize for the best group of cattle, bred by exhibitor and reared out of France" ran the text of the article. "Mr McCombie's successful group numbered six animals … indeed every black polled animal has a ticket of some kind!"

The pedigree cattle breeder from Alford was in good company. The likes of Thomas Edison and Alexander Graham Bell were in attendance to demonstrate advances in communication technology, and the very latest industrial designs filled the giant exhibition halls. Steam ploughs and ice making machines vied with monoplanes and electric arc lamps for the attention of the thirteen million or so visitors to the exhibition. With the notable exception of Germany, which had until 1871 been at war with France and was not invited to exhibit, all of the industrialised countries of the world descended on the French capital to showcase the very best in design and seek out the very latest industrial innovations. Alongside the industrial exhibition halls, the 66-acre central Paris site featured showrings for the judging of the very best in European livestock and the jurors who judged McCombie's prize beasts took almost three days to rank the 1700 cattle, 825 sheep and 380 pigs entered for the various stock competitions.

William McCombie was by then quite used to exhibition success with a track record of wins occupying seventeen pages in the 1875 edition of his book *Cattle and Cattle Breeders*. Gold medals, competition cups and cash prizes came his way by the dozen and by the time of his death in 1880 he had become widely recognised as the "great deliverer of the polled race", a reference to the fact that pure bred Aberdeen Angus beasts are entirely devoid of horns. His success in the show-ring was down to both careful management of his breeding programme plus a flair for publicity on a grand scale. That great showman Buffalo Bill Cody would have admired the man's ability to both create and capitalise on international headlines. His Tillyfour bred bull Black Prince for example was invited to an audience with Queen Victoria at Windsor Royal Farm in recognition of his successive wins at Smithfield and Birmingham Fat Stock Shows. When the animal was finally retired in around 1867, McCombie presented the monarch with a 90kg Baron of Beef, sufficient to feed sixty people, from the carcase. A year or so later when the Queen travelled to Alford from Balmoral Estate to inspect the Tillyfourie herd she was surprised to meet Black Prince again. McCombie had retained the animals head which now hung stuffed and in a prominent position above his dining table. The story, possibly apocryphal, still resonates amongst aficionados of the breed.

The Aberdeen Angus breed has origins from long before William McCombie; indeed, the herd book, or 'bible' of the breed, records Hugh Watson's bull Old Jock from Keillor of Newtyle in Angus as the originator

William McCombie of Tillyfour

of the bloodline we still see today. McCombie is however widely regarded as the great improver of the breed and a life size statue of his legacy stands on the southern approach to Alford in the form of Jeremy-Eric, a Kemnay bred prize winning bull from the 1990s. Unveiled by the Prince of Wales and the late Queen Mother, in perhaps her last Scottish public engagement, artist David Annand's bronze statue of the bull was cast at Edinburgh's Powderhall foundry and is a fitting reminder of the role played by William McCombie in making the town of Alford famous as the home of the Aberdeen Angus. Local preparations for the Paris Exhibition had involved major upgrading of the French railway network and it is fair to assume that McCombie's prize winners travelled in some comfort to Paris by train before alighting at the delightfully named Gare du Champ de Mars, near the site of the present-day Eiffel Tower.

In sharp contrast, the Alford Valley Railway Line linking Alford with Aberdeen had less romantic origins. Built originally to facilitate the export of granite from local quarries such as those at Kemnay and Tillyfourie and the importation of manure via Aberdeen docks, the 16-mile-long spur line opened in 1859. Passenger traffic ended in 1950 and the line finally closed in 1966. As is the case with many settlements in the North East, the railway was instrumental in both growing the existing settlement and re-locating the town centre near the rail head.

There are local tales, possibly apocryphal, of travellers in pre-railway times asking the way to Alford only to be told that they were in the place already! When the railway came everything changed. By the late Nineteenth century Aberdeenshire was producing over 300,000 tons of granite per year and towns such as Alford, which had not benefited much from the cutting of the Inverurie to Aberdeen canal, found a new prosperity with quarried Tillyfourie stone being exported by rail and then ship for use in the likes of London's Thames Embankment, Tower Bridge and His Majesty's Theatre Aberdeen. Dressed Tillyfourie stone even found its way into the piers of the Forth Bridge.

Aberdeenshire writer Norman Harper has a take on it and advises that the original Alford Valley line between Kintore Junction and the Alford terminus involved the steam engines making long and often painfully slow journeys up the steep incline between Whitehouse and Tillyfourie. His mother recalls that some local wag had scrawled "Please do not pick the daisies while the train is in motion!" on the carriage wall. Worse still, Norman can still recall the tale of a railway guard's infamous full volume shout to those travelling on to Alford from Kintore which sounded remarkedly like "Kintore Junction! Change here for AaaFart!" But obviously Norman might just have misheard the expletive.

4
BALLATER – CAPITAL OF ROYAL DEESIDE

Bradshaw's edition of his *Descriptive Railway Hand-Book of Great Britain and Ireland* for 1863 describes Ballater as "the Tunbridge Wells and Keswick of Aberdeenshire, where people go to take the waters." He was of course referring to the Pannanich Wells on the outskirts of the settlement. Medical dissertations of the time recommended the use of mineral spring water in the treatment of diseases of the glands including "the Scurvy, Jaundice, Leprosy and the Glandular Consumption" and intense debate erupted amongst learned men as to the efficacy of spring water versus sea water in the curing of the sick. Some took to verse. Reverend Dr John Ogilvie, minister at Midmar, penned the following lines in 1795:

"I've seen the sick to health return
I've seen the sad forget to mourn
I've seen the lame their crutches burn
And loup and fling at Pannanich

I've seen the auld seem young and frisky
Without the aid of ale or whisky
I've seen the dullest hearts grow brisky
At blithesome, helpful Pannanich."

The curative qualities of Pannanich Wells had been known locally for centuries, but had first attracted national attention in around 1760 when a local Tullich woman by the name of Isabella Michie began bathing in the waters there. She had been suffering from Scrofula – a tuberculosis of the lymphatic glands – also known as the Kings Evil, so called because of a popular belief that the sovereign's touch could effect a cure. Indeed, monarchs including Edward the Confessor and Louis XV of France reportedly "touched" hundreds of victims at a time in the course of grand ceremonies designed to show that the sovereign's right to rule was God-given and that divine intervention in the affairs of man came via the Royal palms. There was little likelihood however that Isabella had been touched by royalty so her recovery, from what was an often-fatal disease, was put down to the curative properties of the Pannanich spring water and word spread like wildfire.

Pannanich Wells

The Ballater of 1760 was however not quite ready to cope with the influx of visitors. In fact, it largely consisted of bleak empty moorland with few dwellings or indeed creature comforts for the visitor. The railways were not to arrive until 1866 and the road system was quite primitive lacking even a bridge over the Dee. Deeside landowner Francis Farquharson of Monaltrie became an unlikely prime mover in the development of the wells as a hub for health tourism. He had fought on the losing side at Culloden and was subsequently taken to London's New Gaol at Southwark in an overcrowded prison ship where, alongside the majority of Jacobite officers, he was condemned to be executed. In November 1746, just days before his scheduled hanging, he was reprieved following the granting of a petition for clemency. Exiled for 20 years, he returned to Ballater in 1766 and began improvements designed to provide employment and prosperity for the area. Impressed by Isabella's miracle cure he built the granite facings which to this day grace the well heads at the upper and lower Pannanich Wells and also set about the construction of lodgings and bath houses to accommodate the needs of the new health tourism industry. As the wells grew in popularity so Ballater grew in stature.

By 1851 the population of the Parishes of Glenmuick, Tullich and Glengairn was recorded at a combined 1,984 with Ballater comprising much of the total. Following the purchase of the Balmoral Estate by the Royal Family in 1848 and the provision of modern transport infrastructure it had reached 2,160 by 1871. The 2011 Census records 1533 inhabitants within the town boundaries. The old ferry crossing the Dee linking Pannanich to Ballater quickly proved inadequate and the first of several bridges was built in 1783 at a cost of £1700. The present bridge dates from 1885 and, opened by Queen Victoria, is the fourth to be built on the site, two previous bridges having been washed away in floods. With the arrival of the Deeside Railway at Aboyne in 1859 and its subsequent extension to Ballater in 1866, tourists seeking the cures offered at the wells and those seeking out the romance of the highlands arrived in droves. Tour companies, such as Thomas Cook, began to offer package holidays and Ballater capitalised on both its Royal and its spa reputation.

In Queen Victoria's time the Royal Train journey from Windsor to Ballater took some two days and involved travelling a total of 589 miles at speeds ranging from 25mph at night to perhaps 35mph during daylight hours. The locomotives of the day were quite capable of reaching speeds in excess of 60mph however the queen had stipulated lower speeds due to her anxiety about the safety of this new mode of transport. In the decades following Prince Albert's death at Windsor in 1861, the grieving monarch's constant companion John Brown was more than once seen on the footplate of the lead engine advising the driver that "Her Majesty cannot gain sleep due to the rumbling of the locomotive at too much speed." The Deeside Railway closed in 1966 and tourists nowadays depend, yet again, on the turnpike road system established in the mid-Nineteenth century. With an estimated figure of 1.3 million tourists visiting Aberdeenshire annually, Ballater has geared up to cope with the influx. Alongside the traditional grocer, butcher and baker, with several holding Royal Warrants, the town sports a wide range of facilities for the tourist.

With over 100 seasonal stances plus 76 touring stances, the Ballater Caravan Park provides a base for exploring the Cairngorms National Park. The caravan park and the adjacent Ballater Golf Club share the distinction of each having had a tree planted by Prince Charles in recent times although neither business sports a 'By Royal Appointment' logo. Bryn Wayte of Deeside Books, an independent bookshop frequented by the Royals, recently commented on the town's dependence on the seasonal trade. "Ballater depends heavily on the tourist trade. In season the visitors provide a steady trade but in winter things go quiet and many businesses struggle with the seasonality of tourism." Bryn's Bridge Street shop specializes in rare and out-of-print books covering topics such as Scottish history, royalty and railway history. With over 10,000 titles available both within the shop and online, including facsimile reprints of long out of print titles as such as McConnochie's *Lochnagar and Ben Muich Dhui & His Neighbours: A Guide to the Cairngorm Mountains* he is perhaps better equipped than many local businesses to survive the winter downturn in visitor numbers, but he is not complacent:

> "The Ballater business association regularly looks for ways to increase the off-season footfall" said Bryn "alongside the summer events such as Victoria Week and the Ballater Highland Games, we now host Ballater Winter Festival in the last week of November."

Perhaps however the most iconic of Ballater's modern day enterprises is The Deeside Water Company. Using mineral water bottled direct from the historic Pannanich Wells Springs and exporting across the globe to countries including Japan, Switzerland and Italy, the enterprise is a source of pride for joint owner Martin Simpson. "Following years of research to confirm the water's quality, purity and properties, hand bottling started in May 1996, a modern bottling line was installed in 2005 and a new warehouse built in 2007, but the charm of the water and its location remain. The company retains its core family values and respect for this gift from nature" says Martin who has recently begun exporting to Russia and also supplies Prince Charles's *Duchy Originals* brand. "Pannanich Spring Water is much more than just mineral water" he says, "When you consider that there was virtually nothing here up until 1760, the springs with their proven health-giving properties made Ballater what it is today."

Author John Buchan once described Walter Scott's 1814 novel *Waverley* as a "riot of fun and eccentricity", an opinion not shared by some commentators who have been known to describe Scott's romanticised tale of wild tartan clad Highlanders, castles and Jacobite insurrection as somewhat dour and humourless. Notwithstanding this, Sir Walter was charged with organising festivities for the 1822 visit of King George IV to Scotland in which "the garb of old Gaul", the kilt and the tartan, featured prominently. The Royal romance with the Highlands had been kindled and in 1848, following some three years of hard-nosed negotiation, Queen Victoria purchased the run-down Balmoral Estate and the Royal connection with Ballater began in earnest. By 1856 the new Balmoral Castle was complete, the original having been completely demolished, and Victoria's "dear paradise in the Highlands" was good to go. The original Balmoral has often been derided as an architectural confusion replete with a jumble of styles complete with a roofline resembling a vast collection of magician's hats.

The new Balmoral, designed by Prince Albert, is similarly odd. The rooms, despite their delightful tartan themed décor, were criticised by some visitors as being tiny, damp and quite cluttered. Lord Clarendon was one such critic. He famously wrote, in 1856, that 'Thistles are in such abundance that they would rejoice the heart of a donkey.' Marie Mallet writes in the 1890s about the "dreadful food and footmen reeking of whisky" while guests often complained that Victoria, a great lover of the outdoors, "had the windows open while we were at dinner". Some guests also objected to the "whisky fuelled evenings of merriment and dancing around piles of newly slain stags", as depicted in Carl Haag's painting *Evening at Balmoral*. Others, such as Liberal Prime Minister Campbell Bannerman, simply hated the place "It is the funniest life conceivable. Like a convent. We meet at meals, breakfast, lunch, dinner and when we have finished each is off to his cell." However, at least the roofline was simplified and the number of architectural styles reduced to a trickle. The 50,000 acres of the Royal Balmoral Estate attracted the good and the great to Deeside to hunt, shoot and fish and in consequence Ballater flourished.

Alongside the re-building of Balmoral, Albert and Victoria commissioned a set of military barracks in Ballater to house the Royal Guard. Anecdotally, these barracks were said to have been built in error to a design intended for use in India. A military architect, runs the story, got the plans mixed up and somewhere in the former British Raj there sits the genuine Deeside Barracks built as intended but on completely the wrong continent. But this, like many such tales probably has no basis in truth. Structurally the buildings are constructed with thick walls and steeply inclined roofs more suited to snowy Deeside winters than to the heat of the North West Frontier. It's a bit like the old chestnut that Glasgow's Kelvingrove Museum was built back to front because someone, a drunken architect who discovering his mistake flung himself from the roof of the building, drew the plans upside down! For the curious, Kelvingrove was built to face the 1901 Great Exhibition site and not Dumbarton Road and the architect got it right first time around and did not throw himself to his death!

The Victoria Barracks, Ballater

Alongside the Royal patronage there were hordes of tourists who flocked to the town by road and rail in the hope of both experiencing the beauty and romance of Sir Walter Scott's tartan Highlands and doing a bit of Royal spotting, a practice which continues to this day. Among Victoria's many visitors were dignitaries such as Robert Peel, Benjamin Disraeli and William Gladstone as well as a wide selection of the crowned heads of Europe and beyond. Perhaps the most infamous, aside from Kaiser Wilhelm II, was Tsar Nicholas II who with his wife Alexandra Feodorovna, grand-daughter of Victoria, visited Balmoral in autumn 1896. He didn't know it yet, but a decade or so later he was to become the last Tsar and along with his family was to meet a bloody end in the course of a new political order which swept the Romanovs from power.

According to the Aberdeen broadsheets, "The heaven's opened as in tears" when the Tsar alighted from the Royal train at Ballater Station and an honour guard of 100 men of the Black Watch stationed at the town's Victoria Barracks stood to attention in drenching rain to welcome the man whom the Aberdeen Town Council of the time seemingly loved to hate.

A regiment of sabre-wielding mounted cavalry accompanied the Royal coach on its journey through Ballater then on to Balmoral, the government of the time fearing an assassination attempt which might lead them into a war with Russia. Leon Trotsky would later refer to the Tsar as "more awful than all the tyrants of ancient and modern history" so the council may not have been too far out in their assessment. Aberdeen's *Bon Accord Magazine* reported "When the Tsar is at home, we do not hesitate to call him a tyrant. Then in heaven's name, why then, when he visits his grand-mother-in-law should we play the hypocrite and fete he whom we at other times curse."

Some years later, on the night of the sixteenth of July 1918, in the small basement room of a mansion in the Russian town of Yekaterinburg, the locals agreed and shot the man dead along with his entire family including Queen Victoria's favourite granddaughter Alexandra who had in fact been well liked in Ballater. The Tsar had fallen and a Royal child was dead. But Victoria's country retreat in the Highlands was still good to go. An ermine laden Sir Walter Scott and his re-imagined plaid and his Anglicised German Geordies had made their mark.

5
BANCHORY – GATEWAY TO ROYAL DEESIDE

Known as the Gateway to Royal Deeside, Banchory has long been a favourite for those seeking escape from the bustle of Aberdeen whether as day trippers or residents. With a population estimated at 7,200 in 2016 and with house prices then around 35 percent above the Aberdeenshire average plus a mere five percent of housing stock in Council Tax Band A, it is clear that Banchory is an affluent town, a fact confirmed by local estate agents who point to an extremely buoyant housing market.

The Banchory Community Action Plan identifies the introduction of the toll roads and the coming of the railway as significant in terms of the local economy, but points to the fact that until the 1970s the town's population remained under 3,500. The exploitation of North Sea oil and gas appears to have been the catalyst for the dramatic increase in both population and development over the past forty or so years. Employers such as Cordiners Sawmills, energy firm PGL Senergy, plus award winning hotels such as Raemoir House provide local jobs but some forty-three percent of the town's working population continue to commute to Aberdeen and beyond each day. In the tourist season, which in lower Deeside is all year round, Banchory more than compensates for the vacuum left by the commuting classes and is often full to bursting point with busloads of tourists from all parts of the world seeking a taste of Deeside heritage.

When novelist and playwright Somerset Maugham published his short story *Sanatorium* in 1928 few residents in Banchory, or indeed anywhere else in Deeside, would have been in much doubt about the identity of the central character Ashenden who relates the tale of secret agent Major John Templeton, slowly dying of pulmonary tuberculosis in a Scottish sanatorium. The plot owes its origins to Maugham's own experiences both as a spy and as a patient at Nordrach-on-Dee Sanatorium on the outskirts of the town. Ashenden is of course Maugham. Alongside his literary endeavours, Maugham worked for British Intelligence and had been involved in plots to stem the outbreak of the Russian Revolution. A secret army of spooks spread tentacles throughout Russia and Asia. Dark schemes to assassinate the likes of Lenin were hatched and a young Arthur Ransome of *Swallows and Amazons* fame was funded by a budding MI6 to wine and dine and finally seduce Trotsky's secretary in a bid to derail the red revolution through pillow-talk. A young Churchill encouraged the sabotage recording in his diary that "we need to strangle the Bolshevik state at birth" before going on to suggest the use of poison gas to exterminate the leading proponents of communism once and for all. The UK security services were, according to Giles Milton, (author of a political history of the times titled *Russian Roulette*) spending the equivalent of three million pounds a month to support the pro-capitalist White Russians and finance a counter revolution. Perhaps it's no wonder that even today, a modern-day Putin views western democracy with deep suspicion.

For his part, and while working as a foreign correspondent and spy in the Russian city of Petrograd in early 1917, Maugham famously caught what he termed "a touch of tuberculosis". A lung specialist recommended a curative stay in a sanatorium and, in November 1917, he booked himself into the Nordrach-on-Dee Sanatorium where he remained until spring 1918 writing *Sanatorium* during his stay and completing his play *Home and Beauty*. Following a second stay during the winter of 1918-19 Maugham was discharged with a clean bill of health.

Glen O'Dee Sanatorium (before the fire)

Better known as Glen O'Dee Hospital, the Banchory Nordrach Sanatorium was founded as a private residential clinic for the treatment of tuberculosis by Dr David Lawson, a local physician who had visited the German Nordrach-in-Baden in order to study the treatment methods employed. The facility opened on Christmas Eve 1900 offering treatment for up to fifty wealthy private patients according to the system developed by Dr Otto Walther. Employing a combination of fresh forest air, complete rest plus a punishing so called "overfeeding diet", involving intake of up to four kilograms of food each day, the Nordrach regime quickly caught on amongst the rich and famous and Nordrach sanatoria sprang up across Europe with the Banchory facility being one of the first to employ X-ray techniques in the diagnosis of lung complaints.

As the incidence of tuberculosis declined during the 1920s, patient numbers declined too, and in 1928 the Nordrach sanitorium became a fashionable hotel, then in 1939 a military hospital. Latterly the building provided care for the elderly before its closure in 1998. A modern purpose-built NHS Grampian, home for the care of the elderly now occupies part of the hospital site in Corsee Road; while the original wooden building, once on the Buildings at Risk Register, stood empty, decaying and neglected until October 2016 when it was completely destroyed by fire. The Deeside climate had been a deciding factor in the decision to site Nordrach-on-Dee in Banchory. Dr Walther's treatment regime required fresh mountain air, low ozone levels and low rainfall. All of which Banchory, sitting in the lee of the Hill of Fare, offers. However, favourable climate is not the first thing to spring to mind when recalling the work of Joseph Farquharson. Born in 1846 and heir to the family estate at nearby Finzean, he is popularly associated with atmospheric paintings of sheep-littered winter landscapes.

Affectionately known locally as The Painting Laird, he studied landscape painting under French Master Carolus-Duran, a contemporary of French Modernist Édouard Manet. In the Paris of the 1880s he became well acquainted with the Barbizan School of Painting. In warm summer weather, Barbizan artists ventured outdoors to paint directly from nature and canvasses would typically be left on site, often for weeks at a time, until completion. On his return to Deeside, Joseph Farquharson adapted this *Plein Air*, or open air, technique for use at northern latitudes. Having designed and built a series of mobile painting huts, complete with thick glazed panels and wood stove, he would sit in reasonable comfort painting Deeside landscapes in almost any weather conditions, returning to part-completed work as and when favourable light and weather allowed.

It was his mastery of snowbound winter landscapes, often including flocks of sheep, which caught the popular imagination. Well known paintings such as his 1883 Christmas card classic *The Joyless Winter Day*, featured a shepherd tending his flock in a raging Deeside blizzard presented Farquharson with technical challenges such as the fact that sheep cannot easily be persuaded to stand still. To solve this difficult problem, Farquharson commissioned a flock of life size plaster sheep from Monymusk born craftsman William Wilson of Kelly's Cats fame, and used these to mark out the positions of the original live subjects in order to preserve the scene as the work progressed. Surprisingly perhaps there is no record of a commission for a plaster shepherd. Seemingly it was quite common at one time for folk, in and around Banchory, to stumble across his painting huts complete with a dozen or so silent and unmoving sheep neatly arranged and awaiting the artist's return.

Popular Scottish artist Jack Vettriano was once quoted as saying that whoever had rejected his paintings for the Royal Academy should "Go and live in a cave." Joseph Farquharson might well have agreed. Despite financial success as an artist during his lifetime and election to the Royal Academy in 1900 he was often sneeringly referred to by fellow artists as Frozen Mutton Farquharson. But despite the sneers his reputation grew and Aberdeen Art Gallery hosted a retrospective of his work in 1985, the fiftieth anniversary of his death. Sadly, his home and studio were destroyed by fire in the 1950s and it seems that the plaster sheep may have perished in the blaze along with a good deal of his artistic work.

Another well kent local character was a lad by the name of Blind Johnnie Moir. In the early years of the Twentieth century, he ran a small grocer shop just down from the old tollhouse. Alongside selling bread and essential supplies, Johnnie wrote verse and was perhaps for a time Banchory's answer to William McGonagall. However instead of penning broadsheets telling of Tay Bridge Disasters and the like, Johnnie maintained a chalkboard outside his shop on which he wrote about local events such a farmer's lost sheep, a local concert party or on one occasion about the local Coal Fund Annual Charity Concert. When local news was scarce, he would promote his wares on the board in verse:

> "Oranges, oranges, luscious and large,
> Oranges, oranges, moderate in charge!"

Reputedly almost completely blind, his output was prolific and new work would appear on a daily basis much to the amusement of his customers. Seemingly, horizontal lengths of string were stretched across the blackboard to keep his chalk hand steady. One immortal stanza reflected on the shop's location beside the local river and ran something like:

> "Hard by Feugh Bridge,
> A little store is kept by one not less than Moir,
> Who shows on blackboards by his door,
> A varied wealth of rhyming lore!"

Then there is the bizarre story of Banchory's eccentric inventor Fleein' Geordie, a pioneer Scottish aviator and designer of the steam driven Davidson Air-Car. Born in 1858 and fourth son of the Laird of Inchmarlo, George Louis Outram Davidson was just one of many early aviation pioneers who in the years prior to the Wright Brothers successful 1903 manned flight experimented, at some personal risk, with heavier than air flying machines. Weighing in at almost eight tons, George's Air-Car concept was certainly ambitious. Between 1883 and 1897 he carried out local testing of early and simpler monoplane designs culminating in a well-publicised flight attempt in Banchory's Burnett Park. In front of assembled press and curious onlookers he took off in a scaled down model of his monoplane only to crash almost immediately. Unhurt, he continued to develop his theory that if birds could fly, man should surely be able to do likewise. An improved version of the Air-Car, renamed the Gyropter, was built in America where George's family had mining interests, but following a disastrous steam boiler explosion in 1906, the project was finally abandoned. He died at Inchmarlo Cottage, Banchory in 1939 aged eighty having lived to see his predictions that airplanes would fly cross the Atlantic and be used to "drop dynamite on our enemies" come true.

Another well-known resident of the town was physiotherapist Sheila Ferres (1923-2017). An accomplished water colourist she contracted polio in her early thirties but overcame this and went on to be recognised as the UK's eldest working physiotherapist during a career which spanned some 75 years. In her autobiography *A Life of Giving*, which she co-wrote with Deeside author Jo Booth, she recalled her life's work with both the rich and famous, and the poor and downtrodden. Folk from the oppressed black suburbs of colonial Rhodesia came under her care and in later life she treated Royals including the late Princess Margaret the Countess of Snowdon.

A highlight described in her memoirs involved meeting and treating Nottinghamshire composer Eric Harrison Coates. Famous for his contribution to the musical score of the film *The Dambusters* and composer of the iconic *By the Sleepy Lagoon* signature tune for Desert Island Discs, Coates also penned occasional orchestral commissions for the Royal Family. Described by Sheila as a shy and retiring man, he would rarely allow visitors into his work space. For her however, he made an exception. "Very often as I was treating him" she writes "he would suddenly say 'Oh, just a minute' and he'd get up and walk next door to his music room. He'd sit down at his piano and I would hear him tinkling away there. Then he would come back and write something on his score and I would then recommence treating him." At the time Sheila treated Coates, he was working on a piece called *Elizabeth of Glamis* in honour of the then

Queen Elizabeth the Queen Mother. Many years later, Sheila recalled attending a concert at Glamis Castle during which the Coates piece was played to celebrate the 100th birthday of the Queen Mother in August of 2000. "It was one of the most moving experiences of my life" she writes "and brought back all those memories of him jumping up, going and adding this bit or that, and then coming back to continue his treatment."

Sheila was married, until his death in 1993, to Echt-born GP Dr Gordon Ferres. An avid hunter in his earlier days, her husband had spent some time living and working on the Indonesian island of Sumatra as a young rubber planter. "One of the things he liked to do" recalled Sheila, "was to go big-game hunting in the jungle." She recounts in chapter eleven of her autobiography how, alongside once being chased up a tree by an enraged elephant, her husband was on one occasion badly injured by an angry tiger. Seemingly the animal had been suspected of eating local villagers and when eventually cornered it lashed out and lacerated his leg with its front paws. There can't be that many folk hailing from Echt who can honestly claim to have been mauled by a tiger!

Surprisingly, given Banchory's position alongside the Royal Deeside Railway line, *Bradshaw's Railway Guide* makes only passing mention of the town. His army of researchers were obviously unimpressed both by the Royal patronage and by the constant flow of politicians and heads of state of Europe and Empire who passed through on their way to meet up with Victoria and Albert. Describing the town as "a small village on the banks of the Dee, at the confluence of the Feugh" Bradshaw was not, in 1863, to know that William Bridges Adams (1797-1872) inventor and locomotive engineer would in later years have a quirky but solid connection with the town. Best known for his patented Adams Axle, a radial axle design in use on railways in Britain up until the end of steam in 1968, and the 1842 invention of the railway fishplate (a small but important metal bar bolted to the ends of two rails to join them together), Adams was also the father of Hope Bridges Adams, first wife of Dr Otto Walther of Nordrach Sanatorium fame.

The railway line from Aberdeen reached Banchory in 1853 and was later extended to Aboyne and finally as far as Ballater in 1866. Although closed down during the 1960s, the stretch between Milton of Crathes and Banchory has experienced something of a revival in recent years due to the efforts of a group of committed volunteers comprising the Royal Deeside Railway Preservation Society. The hard work of restoring Deeside's Royal railway connection commenced in 2003 and there are ambitious plans to extend back into Banchory over the next few years. With a wide range of rolling stock plus both steam and diesel power units in regular use, the line has proved popular with both locals

Royal Deeside Railway Preservation Society

and tourists. Visitor numbers topped 13,000 in 2014 and the Society has taken to laying on special charter trains for events including fashion shows and film shoots. Easter weekend 2015 marked a first for the line in the form of an onboard wedding ceremony complete with mobile registrar and onboard champagne reception.

    No Deeside town would be complete without its castle and just east of Banchory and only a short walk from Milton of Crathes Railway Station lies Crathes Castle and Gardens. Dating from at least the 1550s and the ancestral home of the Burnett of Leys family, Crathes is a classic fairy tale pile complete with spiral staircases, magnificent Jacobean painted ceilings and of course a resident ghost. The original tower house comprises four storeys plus an attic but the building has been much extended over the centuries. One such extension is the two-storey Queen Anne Wing, an addition added by the Third Baronet of Leys, Sir Thomas Burnett (1656-1714) to accommodate his expanding family. Sir Thomas along with his wife Margaret produced a quite staggering twenty-one children in just twenty- two years! Briefly occupied by the Marquis of Montrose in 1644 during the Scottish Civil War, Crathes Castle was acquired by the National Trust for Scotland in 1951 and attracts well over 50,000 visitors each year.

    With its various Royal railway, Somerset Maugham and Davidson Air-Car connections what's not to like about Banchory? Mind you the notion of Joseph Farquharson's plaster sheep takes some getting used to.

6
BANFF – A DELIGHTFUL TOWN ON THE COAST

A recent conservation study commissioned by Aberdeenshire Council identified 234 Listed Buildings, including nineteen listed as Category A within the Banff Town Conservation Area. The 2012 report also highlighted the Scheduled Ancient Monuments of Duff House, Banff Castle and the town's Sixteenth century St. Mary's Churchyard as being particularly archaeologically sensitive. Architectural gems include the quirky Colleonard Doocot which sits somewhat uncomfortably amongst the new-builds at Banff's Doocot Park, the Market Arms on High Shore and the Category A listed Banff Harbour at Guthrie's Haven, nowadays better known as Banff Marina.

Welcome to Banff - the town that hanged Macpherson

The town is a treasure trove of architectural history and features many important buildings which even today would be familiar to the likes of Robert Burns and Dr Samuel Johnson, both of whom passed through during the latter part of the Eighteenth century. Essayist Dr Johnson visited in 1773 and on discovering that the Earl of Fife was not in residence at Duff House was forced to stay overnight at a local inn, an experience which he found quite unpleasant. His long-suffering travelling companion Boswell records that the grumpy Johnson struggled to open the windows in his room and on discovering that they had neither pulleys nor counterweights commented that "this wretched defect was general in the whole of Scotland ... the necessity of ventilating human habitation has not yet been found by our Northern neighbours".

Burns, by contrast, appears to have thoroughly enjoyed his 1787 visit to the coastal town. After breakfasting with the rector of Banff Academy, a linguist and distant acquaintance of Burns' friend and travelling companion William Nicol, he was treated to a tour of Banff guided by thirteen-year-old academy dux George Imlach who recalled many years later, in an article published in *Chambers Journal*, that the bard paid particular attention to the portraits of the exiled Stuarts in Duff House's great drawing room.

Inspired by local tales recounting the November 1700 execution of James Macpherson, possibly the last man to be hanged at Banff, Burns wrote the ballad *Macpherson's Farewell* thus immortalising the final hours of a notorious outlaw who was sentenced "to be taken to the Cross of Banff... to be hanged by the neck to the death, by the hand of the common executioner, upon Friday nixt ... betwixt the hours of two and three in the afternoon". Legend insists that Macpherson played a final lament on his fiddle before being turned off and popular belief insists that the town clock was put forward by fifteen minutes in order to silence forever the infamous fiddler before a pardon could arrive to reprieve the man. Perhaps the wretched outlaw had made the fatal mistake of playing out of tune. Whatever the truth of the matter, Burns was obviously quite taken by the tale:

> "And he took the fiddle intae baith o his hands and he brak it ower a stane
> Sayin, nay other hand shall play on thee when I am dead and gane
> The reprieve was comin ower the Brig o Banff tae set MacPherson free
> But they pit the clock a quarter afore, and they hanged him frae the tree."

Some claim that the clock that hanged Macpherson now graces the clock tower in Dufftown's High Street and a stringed instrument purporting to be his broken fiddle is seemingly preserved at the Clan Macpherson Museum at Newtonmore.

Birthplace of two of Scotland's most successful Nineteenth century sculptors, William Brodie (1815-1881) and John Rhind (1828-1892), Banff was historically an important centre for both gold and silversmithing. Banff Silver features in many collections including that of the National Museums of Scotland which has several examples including the Huntly Race Cup, a horse racing trophy made for the Duke of Gordon by William Scott of Banff around 1695. There are calls to revive the local silver-making industry and

Aberdeenshire Council recently completed a project to convert the derelict Meal Mill on Old Market Place, opposite the town's famous Spotty Bag Shop, into a silversmithing centre funded in part by a Heritage Lottery grant.

Bryan Angus is a visual artist based in Banff. Alongside his 2015 exhibition, Bright Coast Long Shadows at Duff House, he and artist wife Carla Angus were commissioned to produce a permanent installation inspired by the experiences of the local community for Banff's new Deveron Centre. Bryan's studio in the town's St Anns Terrace is the antithesis of William Lamb's (1893-1951) nowadays pristine studio, now a museum, at Montrose. South facing and busy, Bryan's work space is jam packed with equipment, materials, works in progress, empty coffee cups, lino shavings, pastel dust and what can only be described as the welcoming fug of oil paint. There is a rack, with drying paintings and some half-forgotten pastels that are surely part of a gestation period for the making of a picture; a process that can occasionally last a couple of years. Says Bryan "Its where I print, paint and draw. It's the year-round haven in my house that drags me into it every minute I can. Some artists try to work in a clean white space, but I can't imagine being that careful, or having that luxury of space. It must be something like the inside of my head." Often the messiest of minds produce the most memorable of images.

Just down the road from Bryan's studio and nowadays in the care of Historic Scotland, the grandiose Duff House was originally built for William Duff, First Earl of Fife (1696-1763). Completed in 1740 after five years of construction and to a design by William Adam, the Georgian mansion has undergone many changes during the last century. From early beginnings as a stately home, it became a luxury hotel, then a sanatorium for the "scientific treatment of disorders of nutrition excluding inebriation" and briefly a WW2 prisoner of war camp. Currently the building operates as a cultural and artistic hub governed by a unique partnership between Historic Scotland, The National Galleries of Scotland and Aberdeenshire Council. It attracts well over 18,000 visitors each year to a series of art exhibitions plus events including music, story-telling and lectures. In 1939 Duff House was requisitioned by the War Office and housed German prisoners of war. Tragically on the morning of the twenty-second of July 1940 a single German aircraft bombed the property killing a British guard and seven German prisoners. The stonework on the building's frontage still shows damage from the raid.

Banff witnessed many more tragic events related to the war. The Moray Firth coastline was frequently subjected to bombing raids from Luftwaffe planes based in Norway, shipping was attacked and air crashes of both friend and foe became regular occurrences. The flat nature of the coastal farmland made it ideal for the building of aerodromes. From Forres in the west to Peterhead in the east there were, at various times throughout the conflict, at least ten operational airfields home to both defensive and offensive air squadrons.

One of these was RAF Banff. Better known locally as Boyndie Airfield it opened in 1943 as a Flying Training Command Field. A fairly typical airfield for the time it had one long runway of about 1800 metres intersected by two shorter ones. Thirty-six aircraft dispersal areas, a control tower plus several large thirteen-bay aircraft hangers and an array of associated technical and administrative buildings completed the station's complement. At its peak it was manned and operated by around 3,200 RAF personnel. According to census data the population of Banff, just few years after the war in 1951, was a mere 3,357 in comparison. The 2011 Census records 4,082 inhabitants. On RAF leave days, the local police in Banff and at neighbouring Macduff were kept busy keeping a semblance of order as the population of both towns swelled to bursting point with high-spirited young men and women many of whom faced the spectre of imminent death in battle.

In September 1944, 248 Squadron RAF was transferred from England and the base was renamed RAF Banff Strike Wing Coastal Command. The air station was equipped with mainly Beaufighter and Mosquito fighter bombers and even today streets around the airfield perimeter reflect this history in the form of street names such as Beaufighter Road and Beaufighter Crescent. These long-range aircraft were armed with anti-shipping cannon and the daily routine involved attacking convoys off the Norwegian and Danish coastlines. The Strike Wing's primary mission was to disrupt German imports of iron ore and sink shipments of fish oil which was refined in the Lofoten Islands before being shipped south for use in the manufacture of explosives. At first light most days a single reconnaissance aircraft, often crewed by Norwegian airmen, took off from either Boyndie airfield or neighbouring RAF Dallochy to spot enemy convoys in the Norwegian fiords before calling in the affectionately named 'Ship Killers' to attack the cargo ships. Losses among aircrew were high with many dying in training accidents. Mid-air collisions and unexplained crashes were common and graveyards around the North East reflect this carnage in the form of war graves. In addition, a good many young men became combat casualties. In 1989 a memorial to the eighty or so aircrew killed in action during Banff Strike Wing's brief period of operation was unveiled on the Banff to Portsoy Road.

On a lighter wartime note, the sixteenth of August 1941 saw a lone German raider bomb Inverboyndie Distillery just outside Banff. Two bonded warehouses caught fire and despite the best efforts of the Banff fire brigade, the buildings were destroyed with the contents variously going up in flames or running off into a local burn. The German plane went on to machine-gun several local farms and local lore has it that geese from nearby Old Manse Farm became inebriated when they drank the whisky-laden water.

Before the onslaught of the coronavirus pandemic of 2020, VisitScotland estimates indicated that tourism in general contributed around £5.4 billion to the Scottish economy annually and a recent Scottish Marine Recreation and Tourism survey suggested that around £1.3 billion of that spend is on specialist activities. In days past Banff relied heavily on tourism and today little has changed. The fishing industry has long since migrated to neighbouring ports and the coastal harbour trade is also long gone although the Banff Marina remains busy and popular. Today the tourist pound is an important source of revenue for the town. Surfing, dolphin watching, golf, angling and sailing remain stalwarts of the local economy. Banff Links Caravan Site, Surf Scotland and the Duff House Royal Golf Club now compete for tourist cash.

Banff Marina

Banff can even boast a link to Hercules, the son of Zeus. Billed as 'Apollo the Scottish Hercules', Banff born strongman William Bankier (1870-1949) began his performing career at the tender age of twelve, when he ran off to join the circus. He got his big break at the age of fifteen during a spell working in a

Canadian circus. As the tour progressed and the strongman began to miss performances due to a love affair with the bottle, Bankier found himself taking over the lead spot. During his subsequent career he added wrestling, boxing and jujitsu to his repertoire and began to build an international reputation as a stunt man. In one of his most famous death-defying stunts, he lay prone while a car laden with volunteers from the audience drove over him. In another act he lifted a full-grown man with his right hand, juggled plates with his left while balancing on the back of a chair. Bankier went on to publish a bodybuilding guide entitled *Ideal Physical Culture: And the Truth about the Strong Man* and after his retirement from the stage he opened a gymnasium in London. Later he became a leading wrestling promoter and in 1919 was elected King Rat of the show business charity The Grand Order of Water Rats. Bankier is perhaps best remembered though for his Tomb of Hercules feat of strength in which he balanced a grand piano topped with an entire six-man orchestra plus a scantily clad dancer on his back. The Scottish Hercules died in 1949 in a Cheshire nursing home.

But the final word on Banff must surely come from a long-forgotten man by the name of Gordon Stables. A would-be poet and published author of perhaps as many as 130 adventure books for boys, Dr Gordon Stables (1837-1910) was in his later years the first Vice President of The Caravan Club and the author of a book catchily titled *The Cruise of the Land Yacht Wanderer* - an account his 1300-mile-long horse drawn caravan journey around Britain. Perhaps unfairly accused by critics as an author of difficult verse, Stables was unrepentant:

"Oh! Caledonia, stern and wild,
Nurse meet for a poetic child;
Land of brown heath and shaggy wood,
Land of the mountain and the flood."

One reviewer even went so far as to say that his entire writing was replete with "occasional attempts at elaborate description which are not very successful", the Aberchirder-born doctor and *Boys Own Paper* contributor, kept a diary of his horse-drawn tour. His two-ton 30ft caravan, described as "a shed on wheels complete with china cabinet", was drawn by a brace of horses whom he named Captain Cornflower and Polly Pea Blossom.

Despite the accusations of difficult prose, he certainly describes Banff in glowing terms "I have discovered Banff, it is by far and away the most delightful town on the coast … the scenery all round would delight the eyes of poet or artist." The days of the Land Yacht Wanderer are long past but the sentiment expressed by Dr Stables all those years ago remains valid. Banff is indeed a delightful town on the coast.

7
BRAEMAR – HIGHEST PARISH IN SCOTLAND

Braemar, probably the highest parish in Scotland, sits at the heart of the 4500-square kilometre Cairngorms National Park, the largest of Britain's fifteen national parks. With a total of 43 Munros, including five of the six highest mountains in Britain, on the very doorstep, the picturesque village is a natural base for both walkers and climbers. At some 1200 feet above sea level, Braemar Golf Club, founded in 1902, offers visitors the chance to play the highest eighteen-hole golf course in Scotland. Add to this the opportunities for mountain biking, hang-gliding, field sports such as shooting and salmon fishing, and winter sports including skiing and snowboarding, and it's not hard to understand why Braemar is a year-round tourist destination. Seemingly a consumptive Robert Louis Stephenson penned some dozen chapters of *Treasure Island* during an extended stay in the Highland village although the final pages were to be penned at Davos in the Swiss Alps where a high altitude sanitorium plied him with cold showers and freezing mountain air. The cottage he rented at in the village now functions as bed and breakfast establishment.

Welcome to Braemar - home of Treasure Island

Despite the lack of a rail link to the national rail network Braemar had, by the time of the Queen's death in 1901, become a favoured holiday destination. In the process, it had accumulated a housing surplus far in excess of the neighbouring resort towns of Ballater and Aboyne. Compared to the then Scottish average of 1.62 persons to a room, Braemar was at the time recorded as having 0.55 per room and had an impressive overall surplus of 916 rooms catering for the needs of a resident parish population of less than 600, a surplus almost certainly generated by second home ownership and visitor demand.

A survey commissioned in 2013 for the Marr Area Partnership highlighted Braemar's broad dependence on tourism and the Tartan Pound. The resulting Community Action Plan indicated an unmet demand for increased social housing to accommodate the vast army of seasonal workers required to cater for the annual influx of visitors. With an estimated 46 percent of local residents either working from home or self-employed within the retail and hospitality sectors, the local economy remains just as heavily dependent on the tourist pound as it was in Victorian times.

Today's resident population is around 580. However, in high season visitors far outstrip locals, with peaks of 16,000-plus on a typical Braemar Gathering weekend. Recorded as the oldest Friendly Society in Scotland, the Braemar Gathering attracted a record attendance in pre-Coronation 1952, when more than 28,000 spectators descended on the village. The railway never quite made it as far as Braemar. The line was seemingly surveyed but never laid much more than a hundred yards beyond Ballater Station. The travellers of old made the final few miles between the Station at Ballater and the Station at Braemar by coach. Indeed, the original Braemar Station building still sits to this day alongside the Invercauld Arms Hotel leading to a measure of confusion amongst hopeful visitors' intent on travelling by rail but unaware perhaps that the brightly painted clapper-board building, with its hoarding proclaiming "Great North of Scotland Railway", is nowadays a holiday let which was in past days simply the terminus for horse drawn livery coaches and latter day GNSR omnibuses. Nowadays most travellers make the seventeen-mile journey by car, or *in extremis* on foot. The Deeside Railway, such as it is nowadays, runs only for a mile from Milton of Crathes towards Banchory but cannot do much more than transport holidaymakers and tourists there and back at a leisurely 10mph. In Victorian times, things were very different on Deeside and you could steam up the valley at 60mph and for twenty miles or so before stopping at Ballater.

Nowadays, and by road, on the final approach into Braemar, the scrubby roadside silver birch alongside the River Dee gives way to Scots Pine and somefinely tinted purple heather. There are glimpses of soaring birds of prey including the odd buzzard and hen harrier, and an occasional red squirrel can be seen making a suicidal dash across the tarmac. Normally the traffic on the A93 is light, consisting mainly of tourists seeking a bit of Highland romance and a measure of good Scottish hospitality; plus a smattering of bikers and motor caravaners. But on the first Saturday of September each year everything changes as folk focus on the Braemar Gathering. 2015 was the bi-centenary of the founding of the event and 2016 saw the ninetieth birthday of the Chieftain of the Braemar Gathering, Her Majesty the Queen. The Royal Highland Gathering Saturday at Braemar is like no other throughout the year. From first light, lone pipers can be heard practising on every street corner and at regular intervals, parades of pipe bands from all across the North East assemble at the rallying point just outside the Invercauld Arms before marching purposefully through the village centre, then on up to the showground at the Princess Royal and Duke of Fife Memorial Park.

Braemar Gathering - 2015

The Gathering is an athletic meeting and a social affair as well as a big draw for tourists. The programme for the one-day show sets out a long list of events ranging from Highland Dance to tug of war. Throughout the day there's something going on in almost every part of the games field. As the Heavy competitors work through a testing programme of traditional feats of strength in one corner of the field, the teams taking part in the Inter-Service tug of war take up the strain in another. Flat and hill races take place against a backdrop of Highland Fling and Sword Dancing while in a distant corner, far away from the bustle of the main action, a series of lone pipers compete in the Piobaireachd competitions.

The Royal Enclosure at the Braemar Gathering - 2015

Over the past thirty years or so the Glenfiddich Distillery has supported the Highland Games in the North East through the provision of financial support and sponsorship. In 2016 for example, the company provided a five-figure sum to support the Heavy Events at the twelve Highland Games events which make up the Grampian series of Highland Games. Said Jim Brown of the Grampian Games organising committee "Glenfiddich's sponsorship has been invaluable … the distillery's loyal support has helped to ensure that our Highland Games have gone from strength to strength and enabled us to attract some of Scotland's leading heavy athletes to participate and delight the crowds with their incredible feats of strength and skill." Royan Graham of Glenfiddich echoed Jim's view adding that "We are keen to play a part in ensuring that the traditions of this region can continue to flourish and our sponsorship of Highland Games helps us do this." Alongside the field events, the annual Braemar Gathering is an occasion to head off to Deeside and meet up with old friends. Dotted around the park are literally dozens of hospitality marquees ranging from the Overseas

Rotary and Clan Tents to the various beer and catering marques, all buzzing with excited conversation as old friends meet perhaps for the first time since last year's Gathering. When Sunday dawns, all becomes eerily quiet in the village. The Sporran shop alongside The Hungry Highlander café typically opens early for business and a smattering of early tourists stop for sandwiches and selfies. Up at the Gathering field, save perhaps for a lone kilt-clad busker in the shape of the legendary Jake Williams, all is usually fairly quiet. The cabers have been put away for next year and the business of planning for the next Gathering is already underway.

But Braemar has a life beyond the Gathering and local initiatives such as Braemar Community Ltd provide much needed economic support for the local economy on the other 364 days of the year. Set up in 2004 to undertake the development and operation of major projects on behalf of the community, Braemar Community Ltd has been instrumental in coordinating a number of major projects aimed at restoring existing assets and initiating the construction of new bridges and footpaths throughout the town and the surrounding countryside. The charitable trust's ongoing plans include provision of a dedicated visitor centre at Braemar Castle; a local arts hub, housed in the Grade A listed St Margaret's Episcopal Church, and all weather attractions including a swimming pool, indoor tennis court and climbing centre.

Braemar Castle

In 2007, Braemar Community Ltd acquired Braemar Castle, the ancestral home of the Farquharsons of Invercauld on a 50-year lease. Built in 1628, the castle has seen service as a garrison fort for the suppression of post-Culloden Deeside and as a Victorian holiday home, and is now a modern-day visitor attraction. Having featured in Neil Oliver's BBC series *A History of Scotland* and as a backdrop for an Andy Stewart rendering of *A Scottish Soldier*, the castle also hosts re-enactment events featuring rebellious Jacobites led by the troublesome Earl of Mar.

Additionally, in the village centre a £210,000 renovation funded by Aberdeenshire Council and the Cairngorms National Park Authority has enabled the Eleventh century Kindrochit Castle, a ruin near the village centre, to open as a visitor attraction. A further initiative involves the harnessing of hydroelectric power further up the valley of the River Dee. Following extensive preparatory work by Braemar Community Ltd, Braemar Community Hydro Ltd now operates a 100KW hydro-electric scheme designed to generate low-carbon electricity from the Corriemulzie Burn.

Corriemulzie Burn was previously used to generate electricity for nearby Mar Lodge. Built as a hunting lodge for the Duke and Duchess of Fife in 1895, the Lodge, with its stunning main hall dressed with deer skulls, is the fourth to occupy the site and is nowadays owned and operated by The National Trust for Scotland and is a popular setting for Highland weddings, corporate events, family gatherings and private parties. In previous incarnations, the building fell victim to flooding, and indeed the current incumbent almost suffered the same fate when in 2016 Storm Frank sent the River Dee along the driveway and almost to the front door, in a nod to the Muckle Spate of 1829.

Tourism is a double-edged sword however and the thorny question of second homes remains under discussion throughout Scotland as well as in both Braemar and other Deeside settlements. Seen by many as elitist and problematic, as many as fifty percent of Braemar's dwellings fall into this category. Investigative work on the subject by Scottish broadcaster and journalist Lesley Riddoch, together with the work of campaigning group Reforesting Scotland, is currently focusing minds on the arguments both for and against. The jury is still out as to how tourist-dependent settlements such as Braemar can best address the issue and the Scottish 'second home debate' rumbles on.

If the tale of Peter Grant, better known locally as Auld Dubrach, is to be believed in its entirety the Victorian travel writer Reverend Crombie's assertion that Braemar folk are blessed with unrivalled and disease-free longevity may have some justification. Born in 1714, the son of a local crofter, Peter joined the

Jacobite Army during the 1745 Rebellion. Taken prisoner of war following the 1746 Culloden disaster, he somehow escaped from imprisonment at Carlisle and made his way home to Braemar where he married and quietly resumed his trade as a tailor. A curiosity and possibly the last survivor from the final bid to restore the Stuart dynasty, Peter at the advanced age of 108 was, according to local lore, presented to King George IV during the monarch's 1822 state visit to Edinburgh. When the pair met, the King reputedly said "Ah Grant, you are indeed my oldest subject," only to receive the reply: "Na, na, your Majesty, I am your oldest enemy!"

On further questioning regarding his Jacobite sympathies, Peter is said to have advised the king that he would again support the Stuart cause should the need arise. Despite their obvious political differences, King George, thanks perhaps to the intervention of a sympathetic local laird, awarded Peter an annual pension of £50 which the old Jacobite received until his death aged 110 in 1824. His gravestone lies close to the Farquharson family mausoleum in Braemar Cemetery, and the third fairway at Braemar Golf Club is named in Auld Dubrach's memory.

A full thirty years before the '45 Rebellion, Braemar witnessed the raising of the Jacobite Standard during the opening phase of the 1715 Rebellion. Indeed, a preliminary meeting of Jacobite supporters had been held at Invercauld in the August of that year at the behest of the Earl of Mar. However, Farquharson of Invercauld was not completely convinced that the timing was right for a full-scale rebellion and he asked if he could mull over the matter for a few more days. Accordingly, Mar headed over to Aboyne to consult with the Earl of Huntly, before returning to Braemar on the fourth of September, by which time Farquharson had finally committed to the uprising. Two days later, Mar raised the Royal Standard of James Edward Stuart in front of a Jacobite gathering of some two thousand men at arms.

In 2015 a ceremony to celebrate the three-hundredth anniversary of the event took place on the grassy knoll beside the present-day Invercauld Arms Hotel. A small brass plaque on the wall beside the fireplace in the hotel lounge records the exact spot of the raising of the Jacobite flag and just across the road from the hotel, a stone tablet erected by the Deeside Field Club in 1952 also reflects on the event. Tradition asserts that the richly embroidered flag bore the words "Nemo me impune lacessit" and "No Union", alongside the Royal Arms and thistle of Scotland.

As the standard was raised, the gilt finial atop the flagstaff seemingly came loose and fell to the ground; an event which many of those present considered a bad omen.

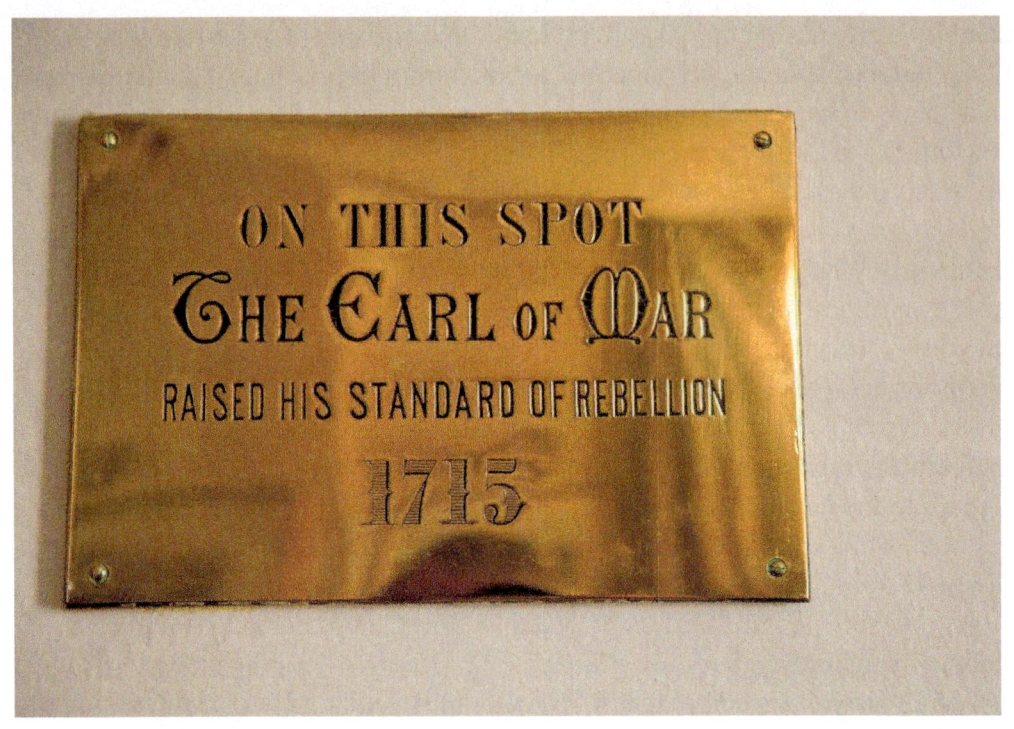

Invercauld Arms Hotel plaque commemorating the raising of the Jacobite flag

The Battle of Sheriffmuir on the thirteenth of November 1715 affirmed the portent. Although neither army gained the upper hand and both winning sides fled, this key engagement proved decisive in the defeat of the Jacobite cause. In his poem The Battle of Sherramuir Robert Burns describes the event thus:

> "Then ye may tell, how pell an mell,
> By red claymores and musket's knell,
> Wi' dying yell, how Tories fell,
> And Whigs to hell,
> Flew off in frighted bands, man."

Following the slaughter at Sheriffmuir, Mar and his army retreated to Perth and the momentum of the uprising was lost. Despite detailed plans for the coronation of the new Stuart king at Scone, it soon became obvious that the uprising had simply fizzled out. Accompanied by James Edward Stuart, the Earl of Mar escaped back to France. The failed king had spent just forty-three days on Scottish soil and he never returned again to claim his throne. In February 1716, his surviving supporters received a message confirming his safe arrival in Europe and advising them to pretty much fend for themselves. Many Scots suffered imprisonment, execution and even transportation to the British penal colonies. Braemar suffered dreadfully during the aftermath, when a vengeful government dispatched troops to the district with strict orders to burn crops and destroy property. When the Government soldiers left, barely a house remained standing.

In the 1875 edition of his popular tourist guidebook *Braemar and Balmoral - A Guide to the Deeside Highlands*, the Reverend James Crombie describes Braemar as the capital of the Deeside Highlands. Crombie goes on to enthusiastically promote the virtues of the ozone-rich high-altitude Highland atmosphere, praising the Braemar climate as "the healthiest probably in all of Great Britain … as is evident from the fact that the inhabitants are long lived and free from all the diseases of cities and low-lying districts." Even today, some 145 years on, few would disagree with the man.

8
BUCKIE – ASK NOT THE PRICE OF FISH

The Moray Firth fisher town of Buckie sits mid-way between Fraserburgh and Inverness. A population count of 9,077 at the 2011 census ranked it the third largest settlement, after Elgin and Forres, within the Moray Council area. Buckie is home to a number of manufacturing, seafood and maritime related businesses. Associated Seafoods, also trading as Moray Seafoods and GlenIsla Shellfish, are major employers in the town and supply UK and international wholesale and retail sectors with langoustine, crab, scallops and squid. On Low Street, family run business Paterson and Sons, with brand-names including 'Cluny Fish' and 'Shetland Smokehouse' process and export salmon, trout and kippers worldwide. March Road Industrial Estate hosts Mairs fish merchants, known throughout Scotland for their innovative advertising strap-line "Eat Mair Fish". Just outside the town the Diageo owned Inchgower Distillery produces fine malt and harbour-side, the workforce at Macduff Shipyards continues the tradition of building and refitting ships.

Buckie Harbour

Then there are the Jags. Better known perhaps as Buckie Thistle FC, the team have (in 2020) eleven Highland League wins to their name and have even made it onto the pages of a Stephen King novel. In the course of investigating a terrorist act in *If It Bleeds*, fictional private investigator Holly Gibney discovers that Buckie Academy is twinned with a bombed US High School. So, pupils in King's fictional Buckie learn about the Pittsburgh Pirates and in return fictional exchange pupils across the Atlantic are brought up to speed on the triumphs and tribulations of the Jags.

The New Town at Buckie with its grand sandstone buildings and fine churches was laid out some 200 years ago when the Gordon family of Cluny commissioned a planned town along the high ridge above the harbour. Cluny Square marks the centre of the new town with West Church Street, East Church Street and High Street running off to the four quarters of the cross. The more traditional fishermen's houses of the Low Town however follow no such geometrical rules. Many of the houses along the A990 Coastal Trail align with the main highway but in common with most traditional fishing settlements, a casual glance behind the frontage reveals a quite different story. Buckie's seafront consists of an amalgamation of the once distinct fishing communities of Buckpool, Seatown, Gordonsburgh, Ianstown and Portessie which lie both east and west of the Burn of Buckie. Many of the houses are sited haphazardly and at every conceivable angle to one another. The Yardie, a designated Conservation Area not far from Cluny Harbour, is a prime example of this wonderfully random style of *laissez-faire* town planning and to this day features communal drying greens right on the seafront.

Visitors to Buckie often remark upon the number of churches in the town. Recently a TripAdvisor reviewer commented that "the most amazing thing about the town is the number of churches and the comparatively small number of pubs." Fishing communities traditionally hold a strong religious bias; however few towns of Buckie's size offer such a broad degree of religious diversification. Many of the local churches are architecturally stunning and the twin-towered, red sandstone, St Peter's in St Andrew's Square must rank as one of the grandest churches in the North East of Scotland. Originally conceived as a cathedral for the Roman Catholic Diocese of Aberdeen, St Peter's opened for business in 1857 to the alarm of seafarers who referred to the twin spires, visible many miles out to sea, as "Yon twa horns o' the Deil!"

Kinder folk referred to the new structure as The Cathedral of the North. In post-reformation Eighteenth century Moray the practising of Catholicism involved secretive worship and in stark contrast to the open grandeur of St Peter's, the RC Church of St Ninian at nearby Tynet makes no pretence whatsoever to architectural greatness. Pugin's weasel words that Gothic architecture is the only true form for Christian worship have no place here. Built around 1755 and enlarged in 1787, the church remains open for worship and closely resembles a long low cow shed. Indeed, few today would give it a second glance. The so-called 'Banffshire Bethlehem' of St Ninian's is probably the oldest Scottish post Reformation chapel still available for worship. Alongside the clandestine congregation at Tynet, Buckie is home to Methodist, Baptist, Church of Scotland, Gospel Hall Brethren, Episcopal and Salvation Army congregations.

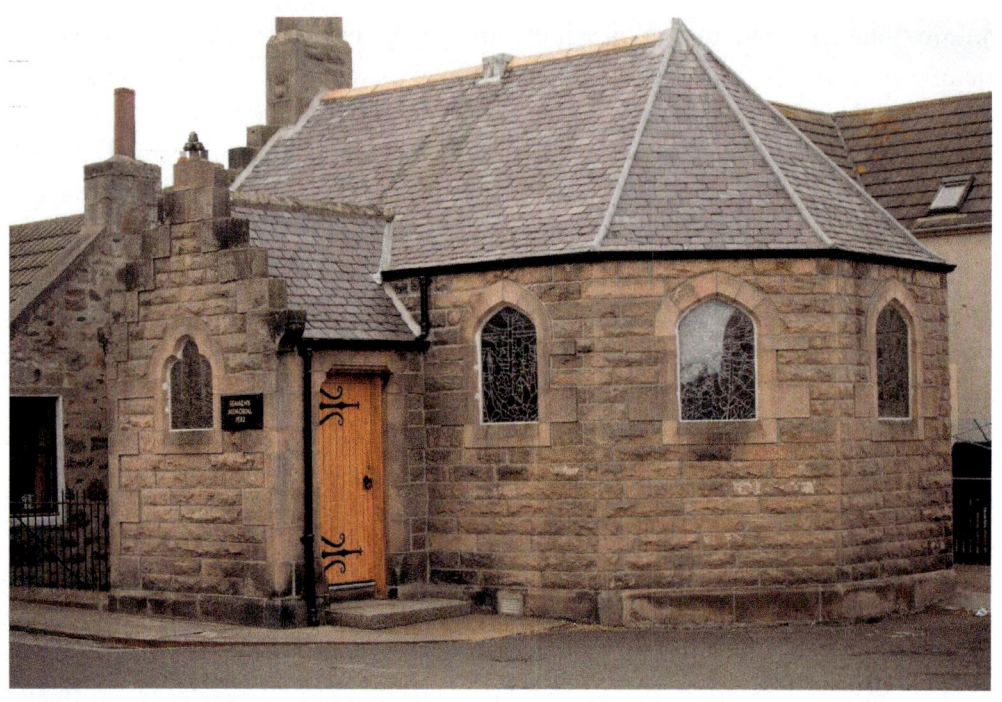

Buckie Seamen's Memorial Chapel

"Ask not the price of fish, for it is measured in men's lives" runs an old adage and even in the Twenty-first century, fishermen in the UK are exposed to an accident rate many times that of construction workers and the folk who work the land. Despite all of the technology and the improved safety regulations fishing remains Scotland's most dangerous industry. Between 1992 and 2006 alone, the Marine Accident and Investigation Board recorded 180 fatal accidents resulting in the deaths of 256 seafarers within the UK fishing industry. One third of these fatalities were attributed to men going overboard. Often no burial is possible and the bereaved are left without closure. One local can recall dropping off a pal at Cluny Harbour a decade or so ago and never seeing him again. "He got on a trawler and that's the last I saw of him, that was just how it was in those days." He continued "you just got used to it as a fact of life, I lost three school-friends that way." Following the loss of the Buckie fishing boats Bounteous off Cornwall in the January of 1980 and Carinthia off the Orkneys in June 1979, three local women decided that a fishermen's memorial might offer comfort to the bereaved of the town. A Memorial Chapel Committee was formed and following eighteen months of fund-raising, the Buckie Seamen's Memorial Chapel, dedicated to all the men of the area who had lost their lives at sea, was opened on Sunday fourth of July 1982 in the town's New Street. The following day the Queen and her husband Prince Philip of Greece and Denmark, who were in Buckie touring the Jones shipyard and the Herd and McKenzie's yard, visited the chapel to chat with the bereaved. The Roll of Honour within the building lists the names of some 190 local men lost between the end of WW2 and the present day. Buckie Fishing Heritage Centre holds keys for those wishing to visit the chapel.

The original harbour at Nether Buckie was completed in 1857 by Edinburgh-based engineers David and Thomas Stevenson, the family firm of writer Robert Louis Stevenson. It was said to be poorly engineered and prone to silting up. By the 1870s it was deemed unusable. Nowadays infilled and landscaped the harbour is a popular stop for walkers on the Speyside Way. In 1877 Cluny Harbour was completed after two years of construction and in 1909 Buckie Town Council took on ownership. Nowadays it is owned and managed by Moray Council. In the early part of the Twentieth century, Buckie played host to the largest steam drifter fleet in Scotland and until quite recently the town boasted several shipyards. The largest of these was Herd and McKenzie. Originating from nearby Findochty, where they built steam drifters, the firm moved to a new site at the east end of Cluny Harbour in 1918.

The First War years had been busy and profitable. Orders included the building of anti-submarine vessels to Admiralty specifications plus the converting of existing drifters from the fishing role to full fighting specification. Post-war, the yard found themselves converting those same boats back to civilian specification but by the 1920s the Scottish fishing industry was in decline. Overseas markets had been lost during the war and the knock-on effect was a sharp decline in demand for fishing boats. Even the repair market was in meltdown with boats being laid up all around the UK. Many Scottish shipyards went to the wall. The Buckie yard clung on and in 1939, with the outbreak of the next global conflict, the company's fortunes revived again due to the Admiralty orders. Anti-shipping mines were the new menace and the yard began building wooden minesweepers and, yet again, converting fishing boats for war service. Post WW2, the yard saw changes in both name and ownership.

In August 2013 it was announced that Buckie Shipbuilders had gone into administration with seventy-four redundancies. In its time the company, alongside its war-time work, had built and refitted everything from pilot boats to landing craft. The RNLI had for many years used the yard for refitting lifeboats and alongside the building of traditional fishing boats, the craftsmen are rumoured to have even turned their hand to the manufacture of fish farm cages for the offshore salmon industry.

Perhaps the most famous vessel to emerge from the Buckie slipway was the 380-ton sail training schooner *Captain Scott*. Named after polar explorer Robert Falcon Scott, she was ordered by the charitable body The Dulverton Trust as an adventure training sailing ship. Timber-built using oak and Scottish larch, the keel was laid in March 1970. The ship, a square-rigged schooner, took just eighteen months to build and was launched in the presence of Falcon Scott's son, naturalist Peter Scott in September 1971 to the accompaniment of a piped rendition of *The Skye Boat Song*. The *Captain Scott* was sold on to the Sultanate of Oman Ministry of Youth in 1977 and her name changed to *Shabab Oman*. In 1979 she became a sail training ship for cadets serving in the Royal Navy of Oman.

The decline of Buckie as a both a fishing and shipbuilding port led the Moray Council to adopt a business plan focused on making Cluny Harbour, and several other harbours along the Moray coast, self-funding by 2021. Currently 100,000 tons of cargo flows through the port annually, ranging from bulk shipments of timber, stone and foodstuffs to fabricated steel modules for the offshore oil industry. Future plans include the seeking out of new markets to increase both cargo traffic and investment in infra-structure to service offshore renewables. Buckie Harbour currently services deep water test turbines and with the prospect of the erection of up to 384 wind turbines in the Moray Firth over the next few years an obvious strategy is to provide engineering support to the offshore power industry. Estimates indicate that the proposed windfarm fields will require some 38,400 routine service visits over the next fifty years.

Today Macduff Shipyards Limited operates a modern fabrication shed at Buckie's Harbour, equipped to accommodate new builds of up to thirty metres long. Recent orders have included a £2.4 million dredger contract awarded to the firm by Moray Council for completion in spring 2016. Other initiatives included the Buckie Drifter Maritime Heritage Centre on Freuchny Road which operated from 1994 to 2004 and told the story of the fishing communities on the Moray Firth coast. Despite plans to turn the derelict building into a performance venue, the council-owned building lay empty for several years. There are rumours that the site may soon be redeveloped for use as a base for the renewable energy sector.

Buckie Fishing Heritage Centre on Buckie's Cluny Place marks the starting-point of the 13-mile Fishwives Path linking the town to inland Keith. A registered charity established in 1986, the centre is committed to preserving "The rich fishing heritage of Buckie and District". Manned by local volunteers, mainly retired fishermen, the centre holds over eight thousand photographs illustrating the fishing industry plus a unique collection of oral history recordings including a 1988 interview with John Gray, one-time Skipper of the Purse Net boat 'Flowing Tide' and also a past President of the Pelagic Fishermen's Federation of the UK. John was obviously a charismatic character and was very well known throughout the entire industry. His premature death in 1991 was a very sad day for the fishing industry. Interviewed shortly before his death by Buchan film maker James Taylor he recalled his early days at sea:

"That rats caused mair trouble in a boat wi their stealing. The likes o' this auld fisherman hid a muffler o admiral cloth, well the rats hid it awa for a nest an him blaming abidy for stealing it aff him. Far's my muffler? He didna ken the rats hid it awa, see that's a fact. Oh ye widna believe some o the stories I could tell. Aye that wis trawlin. Bit noo since we gied intae diesels, aye in my latter life, ye niver see nae rats; whether it is the smell o the diesel ile, I dinna ken bit ye dinna see rats the same noo."

John Gray wasn't the only Buckie fisherman to gain international fame. Captain Dod Osborne (1904 -1957) hailed from Buckie and obtained his Master's ticket aged 21 following five years of service as a Boy Seaman and service in the Dover Patrol with the Royal Navy. In his memoirs he records that his early career involved everything from deep-sea trawling to rum-running but it was his 1936 voyage on the trawler *Girl Pat* which launched him into the international headlines. *Girl Pat* was a 66-foot fishing trawler operating out of Grimsby and on April the second 1936 the boat headed out into the North Sea for what should have been a routine fishing trip working Dogger Bank. What followed became a media sensation and would end with the Buckie skipper and his brother James spending time in Wormwood Scrubs doing hard labour.

Having dropped off one of the crew at Dover, Captain Osborne and his remaining crew members headed not for the fishing grounds of the North Sea but south to Spain and then down the coast of Africa where a further crew member was put ashore. Dod then crossed the Atlantic in the 25-ton trawler eventually ending up in British Guiana where the skipper and his remaining crew were arrested, with both Dod and his brother being returned to Britain for trial. At the Old Bailey in October 1936, it emerged that there were no international maritime charts on the boat and that all Dod and his crew had in the way of navigation equipment was a basic ship's compass and a school atlas. There was no radio on board, no charts and no sextant. The press lapped up the story especially when allegations of insurance fraud emerged. The defence, funded in part by The Anglo-Continental Newspaper Company and the *Sunday People,* who in total paid five thousand pounds for exclusive rights to the tale, alleged that far from stealing the vessel (which was stated in court to be worth £3,600) Dod and his crew had actually conspired with the owners to sell the boat abroad and divide up the proceeds. The owner would claim the insurance value while the crew would each gain a sizeable sum on the sale.

Now, the fly in the ointment was the fact that at various points the Buckie-born skipper had taken on supplies and left the bills for the Grimsby owners to pick up. After the sixteen-day voyage across the Atlantic he had resupplied at Devil's Island and before that, stores and fuel had been replenished at Tenerife and at other ports on the African coast. If the serious matter of insurance fraud could not be proved then the unauthorised supply fraud could easily be proved. Dod had for example run up a bill of £235 for supplies and essential repairs at the Spanish port of Corcubion instructing suppliers that the bill be sent to the owners. The same happened at Dakar and the paper trail was indisputable. Despite the defence insisting that the voyage of the *Girl Pat* was purely a joy ride and not a serious case of theft of someone else's property, the jury obviously thought otherwise. Captain Dod Osborne got eighteen months with hard labour; his brother received twelve of the same.

Interviewed at his wife's aunt's house in Portsoy for the *Aberdeen Journal* following his release, Dod showed no remorse and in fact claimed to have enjoyed his prison time. He had been well treated he said and had met many interesting inmates including a convicted murderer named Frederick Nodder. Nodder was already in the headlines as the only person in British legal history to be convicted at two trials in different towns of the same offence and was subsequently hanged for the murder of ten-year-old Mona Tinsley. Dod recalled that "he was sewing mailbags with about a hundred other prisoners when I met him and I can't say I liked the look of him at all." Dod Osborne died at sea in 1957 during a voyage from the south of France to the UK. In his autobiography *Master of the Girl Pat,* he records his thoughts about crossing the Atlantic in a small fishing boat:

"It seemed silly to attempt a crossing of the Atlantic from a position so close to Africa but I realised that actually it would not be so silly. That is one of the narrowest parts of the Atlantic. We were about twenty-two hundred miles from British Guiana and less than three thousand miles from Trinidad and Barbados. And, most important of all we would have the trade winds at our back. If we had luck, we might be able to make the crossing in two weeks. Furthermore, I had friends in the West Indies."

And all that with his son's school atlas and a lucky-bag compass! They obviously breed them well in Buckie.

9
COVE - HOME OF THE LAST FISHWIFE

An 1882 entry in the *Ordnance Gazetteer of Scotland* describes Cove as a fishing village in Nigg parish with a railway station, Post Office and a harbour where locals engaged in the drying and smoking of haddock. The population was stated to be 550. The village sported a busy public harbour, an Episcopal church and a hotel. Just five miles south of Aberdeen the village has been variously known as Cove, 'The Cove' and more recently as Cove Bay. Some older folk remember the place as the home of 'The Stinker'.

The village was designated as a conservation area in 1975 and, like many such settlements on the Kincardineshire coastline, grew and prospered mainly due to the shelter of a natural harbour which allowed fishing boats to be launched from the shingle beach at the foot of the cliffs. A set of stone breakwater piers were constructed in around 1880 and the rusted remains of a hand operated crane can be seen on the single pier which survives today. Alongside the fishing, Cove also featured a granite quarry dating from around 1790 and for some 140 years was home to a fish meal factory affectionately known locally as The Stinker. The factory latterly employed around twenty-five men and the business, The Aberdeen Fish Manure and Oil Company, was re-located to Aberdeen sometime around 1930. Famously or infamously, depending on your view, Aberdeen music hall entertainer and Laird of Inversnecky, Harry Gordon (1893-1957) parodied the Stinker in *Tak' Me Back Tae Cove - A Song of Cove* and there are tales, probably not apocryphal, that folk passing through the village on the railways never really forgot the experience even with the carriage windows firmly closed. Perhaps the smell was best summed up in Harry Gordon's chorus "Oh Tak' me back to Cove, tak' me back to Cove, far the air is as strong as can be!"

By 1833, when the *Second Statistical Account of Scotland* was published, the fisherfolk at Cove were engaged in both herring and salmon fishing with catches later being exported both north and south when the railways arrived in around 1850. Writer Peter Anson records in his classic *Fishing Boats and Fisher Folk on the East Coast of Scotland* that in 1838 there were nine large sail-boats each crewed by six men working out of Cove. He writes "From January to May, the local fishermen ... worked on grounds known as the Long Forties where at a depth of 33 to 35 fathoms they were sure of finding plenty of haddock. But they were often troubled by dogfish, which destroyed their lines and often ate the haddock off their hooks." Anson goes on to record that the men went out fishing from midnight to dawn, while the women - who had perhaps been up since 4 am - took the fish to Aberdeen market on foot (some five miles north of the village) and then returned home to attend to domestic affairs.

By the Twentieth century Cove was in economic decline and the area was becoming run down due to the waning of both the fishing and quarrying industries. Indeed, nowadays the village, although greatly expanded to host a population of some 7,000, is fast becoming a residential suburb of Aberdeen. There are vestiges of the fishing industry still remaining however. The harbour until quite recently boasted some dozen small craft and, until a disastrous dispute took hold involving a group of boat owners and a local landowner, it was quite common to see drying nets and fishing gear piled up on the foreshore alongside fishermen and their boats waiting for the incoming tide. The dispute led to boulders being placed along the access road obstructing vehicular access to the harbour and a long running court case fed the flames with no real victor other than the lawyers. And then, in a final tragedy worthy of an episode of Inspector Morse, the wooden fishing boats on the shingle shore at Cove fell victim to an arsonist.

Cove Harbour

But times change and the community is nowadays keen to maintain links with the past in the form of a fisher-themed white marble sculpture along with interpretation boards relating the long history of the settlement. In 2017 Brazilian sculptor Albertino Costa with the backing of several local conservation groups including Cove in Bloom was engaged to carve a sculpture commemorating Cove's fishing heritage. It featured as inspiration a long gone local resident known as Isie Caie who may very well have been the very last Mearns fish wife engaged in the daily export of fish from the coastal village all the way to Aberdeen. Isabella Catto Caie was well known in Cove and well known in Aberdeen. In the days when catches were bountiful, she could be seen hawking her wares at The Green. Later, as landings of fish at Cove declined, she took to buying from middlemen at the Market in Aberdeen before taking up her usual stance on the cobbles. She had her regulars and, in the early days at least, could be easily spotted walking the six miles into Aberdeen, carrying a creel loaded with fish on her back to sell. Latterly, in old age, she took the bus to town. According to legend, it might take two men to lift the heavy creel laden with fish on to her back before she set out on her journey into the city centre. Latterly, folklore led to some late fame and alongside a few pictures in the press she featured, at least the once, in a *Press and Journal* calendar celebrating the heritage of the North East. Rather than simply create a romanticised studio-based life sculpture of Cove's most famous fishwife, Albertino's approach was

'The Spirit of the Fishwife sculpture (with Wendy Suttar and Albertino Costa)

much more radical; he would work in public in the open air alongside the very harbour where the fishwife's journey began. Permission to site the project on the harbour front was readily granted by landowner Pralhad Kolhe and in summer 2016 work began on the quayside at Cove's little harbour where a large block of white Italian marble began to slowly morph into a vibrant piece of community led sculpture. From the very beginning visitors to Cove Harbour took a keen interest. "People cannot resist watching someone doing something creative. The work is open for everyone to come and contribute and with no preconceived idea of the final form, it is easy to get people involved" recalled Albertino. "From the very start" he said, "creating the work live at Cove Bay gave the people a sense of ownership and a sense of deep connection both with each other and with the past." Wendy Suttar of Cove in Bloom agreed. "We had heard about Albertino's previous work and although when we started speaking to him, we hadn't got a rigid idea of what we wanted; we knew however that he was the artist we wanted and we immediately started the ongoing process of fundraising the £20,000 needed to finance the project." As the work progressed, the conversations with passers-by gave Albertino a breadth of knowledge which he has embodied in the various elements of the sculpture. The creel, the net, the wild sea and the harvest of the sea are vividly portrayed along with the spirit of Isie Caie herself.

Isie Caie died in May 1966 aged 86. Her grand-daughter, Chirsty MacSween recalls that "she sold at the Green to the end" and that she "had a reputation for always having a smile on her face, a happy woman." The completed Cove sculpture now sits on a grassy knoll high above the harbour and is known locally as 'The Spirit of the Fishwife'.

10
CROVIE – HOUSES FOR JELLYBEANS

Pandemics and disasters come and go. Witness both the 1919 and the 1957 flu outbreaks. 1919 saw a global pandemic widely rumoured to have killed tens of millions. In 1957 a government led by Harold MacMillan allegedly hushed up a winter flu epidemic which killed perhaps thirty thousand UK citizens. On a local level the death toll hit hard although it never much made the national headlines. The so-called 'Victory at Dunkirk' was another such piece of state spin where military disaster was portrayed as victory in the national press. Imagine if you will how different these histories might have been in a modern age where news travels at the speed of light on the back of digital technology. Things have changed of course due to smartphones and social media. The global nature of news gathering in the Twenty-first century allows the sharing within hours, or in some cases even minutes, of events occurring halfway around the globe.

The days of news stories travelling at 25 knots across the Atlantic by steamship to feed the news presses of Gordon Bennett Junior's *New York Herald* are long gone, and the latest news about earthquakes, floods and storms can be read on our tablets and laptops almost as they occur. The Arab Spring of 2011 and that very public murder of Drummer Rigby in May 2013 also highlighted the phenomenon of citizen journalism, whereby anyone armed with a smart phone has the power to capture events as they happen and then upload to social media to share instantly with a global audience.

In the post-Second World War years, commercial news distribution was mainly via printed media such as newspapers and magazines with cinema newsreels not far behind. Radio was well-established as a source of information about world events; and television, although in its infancy, was fast catching up, as the BBC broadcast of the Coronation of Queen Elizabeth in 1953 was to vividly illustrate. Several million new viewers crowded around rented black and white television sets to watch the event live. And, although few perhaps realised it at the time, the Coronation broadcast heralded the start of a brand-new era of information distribution. For the first time both Roy Rogers and the British Prime Minister of the day could sit with you at the fireside as you picked away at your austerity (rationing was in place until 1954) mock-goose-lentil-pie with two veg. The irony was that folk could obtain the new television sets on the never-never, but essential foodstuffs such as sugar, cheese and bacon remained in short supply.

As well as being Coronation year, 1953 saw the conquest of Mount Everest. Bill Haley gave his first public performance of *Rock Around the Clock* and although the war in Europe had ended some eight years before, Britain's towns and cities still bore deep scars left over from the German bombing offensive. More than two million homes, perhaps twenty per-cent of the national housing stock, had been damaged by enemy action and it would take decades for the various post-war governments to repair the damage. Then, and just as things were improving, nature was to play its own destructive hand.

Crovie - home of Scotland's North Pole

1953 had begun well, with a few fine days and some sleet. There was nothing unexpected weatherwise and folk got on with daily life in what seemed to be a typical Scottish winter. The winter storms hammered the Moray and Aberdeenshire coast but there was nothing that folk had not seen before. Described as perhaps the best-preserved Nineteenth century fishing village in Scotland, Crovie, locally (pronounced Crivvy) lies seven miles east of Banff. Nowadays a holiday destination, the township is just one of several 'brae set' villages in the North East. Places such as Pennan, Gardenstown and Crovie are typical of the genre. There are high cliffs with good fishing below, and the villages hold a few hardy folk willing to work hard to make a basic living – or more likely in present times having to commute to Aberdeen for work. Up the coast at places like Findhorn and Burghead sea temperatures were dropping with ice forming in the shallows. In Aberdeen and Peterhead, the fish markets and harbours functioned as normal. Inland folk in towns such as Inverurie and Elgin battened down for what they thought would be a typical winter. Then the January winter storms began in earnest.

A full moon, combined with low pressure in the North Sea, swelling tides and high winds mixed to form a lethal situation which claimed lives and flooded thousands of homes on low-lying land all along the east coast and south as far as Holland. In fact, the North Sea flood of 1953 is reckoned to be one of the most devastating natural disasters ever recorded in the United Kingdom. Over 1,600 km of coastline was damaged, with sea walls and harbour defences being breached over a huge area. Flooding forced around 30,000 people to be evacuated from their homes and an estimated 24,000 properties were seriously damaged. The storm surge raced down the east coast into the southern North Sea, where it was accentuated by the shallower waters. In Lincolnshire, flooding occurred from Mablethorpe to Skegness, reaching as far as two miles inland. At the time of the flood, none of the local radio stations broadcast at night, and many of the smaller weather monitoring stations operated only by day. People were generally unaware of the threatening storm. Additionally, since the storm struck on a Saturday, many local government offices in the affected areas were unstaffed and unable to respond quickly to the disaster. Around thirty-eight died at Felixstowe in Suffolk, when wooden prefabricated homes in the West End area of the town were flooded. In Essex, Canvey Island was inundated, with the loss of over fifty-eight lives. Another thirty-seven died when the seafront village of Jaywick near Clacton was flooded. Thousands of people perished on the continent, with the Low Countries of Holland and Belgium suffering the worst. Off County Down, the Larne to Stranraer ferry *Princess Victoria* went down with the loss of 133 lives and on land, both roads and railways were blocked as trees were blown down across the length and breadth of the UK east coast.

At Keith in Morayshire the 7:10 a.m. train from Keith to Elgin became trapped by fallen trees on the line near Drummuir and was then virtually buried in trunks when further trees collapsed onto the engine and tender. It took more than two days for railway engineers to free the locomotive which local wags nicknamed The Jungle Express! The gas works at Banff was completely destroyed by the waves and many coastal towns along the North East coast suffered severe flooding and destruction of houses. The *Aberdeen Press and Journal* headline told of 'The Weekend of Terror' and described a countrywide scene of devastation and death: "360 Dead or Missing in Britain's Worst Floods" read one header while another claimed that the captain of the stricken

Princess Victoria had "gone down with his ship his hand at salute" although how this heroic last stand came to the attention of the journalists was not made clear. At Inverurie, the town hall cupola was seen to sway wildly in the wind for two hours before crashing 50 feet to the road below and an Elgin hotel worker was injured when a chimney stack plunged through a roof as she laid table for a wedding reception at the Station Hotel. At Mintlaw, the war memorial blew down and folk talked of a slaters' paradise as roofs were wrecked across the country.

Alongside the devastation on the coastline, entire forests were blown down all over Scotland and some estimates at the time put the losses at some twenty million cubic feet of timber in the area between Fife and Forres. At Glentanar two hundred acres were levelled, at Crathes 750 acres and Haddo Estate recorded a loss to windblow of 600 acres. In the clear-up which followed, road gangs braved blizzards and frost to clear the roads and an Inverurie forester of the time commented that his squad "started at Inveramsay near Pitcaple then cut their way up past Chapel of Garioch, ending up in Monymusk some four days later. We not only had to cut through big tangles of timber along the roads, but we had to dig our way through frost and snowdrifts to get to them." Over the course of the three-year long clean-up operation, some twenty three steam-powered and diesel operated portable sawmills were brought into Deeside and Speyside to deal with the windblow although many of the roadside trunks were simply left in piles beside the roads for councils to clear and the effects of those fallen roadside trees can still be observed in repairs to dykes all over the North East.

The effect of the 1953 gale on the coastal village of Crovie however was potentially terminal. Established probably by folk driven to the fishing by Eighteenth century land clearances, the tiny village sits only a few feet from the high tide mark and many of the cottages sit precariously perched above the waves at the foot of a grassy cliff. In Crovie, the fisher folk were quite used to the effects of the sea. They had, for generations, lived with the seasons and felt that they knew how to survive the furies of the winter storms. These were hardy folk. In February 1906 they had risked life and limb to rescue the crew of the timber-built cargo steamer *SS Vigilant* when, after an engine failure, the ship was driven ashore on the Rotten Beach just down from the village. A joint effort with the folk of nearby Gardenstown enabled the rescue of all six crew members despite terrible sea conditions during a severe winter storm. There is a memorial to the event - featuring plates from the steamer's boiler - on the coastal path between Crovie and Gardenstown.

When the *SS Vigilant* was driven aground, the inhabitants saved all aboard.

But when the great storm of 1953 made landfall, the community all but abandoned the shoreside village, since nothing could have prepared them for what was to come. The storm surge emerged from the North Sea reaching Crovie at around midday, and at full force. Windows were shattered and roofs destroyed. Wooden shutters, made to withstand the worst the sea could throw at them, proved ineffective. Anything loose was swept out to sea and the path along the Rotten Shore leading to Gardenstown was washed away. The seawall and pier were badly damaged and the bridge over the burn was destroyed. Frightened villagers climbed to safety up the cliff behind the seafront as the storm surged over the village but could do little aside from huddle and pray. By dawn the next day, the worst was past. In the re-telling, Crovie folk recall the disappearance of coal stores into the waves, the sight of Eider ducks in the flooded kitchens and the smell of paraffin from the wrecked tank outside the village store. By some miracle, the fishing boats on the Greenie survived but Crovie folk were scared in case it could happen again. Then came the big clear-up.

Crovie from the high road

After the storm many locals wondered if Crovie was worth saving. Indeed, the local council was also wondering about that issue. At a meeting in Banff just a few weeks after the disaster, the County Architect suggested that since the fishing village lacked basic facilities such as sewage, shops or now even a footpath to connect it with nearby Gardenstown, it should be abandoned and housing provision for the inhabitants be provided elsewhere. Costs of twenty thousand pounds just for repair of the sea defences were seen as unjustified and proposals included removing the roofs and abandoning the village to the elements. The future of Crovie seemed in doubt. The young folk had already left for the bigger towns. The fishing was in decline after all, and the place was under threat from the very thing that had birthed it, the sea. In the aftermath, houses seemingly sold for buttons. One is reported by local author Eirwen Watt to have fetched a paltry £13. The rest are said to have been sold for jellybeans with most being taken on for renovation as holiday homes. Eventually in 1962, and after sustained local campaigning, the entire village was listed Grade B by the Secretary of State for Scotland which put an abrupt stop to the council's demolition plans. Ten years later the individual houses were re-listed along with a shoreside footpath majestically described in the official classification as the 'Crovie Promenade'. If you visit the place nowadays however, you may find a very few locals. Only a few of the original families have a hold on the place. The rest are maybe incomers from Belgium or France or from other parts of the United Kingdom.

Then there were those German spies. There are numerous instances of wartime spies being landed all along the east coast of Aberdeenshire. For example, a trio of would-be German agents landed at Portgordon in the September of 1940. One, a mysterious lady named as Vera Schalburg, or in some accounts Vera Erikson, played the role of the long-lost niece of an Italian noble. She was rumoured to be a double agent and survived the war. Her companions, Karl Theo Drucke and Werner Henrich Walti (a Swiss National) were less fortunate. Arrested at Portgordon by the local bobby, Police Constable Grieve, the pair were tried, convicted and hung as spies at Wandsworth in the August of 1941. Another instance in 1943 featured a Norwegian petty criminal by the name of Nikolai Hansen and mirrored the 1941 so-called 'Mission of Peace' when Hitler's Deputy Rudolph Hess flew to Eaglesham in a bid to meet with fascist members of the British aristocracy. Hansen was dropped by parachute at Boyndie near Banff in September 1943 tasked with monitoring troop movements. He immediately gave himself up and following interrogation spent the remainder of the conflict as a guest of His Majesty at Brixton Prison.

There are many more such instances including the bizarre tale of Mutt and Jeff's arrival at Crovie. It was April 1941 and the press reported that two armed men landed at Crovie pier from a rubber dinghy having been dropped off at sea by the panicked crew of a Luftwaffe flying boat who in their hurry to take off back to Norway threw the men's bicycles into the North Sea. It was a time of distrust. Road signs all over the North East had been removed and emergency coastal defences, including pill-boxes and even an armoured train were in place to counter an expected seaborne attack by the Germans. The Gordon Highlander Museum in Aberdeen has no record of these steam-powered weapons in the archives but local military history author Alan Stewart records in his book *North East Scotland at War* that:

"During WW2, armoured trains were used in the North East of Scotland. The trains were built in Derby in July 1940 and consisted of two wagons pushed by a locomotive. There were crewed by Royal Engineers and Royal Armoured Corps personnel and were armed with a quick firing 6 pounder CWT Hotchkiss gun and six Bren-guns. In October 1940, the Polish Armoured Train Battalions were formed where trains were handed over to the Polish forces to operate. Of the 12 trains, the last was decommissioned in Scotland in 1944. Records in the National Archives show at least one train being at Kittybrewster Station and being used often on coastal rail routes up to the Moray Firth and Buchan areas."

Both the armoured trains and indeed General Ironside's Innes Links Coastal Battery over at Lossiemouth were yet to fire a shot in anger, but the general mood was fear of invasion and distrust of any foreigners. The two Crovie spies - Mutt and Jeff - were in fact Norwegians, John Moe and Tor Glad, who had been recruited by the German security services to report on the Moray coastal defences. It's a well-worn story and details differ depending on the source. One version of the tale insists that having rowed ashore to Crovie pier and asked the occupant of number 27, a lad by the name of Charles 'Cheelie' Reid, how to get to Banff by bus. Very few locals spoke a foreign language despite the influx of Polish personnel into the Moray area. The local seemingly contacted the police who promptly arrested the two. Used as double agents, the two Norwegians fooled their German masters for a few months at the very most before being allowed, in one case, to join the Norwegian Army in Exile and in the case of the second agent to live out the rest of the war in an internment camp on Dartmoor. They were nicknamed Mutt and Jeff after two US newspaper cartoon characters of the time whom they were thought to resemble. Moe was to record a tragedy, which resulted from his wartime work, in his 1986 book *John Moe Double Agent*. Seemingly, as part of a diversion to cloak a Luftwaffe re-supply mission for the two turncoat spies, a bombing raid was carried out on Fraserburgh in February 1943. Tragically a young lad, eleven-year-old Laurence Kerr, was killed in the raid. After hostilities ceased, Moe worked for Scandinavian

Airlines in Sweden but he never returned to Crovie. He died aged 82 in 2001.

So, despite its size, there are perhaps less than seventy buildings in the entire village, Crovie has a good few tales to its pedigree and a quite a few claims to fame. Although not quite on a par with the bright red-liveried telephone box of *Local Hero* fame over at Pennan, the public telephone box at Crovie pier, probably the very same one used by 'Cheelie' Reid to report those German spies, also has a tale to tell. In 1989, the 1940s era British Telecom box was subject of a dispute between local residents and BT, who had offered the phone box for sale to the local Preservation Society at a token price of £1. The offer was subject to an upkeep clause which the locals strongly objected to; after a series of terse exchanges and listing as a Grade B Scheduled Monument, BT eventually agreed to continue service to the small community, meaning that anyone who wishes to call Australia or maybe Canada from the coastal phone-box at Crovie can still choose to do so.

Additionally, and perhaps uniquely, Crovie claims to be one of only two places in the entire Northern Hemisphere to be blessed with a North Pole. To get there, the visitor can simply walk the seafront path from the car park to the far end of the village, as far as the drying green beside the Mission Hall. There they will find a green painted metal clothes pole bearing the inscription *The North Pole*. Tourists and casual visitors are seemingly advised that "if you don't walk around the North Pole, then you haven't done Crovie."

11
CULLEN – HOME OF SKINK

Ask pretty much any Scot what they associate with the Moray seaside town of Cullen and the conversation will invariably turn to Skink. Cullen Skink to be precise. A hearty chowder-like soup whose main ingredients are smoked haddock, potatoes and milk with maybe a leek and some onion thrown in for good measure, the town is famous for it and rightly so. Even the road signs on the outskirts of town proclaim "Welcome to the Royal Burgh of Cullen. Home of Cullen Skink" and the local Cullen Bay Hotel proudly hosts the annual 'Cullen Skink World Championship'. In 2013 the event was won by local chef Tracey Fuller using her very own recipe which included some top-secret ingredients, prompting the judging panel to award her the winner's crown against stiff opposition from Portsoy, Mallaig and Aberdeen.

Cullen Viaduct

The popular tourist destination is well known for its history and connections to Robert the Bruce and William the Lion. There is also the Three Kings rock stack which is reputed to mark the graves of a trio of Norse pirate kings who died in battle at nearby Bauds in the year 962. The writer Doris Davidson based her romantic novel *The Three Kings* in the town with the lead character, the orphaned Katie Mair, renaming the rock stacks as 'The Three Wise Men', her trusted friends and the only ones to whom she could tell her troubles.

William the Lion granted Cullen a Royal Charter during his reign and Robert the Bruce granted a further charter in 1327. Although effectively abolished during the reorganisation of local government in 1975, the term Royal Burgh is still used by many former burghs, including Cullen, Kintore and Huntly as a reminder of a prestigious past including the right to be represented in the Parliament of Scotland and rights to appoint bailies with wide powers in civil and criminal justice matters. The Bruce connection goes far beyond the granting of a charter however. St Mary's Church lies just outside the town and sits within the policies of Cullen House. Dating from 1236 the building is situated in what would have been, until the rebuilding of Cullen in the 1820s, the centre of town. However, in a bold move the Fifth Earl of Seafield had the old town demolished and he then constructed an imposing wall around his estate. Fortunately, the Mercat Cross was preserved and re-located in the new town square but St Mary's and the Mercat Cross are virtually all that remain of the original Cullen. St Mary's was described by the late Regional Archaeologist Ian Shepherd as characteristic of the last phase of the medieval church in Scotland with "several later additions the building boasts a fine example of a Lairds Loft dating from 1602 plus both Gothic and Renaissance features."

Raised to collegiate status in 1543 the ornate tomb of Alexander Ogilvie of Findlater and Deskford, one of the principal funders of the extensions to the building, sits in the chancel within an ornate stone sarcophagus sculpted to represent the benefactor clad in knight's armour and with weeping figures carved on the front. The building's most prominent claim to fame however is as the reputed burial place of some gruesome relics of Elizabeth de Burgh. Born in Dunfermline in circa 1289 she had married Robert the Bruce in 1302 at the age of just thirteen. Crowned Queen of the Scots at Scone in March of 1306 her tenure as queen was short lived. Her husband was engaged in a full-scale civil war with the family and friends of John Comyn, whom he had murdered at the altar of Greyfriars Kirk in Dumfries, and was under threat by the forces of Edward I, so although the coronation at Scone had given him some legitimacy his overall position was quite uncertain.

Elizabeth de Burgh became concerned for the family's future and after the coronation she is reported to have said "It seems to me we are but a summer king and queen whom children crown in their support". After taking refuge in Kildrummy Castle for a period, she fled to Tain following the Bruce's defeat at the battle of Methven. She was then imprisoned in England for eight years until a prisoner exchange allowed her return to Scotland in 1314. Elizabeth died at Cullen Castle in 1327 and her entrails were removed for burial in St Mary's Church prior to her embalmed body being taken south to Dunfermline for proper burial. Her husband outlived her by less than two years but is said to have ensured an annual payment be made in perpetuity in gratitude for his wife's kind and respectful treatment by the people of Cullen. There is no record of any recent payments however and it seems likely that the accumulated debt is nowadays unenforceable in law. St Mary's is still in regular ecclesiastical use and in summer visitors can gain access on weekday afternoons.

Cullen's Seatown - underneath the arches

In the Nineteenth century, railway mania swept the United Kingdom and the railway reached Cullen in the 1880s with the extension of the Great North of Scotland Railway via Tochieneal and Garmouth. The most direct route through the town would have seen trains running through Cullen House policies but since the then Countess of Seafield objected to the prospect of noisy steam trains rumbling past her windows, the inhabitants of the town had to put up with the locomotives thundering over their rooftops instead via the Cullen Viaducts. The line through Cullen therefore opened in April 1886 following the lengthy and expensive construction of an elevated section of line incorporating the multi-arched viaducts which still dominate the town.

The Banffshire Reporter headlined with "Portsoy to Elgin Passenger Rail Service Opened" and proclaimed: "The Chairman of the Great North of Scotland Railway proposed the toast of the day, Success to the Moray Coast Railway. Many towns along the coast which have not hitherto had railway communications are now united to the great highways of commerce." There were some teething problems however, including a partial collapse of three of the bridge arches, necessitating the line's closure for three weeks while emergency repairs were made.

Fortunately, no trains were wrecked in the collapse and the viaducts stand to this day providing an insight into the skill and determination of the Victorian engineers. Keith-born railway engineer Joe Strachan (1933-2021) of Inverurie doubts if such a triumph of railway engineering could be built today. Commenting on the sheer volume of both dressed stone and limestone infill required for each pillar, and there are fourteen in the main span alone, he said "The skills to design these structures still exist but the skills to actually construct them are probably long gone." Nowadays the nearest railway station to Cullen is some fourteen miles south at Keith, but the town still benefits from the efforts of those Nineteenth century navvies and engineers both in terms of the visual impact of the viaducts and through their incorporation into the fifty-mile-long Moray Coastal Trail, linking Cullen with Forres.

Somewhat inevitably, Mary Queen of Scots passed through Cullen in 1562 during one of her extensive Scottish tours. Known in polite circles as Progressions, these tours often spanned months at a time. There were nine of these beginning in September 1561 and commentators have pointed to the fact that for someone who had previously spent such a short portion of her life in Scotland, she probably ended up seeing more of the country than almost any other monarch before or since. And it was these 'Progressions' that are largely responsible for the claims that "Mary Queen of Scots stayed here" in the guidebooks to historic houses all across Scotland.

In later years both Burns and Boswell visited the town. Robert Burns and Willie Nicol, his travelling companion, seemingly stayed for just one night in the August of 1787 before travelling on to Aberdeen via Slains Castle. Boswell commented that Cullen had "a comfortable appearance, though but a very small town, and the houses mostly poor buildings". Dr Johnson's take on Cullen was less charitable however and he wrote that he was "disgusted by the sight of dried haddocks broiled that they were served for breakfast".

In common with many Moray towns, Cullen has had to reinvent itself to meet the needs of the Twenty-first century. In summer the population of around thirteen hundred is swelled to well over two thousand by the seasonal influx of folk who flock to the area to enjoy both the mild climate and the wide range of attractions on offer. Alongside golf, fine sandy beaches and history the town has become a hub of the antique trade with a number of businesses offering a wide selection of books, jewellery and memorabilia. The regeneration of the town is a cause which Allan Milne of Cullen Antiques has committed to promote. Trading from converted church premises on the town's busy Seafield Street, Allan has plans to convert previously derelict buildings into an array of workshops, retail units and a garden centre stocking herbal and medicinal plants. Speaking in March 2014 he revealed that several entrepreneurs including a New Age shaman and a specialist bookshop had expressed interest in setting up in the town and that several other small businesses including a film workshop had expressed interest in what Allan said will be a "vibrant and welcome initiative which will add further feel-good factor to the town. Cullen needs new business ideas and we will ensure that premises are available for start-ups" he reflected "It's not Dragons Den, just good sense and good for the town." More recently local artist Carol Anne Taylor has opened a gallery in the town selling prints and original works of art.

Cullen is also home to a last resting place for pets. It all started in around 1992 when local lad Stephen Findlay buried Bruce, his young Alsatian, on scrubland owned by the Earl of Seafield just off the coastal path east of the harbour. Other folk followed his lead and within a short space of time the Cullen Pet Cemetery began filling up with not only dogs and cats, but also pet rabbits and budgies. There's even a grave dedicated to a Moray Firth dolphin washed ashore on the nearby beach. Stephen for his part, took on the unpaid role of caretaker and spent much of his spare time maintaining the graveyard. Inevitably over the years the site has attracted attention from officialdom intent on legalising the disposal of 'animal waste' and worse still, threatening fines for non-compliance with European Union regulations. Press coverage combined with local outrage eventually forced the authorities to reach a compromise and the place still exists to commemorate the lives of our furry friends. There are those who say that Her Majesty the Queen - herself a pet lover - intervened in the affair to sort things out and that she maybe had a discrete word with the Earl of Seafield. But that is of course an entirely unconfirmed story.

Just round from the pet graveyard is a largely forgotten cave which once housed a hermit named Charlie Marioni. Charlie, if indeed that was his real name, lived in the seaside-cave for some thirteen years during the 1920s and 1930s. A Frenchman by some accounts, or an Italian according to others, he was an affable sort of hermit who welcomed local walkers with an open smile and an open palm. Known locally as 'Charlie the Hermit' he scraped a living snaring rabbits and flogging postcards of himself posing alongside his ragged dwelling on the cliffs. The local chemist seemingly funded the printing of his postcards and promoted the hermit myth to tourists. In 1933 Charlie was arrested for some crime or other involving failing to register as an alien. Fined twenty shillings at Banff Sheriff Court, he seemingly took umbrage at this slight and headed off to pursue an itinerant life elsewhere. Local lore says that he ended up in a WW2 internment camp for enemy aliens where he died from typhoid or something equally awful. The truth of the matter will never be known. But some wonder to this day if Charlie Marioni was the original inspiration for Ben Knox, the hermit in Bill Forsyth's film *Local Hero*.

Cullen is certainly quirky in terms of its history and, as the staff of Cullen Golf Club will tell you, the place has one of the most remarkable golf courses in Europe with the outward nine being played along the cliff while the back nine are played at beach level. *Golf Monthly* once described the course as "the epitome of quirky, a course like no other." One wonders what Dr Johnson would have made of it all.

12
DUFFTOWN – MALT WHISKY CAPITAL OF THE WORLD

In a 1998 interview, Harry Potter author J. K. Rowling advised reporters from Scottish television that Hogwarts School of Witchcraft and Wizardry is located in the Highlands of Scotland. She declined to elaborate further despite the fact that *The Daily Prophet*, the UK's leading wizarding newspaper, had reported in the September of 1993 that "Sirius Black, that most infamous prisoner from Azkaban, has been sighted in Dufftown by an astute Muggle". International speculation grew and before long fans of the genre concluded that Hogwarts School, whose motto is of course 'Never tickle a sleeping dragon', might just be a short broomstick hop from the Speyside town of Dufftown!

Dufftown - Fife Street and Clock Tower

Bounded by both the River Fiddich and the Dullan Water, Dufftown sits fifty miles north west of Aberdeen and some seventeen miles south of Elgin. Home to the Speyside Whisky Festival and with a population heading towards the 1700 mark the place is, for good reason, internationally known as 'The Malt Whisky Capital of the World'. With a good few whisky distilleries plus a couple of busy cooperages situated in the vicinity, locals claim that the settlement - an important stop on both the Malt Whisky Trail and the thirteen-mile Isla Way path linking Dufftown with Keith - produces more malt whisky annually than any other mainland Scottish town and is a major player in a global industry which annually generates more than £3.3 billion for the UK economy. A popular tourist destination on the iconic Speyside Way, Dufftown offers visitors a wide range of activities ranging from guided distillery tours at the Glenfiddich Distillery to heritage railway journeys courtesy of the Keith & Dufftown Railway's Whisky Line.

On the southern outskirts of the town lies the historic Thirteenth century Mortlach Kirk. Ranked as one of the oldest sites of continuous Christian worship in Scotland, Mortlach has been in use continuously as a place of worship from around 566 AD when it was founded by Moluag of Bangor, a Christian missionary and contemporary of St. Columba. Expanded and renovated at various points in its history, the church features both a leper's window and a mort house. A weathered Pictish cross stands in the graveyard and an ancient symbol stone, uncovered by gravediggers in 1925 and bearing what some claim is an image of a hairy mammoth, guards the vestibule.

At the northern end of town, the massive battlements of Balvenie Castle guard the road as it crosses over the River Fiddich. Moated on three sides and currently in the care of Historic Scotland the castle overlooks Glenfiddich Distillery and is nowadays roofless and in ruins. Strategically sited to control movement through the mountain passes at Glen Rinnes, the Cabrach and Glen Fiddich, Balvenie was once the seat of power of the Comyns, one of the dominant families of Scotland during the Wars of Scottish Independence. Garrisoned by red-coated government troops during the bloody aftermath of the 1745 Rebellion, the castle is partially constructed using recycled stone removed from nearby Auchendoun Castle high up on the Cabrach. Predictably perhaps, Mary Queen of Scots spent a night at Balvenie and in 1644 the fortification briefly sheltered James Graham, the doomed Marquis of Montrose. All decent castles need a resident ghost and Balvenie is reputedly haunted by a White Lady accompanied by her groom and two dappled horses.

Until his death in 2009, Charles Beck Harman Nicholson, a US-born Coca Cola executive with distant Scottish roots who made his fortune marketing sugary drinks throughout the Italian mainland, held the title of Baron of Balvenie. A Princeton graduate and a native of Columbus Georgia, he acquired the Balvenie title in 1998 and went on to become honorary president of Dufftown and District Highland Games. An avid collector of ancient Greek coins he was a keen supporter of the arts and was a patron of Dufftown

Horticultural Society and a benefactor of Mortlach Kirk. On his death, both the Barony and his ownership of Balvenie passed to his nephew Jeremy Duncan Nicholson, a resident of Atlanta Georgia.

The Dufftown we see today was founded in 1817 by James Duff, Fourth Earl of Fife, and was conceived as a planned village. Historian Douglas G. Lockhart concluded that some 490 Scottish planned villages, including around a hundred in North East Scotland, were laid out between 1750 and the late 1850s. He writes that "Typically, the ground plan and provision of the basic infrastructure of streets, drainage and water supply, and the construction of a few public buildings was undertaken by the landowner. Incoming families normally built their own homes or contracted with tradesmen to build for them." Built to a rigidly defined grid pattern reminiscent of the likes of Tomintoul, Monymusk and Buckie, all roads through Dufftown run past the iconic four storey grey granite Category B listed Clock Tower at the junction of Church Street, Fife Street, Balvenie Street and Conval Street where the principal routes to Elgin, Keith, Tomintoul, Rhynie and Maggieknockater fan out to the north, east, south and west.

Dufftown's Clock Tower doubled formerly as the town gaol. At one time it seemingly housed an illicit still and has a quirky link with the coastal town of Banff. The Burns ballad 'MacPherson's Farewell' recounted in romantic detail the November 1700 execution of Kingussie-born bandit James MacPherson (1675-1700). As recounted in a previous chapter, the man was found guilty of being an 'Egyptian and a vagabond' and hung at Banff. Thereafter the history of the event becomes curiously unclear. A common thread though is the assertion that a pardon was on its way from the High Court at Edinburgh and that the Sheriff at Banff ordered the town clock put forward to ensure that the hanging could go ahead before the pardon arrived. Presumably the good folk of Banff were uneasy regarding the sheriff's murky deceit and at some point, the deadly timepiece was quietly sold off to the unsuspecting citizens of Dufftown. Mysteriously, there are claims that the infamous time piece once also graced the clock-tower of the old townhouse at Inverurie leading to speculation that Banff folk were quite adept at selling off dodgy timepieces.

In addition to the dubious tale of MacPherson's clock, the circa 1839 town centre clock tower sports interpretation plaques commemorating local laird Alexander Duff the Sixth Duke of Fife and also George Stephen (1829-1921), a local man and eldest of eight children. He was instrumental in financing and building the transcontinental Canadian Pacific Railway line linking the Atlantic and the Pacific coasts of Canada. In addition to the Dufftown plaque there is a high-altitude station on the line, Mount Stephen (5337ft), named after him. He later accepted a British peerage as Baron Stephen of Mount Stephen. Other famous folk associated with the town include Leslie Benzies a former CEO of Edinburgh based game developer Rockstar North, makers of the internationally popular Grand Theft Auto Series; and there is the important William Grant whisky link.

An essential port of call in Dufftown is the Whisky Museum on Conval Street. Established in 2002 and operated by registered charity Dufftown 2000, the museum doubles as both the local Tourist Information Centre and also as a well-informed local heritage centre. Over a latte supplied by the nearby Glassworks Gallery coffee shop, local historian Robin MacLennan, a fully paid-up, 'Lifetime Mate' of the Whisky Museum, related the strange but true tale of Glenfiddich founder William Grant. Amazingly perhaps, the man had never really set out to make a career out of whisky. "Dufftown, alongside having pure sources of water essential for the distilling of whisky also sits on a rich seam of limestone running through Glen Rinnes" said Robin. "William Grant started off his career as a clerk at the Tininver Lime Works at Crachie in 1863 and he wouldn't have been a distiller at all if the local laird had not refused to sell him land for a limestone quarry over near Drummuir. It was all down to pure chance that he began making whisky you see. The deal for purchasing the lime quarry was all but done and signed when the laird, seemingly on the advice of his head forester, pulled out". Apparently fear of damage to the estate timber resources made the landowner renege on the agreement. That failed land deal put an end to William's ambitions to become a limestone magnate, but after considering his options - which included emigrating to Jamaica to become a sugar planter - he started to build up a distillery business. He had by that time moved from the lime-works at Tininver to take up a post as head bookkeeper at Mortlach Distillery and had begun to accumulate funds with the intention of manufacturing malt whisky.

Eventually in 1886, exactly twenty years to the day since he started working at Mortlach and having purchased second-hand stills and mash-tuns from the Cardow Distillery at Knockando, he realised his dream with the building of a distilling plant on farmland at Mains of Balvenie. The rest is history. William Grant & Sons, makers of the single malt brands Glenfiddich and Balvenie, remains firmly in family ownership to this day and in 2014 recorded post-tax profits of £139.8 million. William Grant would certainly have been proud of his heritage.

Dufftown's railway history is closely tied up with its distilling history. Most of the North East distilleries are situated in fairly isolated parts of the countryside and during the nineteenth and twentieth centuries the rail network offered easy access to supplies of inputs such as barley and peat and an efficient means of transport for finished goods to distant markets. Indeed, many distilleries such as Dufftown's Mortlach and Towiemore were provided, by the Great North of Scotland Railway, with their very own private goods lines. Following the post-Beeching withdrawal of British Rail passenger and goods services the line through Dufftown fell into disuse and was partially saved when a heritage railway association intervened.

Dufftown Station

The Keith and Dufftown Railway Association took over possession of the Keith to Dufftown section of the line and the first heritage train service ran in July 2000 along the eleven-mile route between the two towns. Known as the Whisky Line and nowadays operated exclusively by volunteer staff, the association's stated aim is to run steam trains along the route and to re-establish the rail link with the national ScotRail network at Keith Station. Open for most of the year the line currently offers a 38-minute weekend and holiday service to Keith utilising nostalgic green and yellow liveried Diesel Multiples such as 'The Spirit of Banffshire'. Rolling stock on display at Dufftown Station includes a restored Canadian Sprinter track inspection locomotive and the association operates regular railroad specials including Scotch Nights, Whisky Runs and Santa Specials. During the 2014 season the line recorded 13,048 individual passenger journeys.

An old Dufftown saying claims that "Rome was built on seven hills but Dufftown stands on seven stills". The exact number of stills in the Whisky Capital of the World may have altered considerably since the rhyme was composed but since the majority of distillery tours involve tasters, the option of sampling whisky on the hoof is a pretty realistic plan. Local trekking specialists offer a guided Dufftown Distilleries Walk which includes exclusive access to the distillery sites at Pittyvaich, Mortlach, Glendullan, Parkmore, Glenfiddich, Balvenie, Dufftown, Kininvie and Convalmore. Dedicated whisky buffs, intent on drinking in a wee bit more local history, might be tempted to include stops at the various hostelries along the way ending up perhaps with a wee look at the 600 or so bottles of malt on display at the local Whisky Shop on Fife Street. A pair of sensible shoes and a pre-arranged lift home might well be the order of the day!

13
ELGIN – LANTERN OF THE NORTH

Despite the Wolf of Badenoch association, Elgin is a grand town full of rich history. Both English-born fascist Oswald Mosely and London-born writer Daniel Defoe visited, though at different times. Defoe thought highly of Elgin. In the journal of his 1724 tour of Great Britain, he writes: "In this rich country is the city, or town rather, of Elgin; I say city, because in antient time the monks claim'd it for a city; and the cathedral shews, by its ruins, that it was a place of great magnificence!"

Mosley, at least according to local lore, was heckled and maybe pelted by a crowd of anti-fascists and then run out of town. In more recent years the Beatles (billed as the Love Me Do Boys) began their 1963 Scottish tour in the town. They shared the bill with The Alex Sutherland Sextet at the Two Red Shoes Ballroom in January during a blizzard. They were not well known and admission was six shillings in old money. Takings were disappointing, according to Elgin music historian David Dills, and one local tale has a skint McCartney playing for his supper at a local wedding before the night's gig to raise petrol money for the journey to Dingwall the next day.

The debate surrounding Elgin's ancient Cathedral City status is ongoing, but for most of the twenty-three thousand residents, the road signs on the outskirts proclaiming Elgin a "Historic Cathedral City" plus the fact that the local football club is named Elgin City FC are perhaps proof enough. Situated five miles from the seaport of Lossiemouth, the Moray capital nowadays appears quite landlocked but this was not always the case. On the northern edge of town lies Spynie Palace. Once the principal residence of the Bishops of Moray and nowadays surrounded by dense woodland it sits on the edge of a partially drained sea loch. On close inspection, the visitor will discover that the palace ruins incorporate a water gate which at one time led to a fully functional harbour at the head of the five-mile long Spynie Loch. Until drained for agricultural purposes in the early Nineteenth century, the loch offered safe anchorage at the now vanished medieval town of Spynie for both fishing boats and small merchant ships trading up and down the Moray coast. Piecemeal attempts to drain the loch date from the Middle Ages but it was only with the completion of the Spynie Canal in 1812, to a plan prepared by Thomas Telford and Company, that the land occupied by the loch was successfully reclaimed.

Badly damaged in the 'Muckle Spate' floods of 1829 and redesigned at a cost of eight thousand pounds under the supervision of local engineer Peter MacBey the seven-mile-long Spynie Canal reopened without much fanfare in

Spynie Palace

1863 linking Spynie Loch to the sea outfall at Lossiemouth. Visitors however are unlikely to encounter either narrow boats or gondolas on the waterway since it was dug for land drainage purposes only; however, the watercourse must surely rate as the northernmost canal on mainland Scotland. Flooding in and around Elgin is not a new issue and the River Lossie has a well-documented history of bursting its banks. With eleven major floods recorded during the past fifty years alone, including the infamous 2002 event which caused considerable disruption including the closure of the Aberdeen to Inverness rail line, Moray Council quickly set in motion Scotland's biggest ever flood prevention scheme. Construction started on the £86 million Elgin Flood Alleviation Scheme in the April of 2011 and by August 2014, whilst only partially completed, the project was protecting over 270 low-lying residential and seventy-five business premises from the prospect of further flood damage. The works were finally completed in January 2016.

Created a Royal Burgh in the Twelfth century by King David I of Scotland, Elgin at that time boasted a castle perched on top of Lady Hill to the western side of the town. This may have been where King Duncan I died in August 1040 following his defeat by Macbeth at Pitgaveny on the outskirts of Elgin. Although unproven, he is popularly thought to have been temporarily buried in Elgin prior to his removal to Iona to be reburied amongst a veritable army of fellow Scottish Kings. The castle ruins on Lady Hill are still in evidence although the memorial to the Fifth Duke of Gordon nowadays dominates both the hilltop and the surrounding landscape. Erected in 1839 to a design by Edinburgh architect William Burn, the ninety-foot-tall Tuscan column commands stunning views over the Moray Firth from Covesea Lighthouse right across to Cullen, via a small north facing window accessed by a narrow spiral staircase. The statue of the Duke, designed by Scottish sculptor Handyside Ritchie and carved by Elgin sculptor Thomas Goodwillie, was added much later in 1855 and portrays the Duke in all of his finery as Chancellor of Marischal College in Aberdeen. Educated at Eton, the Fifth Duke raised the 92nd Highlanders commanding the regiment in Spain, Ireland and the Netherlands. He died heirless although rumour suggests that he sired at least three illegitimate children. A plaque on the base of the memorial column records that the monument was "Erected by public subscription in memory of George, the Fifth (and last) Duke of Gordon".

Bradshaw's Railway Guide for 1863 records that Elgin had a population of 7,277. Industry, Bradshaw wrote, included a woollen factory, several breweries, gas and water works. There were, he says, "five chapels, three schools, a prison and a fine library". Nowadays the railway continues to provide much needed transport links to both Inverness and the Central Belt. Commercial rail traffic has declined although Elgin still retains a goods yard and until recently boasted the most northerly manual signal box still in operation on the UK railway network. The lines to Lossiemouth and Craigellachie closed in the mid-1960s in line with the reorganisation of the railways following the Beeching Reports. Elgin's former West Station was modernised in 1990, Elgin East Station having closed for good in 1968.

The recent announcement by the Scottish Government that it intends to dual the entire length of the A96 from Aberdeen to Inverness by 2030 has renewed calls for a new Elgin bypass to be constructed and there are development plans in place to provide around 2,500 new houses plus a new industrial park to meet the needs of a fast-growing population. The food and drink sector is seen by planners as being critical to the local economy with brands such as Baxters, Walkers and global drinks giant Diageo providing significant economic benefit to the area. The recent opening of the Alexander Graham Bell Centre at Moray College campus has highlighted the ability of Elgin and indeed Moray's ability to diversify the local economy to meet the demands of the Twenty-first century. Jointly funded by Moray College, Highlands and Islands Enterprise, NHS Grampian and the EU, the centre provides facilities for research, education and continuing professional development (CPD) for the life science sector in the North East of Scotland. Telecommunications guru Alexander Graham Bell

(1847-1922), although not a son of Elgin, famously spent an early part of his career teaching music and elocution at the Weston House School for Young Gentlemen in the town's Gordon Street. Better known for his telecommunications work, Bell specialised in the provision of speech therapy for the profoundly deaf and while in Elgin he is said to have developed a phonetic alphabet for the deaf and begun experiments using tuning forks which probably influenced his development of the telephone.

Johnstons of Elgin are perhaps the oldest established employers in the area with 450 local employees and a further 600 nationwide, engaged in the production of yarns and woven fabrics. Owned by the Urquhart and Harrison families, annual turnover for the 220-year-old firm peaked at £77 million in 2019. Established in 1797, the family owned firm have been weaving luxury vicuna and cashmere fabrics since 1851 and operates the only remaining vertical woollen mill in Scotland. The factory has a visitor centre offering conducted tours to visitors. Offices in Paris, Dusseldorf, New York and Tokyo enhance the brand and there are shops in London, St Andrews and in Edinburgh.

But all is not about tartan yarn or Bakelite phones in Elgin. Just as staff at the Mearns based Lewis Grassic Gibbon Centre are seemingly plagued by tourists enquiring about the apes, the good folk of Elgin are, in a similar vein, often asked about the Elgin Marbles.

Fife-born Thomas Bruce, Seventh Earl of Elgin and Eleventh Earl of Kincardine appears to have started the ball rolling when, in about 1801 and using his authority as British Ambassador to the Ottoman Empire, he removed a set of classical Greek marble sculptures from the Parthenon and from other buildings on the Acropolis above Athens. After shipping the antiquities home to decorate his mansion in Scotland he sold them off to the British Museum in 1816 for £35,000 in an attempt to settle his debts. Also known as the Parthenon Marbles, the Elgin Marbles have little to do with Elgin although Elgin Museum have a scale replica by Scottish artist David Henning on public display.

Recently shortlisted from eight hundred museums in the Telegraph Family Friendly Museum Awards, Elgin Museum is owned and managed by The Moray Society and dates from 1843 making it Scotland's oldest independent museum. Staffed largely by volunteers and sponsored by local businesses including Baxters, Walkers and Johnstons of Elgin, the Grade A listed museum building sits at the east end of the High Street. Exhibits include coins from the Birnie Hoard, a Bronze Age cist from Roseisle plus finds from the Sculptor's Cave at Covesea. There are also some nine hundred fish and reptile fossils dating back 370 million years including specimens of footprints left by Permian reptiles fossilised in the sandstone rocks along the nearby Hopeman coast. The collection has been recognised by the Scottish Government as being of National Significance. A more modern local historic Elgin exhibit sits outside the Jet petrol station on the Elgin to Lossiemouth road, where a retired Blackburn Buccaneer military jet, which last saw action in the 1991 Gulf War, waits patiently for refuelling in the forecourt. Quite what Daniel Defoe would have made of that is anyone's guess.

The centre of town, or city, depending on your world view, is nowadays lined with modern shops but still manages to retain a distinctly old-world atmosphere. Elgin High Street, for example, sports many architecturally fine buildings such as St Giles Church, Thunderton House and the magnificently arcaded Braco Banking House all of which vie for attention with the old Muckle Cross, Dr Gray's Hospital and local architect Thomas Mackenzie's delightfully decorated three-tiered 1846 fountain. Thunderton House is today a mere shadow of its former self having been altered extensively over the past four hundred or so years. Formerly the town residence of the Earls of Moray, it seemingly housed Charles Edward Stuart prior to Culloden in 1746, and hosted the funeral banquet for the Jacobite First Duke of Gordon in 1716. It has seen service as a Haldanite Church, a furniture warehouse and until quite recently a public house. Local lore suggests that the building at one time sported a windmill but no vestige of this remains above ground. St Giles's Church is by contrast a much more modern structure. Dating from 1826 and by Aberdeen architect Archibald Simpson, the Doric columned building houses a fine Art Deco-style pipe organ in the west gallery. There is no trace of the original church which, like the cathedral, suffered various trials including being burnt by the Wolf of Badenoch in 1390. On the very day that the Battle of Bothwell Bridge was fought, Sunday the twenty-second of June 1679, St Giles suffered a partial roof collapse following morning service, leading some commentators of the time to wonder if the forces of divine retribution were at work.

Elgin is popularly known as a cathedral town and, despite the rack and ruin, Elgin's roofless cathedral remains a major tourist draw and a mainstay of the town's claim to city status. By most accounts Alexander Stewart was a fearsome character. Even 600 years after his death, his reputation as the Wolf of Badenoch is indelibly associated with the destruction of Elgin Cathedral. In truth however, his burning of the cathedral was just one episode in a series of destructive events leading to the ruinous state of the structure today. Established in 1224, the cathedral was damaged by fire in 1270, a full 120 years before Alexander Stewart vented his rage on the building. A third incendiary attack is recorded as having been carried out in 1402 by Alexander, Lord of the Isles.

Elgin Cathedral

With the coming of the Reformation in 1560, Elgin Cathedral's status as 'The Lantern of the North' rapidly declined. The Kirk of St Giles became the dominant parish church in Elgin and the cathedral fell into disuse and abandonment. The final indignity came when in 1567 an Act of Parliament authorised the removal of the lead from the cathedral roof in order to pay for the upkeep of the army. In due course, the stripped lead made its way to Aberdeen harbour to be loaded, alongside lead from the roof of Aberdeen's St Machar Cathedral, onto a ship bound for some scrapyard in Holland. Now, by the time Dr Samuel Johnson visited the cathedral in 1773 during one of his road trips around Scotland, the central tower had collapsed taking with it much of the north transept. Surveying the sorry state of the buildings Johnson wrote that "A Scotch army in those times was very cheaply kept; yet the lead must have borne so small proportion to any military expense that it is hard not to believe the reason to be merely popular and the money intended for some private purse." On hearing that the ship carrying the cargo of lead had foundered in a squall just off Aberdeen Harbour, he concluded "I hope every reader will rejoice … that this ship of sacrilege was lost at sea!"

In the Scotland of the sixteenth and seventeenth centuries literally anyone could be accused of dealing with the Devil and practising the black arts. These were times of great superstition, backed up by the force of what nowadays might appear to be a cruel and brutal legal system which routinely employed torture to determine the guilt or innocence of those unfortunates accused of consorting with the devil. Taking her lead from a Europe-wide Inquisition leading to the mass burning of heretics and those thought guilty of witchcraft, Mary Queen of Scots had officially banned witchcraft in Scotland in 1563. Known as Mary's Law, the Witchcraft Act of 1563 defined witchcraft as sorcery and described a witch as a person considered to have supernatural powers granted by Satan in exchange for the giving up of their soul. Under Mary's Law, both the practice of witchcraft and the act of consorting with witches were capital offences. Although repealed in 1735, at which time the House of Lords considered the crime of witchcraft to be "an impossible offence", witchcraft in fact remained on the United Kingdom statute books in various forms up until 1951. Estimates of the numbers of people executed in Scotland during the period 1563 to 1735 vary widely, but the figures are likely to be in the thousands and most towns and cities have both tales and historic sites related to this period of terror.

In Keith for example there is the notorious Gaun's Pot, a pool just under the Auld Bridge where those accused of witchcraft were once drowned. Forres has the Witches Stone where according to the Royal Commission on the Ancient and Historical Monuments of Scotland "from Cluny Hill witches were rolled in stout barrels through which spikes were driven. Where the barrels stopped, they were burned along with their mangled contents." It may be no accident that Shakespeare placed his three witches in Macbeth on a heath near Forres. However, it wasn't just the ordinary mortal who could be accused of doing the Devils work as the slightly romanticised tale of Robert Gordon illustrates. Gordonstoun School lies just a few miles northwest of Elgin at Duffus. A co-educational independent school for boarding and day pupils, famous past pupils have included the likes of Prince Charles and the establishment is named after a Seventeenth century aristocrat by the name of Sir Robert Gordon. Better known as the Wizard of Gordonstoun, Sir Robert, the Third Baronet of Gordonstoun, was born in 1647 and lived out his fifty-seven years during a highly superstitious period in Scottish history. Educated in Italy where he studied both chemistry and mechanics, he had somehow acquired the reputation of being a wizard. It was said he "gave himself away" in order to gain unnatural knowledge. Some said that, like Faustus, he had sold his soul to the Devil in exchange for an additional thirty years of life.

The rumours followed him home to Gordonstoun, where he was said to have become involved in conducting occult experiments in a round house connected to the sea caves at nearby Covesea beach via a secret tunnel. Locals asserted that he was a necromancer who supped with the Devil and danced wildly with naked witches. He was said to cast no shadow and was rumoured to have learned the mysteries of necromancy during his residence at the University of Padua. Many other dark rumours circulated and Sir Robert's reputation was perhaps not enhanced when an unlikely tale emerged alleging that he had slowly cooked a Salamander over the course of seven years in order to persuade it to reveal scientific secrets. Fortunately for Sir Robert his great wealth and not a few high connections meant that those who would try him for wizardry were pretty much powerless to act against him. In reality he was probably just a rather eccentric but dedicated scientist who lived in a highly superstitious age.

One of Sir Robert's scientific achievements was the design of a "better sea pump" for the British Navy. Samuel Pepys, who was Secretary to the Navy at the time, obtained a warrant from King James II to pay Sir Robert £318 in recompense for the new and improved pump design which was according to Pepys "Tried in the fleet and highly approved of and found to far exceed anything of the kind then known both for the facility of working and for the amount of water it discharged being beyond what has ever been achieved by the present ordinary chain pump." Praise indeed.

The Wizard of Gordonstoun, aka Sir Robert the Warlock, met a natural death in 1704 and the last convicted witch in Scotland, an unfortunate lady by the name of Janet Horne, was burned at the stake in Dornoch in 1722. Oddly though, further prosecutions under what had by then become known as The Fraudulent Mediums Act occurred in 1944 when two separate cases involving mediums were brought resulting in the convictions of Jane Rebecca York and Helen Duncan. Ms York was fortunate in being subjected to a mere fine amounting to five pounds after being convicted of falsely claiming that her spirit guide, a Zulu warrior known as Guide Spirit Zulu, could contact the dead. The unfortunate Ms Duncan received a nine-month prison sentence following her detailed revelations regarding a highly censored and extremely secret report about the wartime sinking with great loss of life of the battleship HMS Barham off Dakar in 1941. Seemingly the authorities viewed her powers as a medium as a threat to national security during the run up to the invasion of Europe and felt the need to silence her. But back to Sir Robert Gordon. Whatever the truth about mediums, warlocks and witches Sir Robert was probably not in league with Devil. He probably did cast a shadow and almost certainly was endowed with scientific knowledge far advanced for the times he lived in. And of course, he invented that improved bilge pump for the British Navy.

14
ELLON – PEARL OF BUCHAN

With a population of around 9,900, half of whom probably commute to work elsewhere, Ellon is often viewed as a mere dormitory town serving the industrial and commercial needs of Aberdeen and the offshore oil and gas industry. However, the town has a rich history much of which is intimately connected with that of the River Ythan. At a mere twelve metres above sea level and standing astride the lowest fording point on the river, the town has grown in stature over the centuries in line with the general improvements in transport infrastructure. Although bypassed by road improvements during the latter part of the Twentieth century, the settlement at Ellon has been, since pre-Roman times, a strategic crossing point allowing easy access south to Aberdeen and north to Moray and the Aberdeenshire coast. The creation of the Aberdeen to Peterhead turnpike road, the building of bridges across the Ythan and the arrival of the railways have each in their time provided an economic boost to the town. Roman Legions, the armies of Robert the Bruce and more recently Lord George Murray's Jacobite army on the long march to Culloden all passed through the town crossing the Ythan via the old ford.

What impact the Romans had on Ellon is little known although the legions were certainly in the area in the time of Julius Agricola in AD 84 and in the later reign of Septimus Severis. Bruce's armies however changed the face of Ellon completely during what came to be known as the Harrying of Buchan, also known as the Herschip of Buchaine. In a calculated and cruel move, Bruce's soldiers burned the township of Ellon to the ground and put the inhabitants to the sword. This brutal act of reprisal against the supposed supporters of the Clan Comyn took place in 1308 during the Wars of Scottish Independence. Virtually the whole of Buchan was laid waste by The Bruce's army under the command of his brother Edward following the May 1308 victory at the Battle of Barra near Inverurie. Bruce's men put to the sword all those deemed disloyal. Farms, homes and crops were burned and livestock slaughtered. By terrorising the population, Bruce ensured that the folk of Buchan lost all loyalty to the Comyn clan who had dominated Buchan for almost a century. A redistribution of former Comyn wealth to families such as the Hays completed the process and the Comyn never again gained the strength to rally against Bruce's supporters. John Barbour the Scottish poet and churchman (1320-1395) describes the events:

"And gert his men bryn all Buchaine,
Fra end till end and sparyt nane,
And heryit thaim in sic maneir,
That eftre that weile fifty year,
Men meynt the hership of Buchaine."

The New Bridge over the Ythan at Ellon

In more peaceful and perhaps more civilised times, improvements in agriculture and communication revived Ellon's fortunes and when the railway arrived in 1861 the Buchan capital's position as a prosperous market town crystallised. Nowadays only the Station Hotel survives to remind of the heady days when the area around the rail station bustled with both passenger and freight traffic and it is difficult to appreciate the effect that rail transportation had on the local economy. Royal Mail, livestock, coal, crops, eggs and even newspapers moved swiftly over the rail network. New markets opened up and Ellon prospered. As always however, technology moved on and by the 1920s trunk roads throughout the North East had improved to the point where the motor truck and local buses could compete with the railways. By then, the old road bridge over the River Ythan was in urgent need of replacement. With a roadway a mere 16ft wide it was quite unsuited to the needs of modern motor transport. Retained as a pedestrian bridge running alongside the modern road bridge it had been completed in 1793, after two years of construction and remains today the last surviving example of the work of the Banff mason James Robertson. It is similar in design to his 1791 bridge over the Don in Inverurie which was demolished in 1924 to be replaced by a modern reinforced concrete crossing.

Records held by the Royal Commission on the Ancient and Historical Monuments of Scotland indicate that following Robertson's completion of the Inverurie bridge in 1791, the timber shuttering used to form the arches was floated down the River Don, shipped north to Newburgh then floated up the River Ythan for use in the construction of Ellon's Auld Brig. River traffic had in fact been navigating the Ythan between the port of Newburgh and the Meadows four miles upstream since at least the Fifteenth century and the river remained navigable to medium sized coastal boats until fairly recent times. In both Victorian and Edwardian times, barges laden with agricultural lime, guano and coal were towed upstream from Newburgh to the pier at The Meadows just south of Ellon by shallow draft steam driven paddle tugs such as the wonderfully named SS Despatch.

However, just as Dr Beeching's report *The Reshaping of British Railways* would later close Ellon's rail links with the North East, the tide of economic change eventually killed off the coastal steamer trade and the Ythan has nowadays become a haven for wildlife including otters, wildfowl and perhaps even fresh water mussels. In past centuries there was unrelenting commercial exploitation of Scottish fresh water pearl mussels and the creatures, which can live for 100 years and are nowadays protected under the Nature Conservation (Scotland) Act, remain under threat across the entire Scottish river network. The Twelfth century Scottish monarch Alexander I, King of Scots, was said to have amassed the finest pearl collection of any man living and Julius Caesar's biographer, Suetonius, records that Caesar's lust for pearls was just one of the many reasons for the Roman invasion of Britain in the August of 55BC. The Scottish Crown Jewels, nowadays displayed at Edinburgh Castle, are said to include a large Buchan pearl found during the early Seventeenth century in the Kelly Burn, a tributary of the River Ythan.

Ellon nowadays retains many reminders of the past in the form of buildings such as the Tudor Gothic 'Victoria Hall' in Station Road. The hall's foundation stone, complete with a time capsule including various coins and newspapers of the day, was laid in September 1900. Completed in 1901, it remains in regular use hosting events as diverse as Wrestle Zone and the Ythan Hairst Reel Nicht. Further buildings of note include the quite stunning 1870 Early English style St Mary on the Rock church and the ruins of Ellon Castle which sit enclosed

St Mary on the Rock, Ellon

within a twelve-foot-high wall known locally as the Deer Dyke. The short walk from the river to the top of Bridge Street reveals a mixture of the old and new including the site of Neil Ross's Garage and The Chestnuts which was formerly the residence of Sir James Reid. Sir James served for much of his life as not only Queen Victoria's physician but also her confidant. After Victoria's death in 1901 he continued to serve the Royal Family, attending to both Edward VII and George V before dying in 1923.

Local entrepreneur Neil Ross must have been quite a character. Originally a fee'd farm labourer he opened a bike shop in the town in 1917 and later moved into the old McGlashan's Brewery on the west side of Bridge Street where he built up a highly successful garage and tractor repair business. Known to work from dawn until well after midnight he is remembered as having put down his success to his hatred of the 24/7 drudgery of farm work. Neil's workshop and indeed the brewery are long gone but in modern times brewing has returned to the town in the shape of the BrewDog production plant sited in the town's Balmacassie Industrial Estate. With a staff of around ninety and big plans for expansion, the state-of-the-art craft brewery supplies BrewDog pub outlets across the UK including DogTap which is the brewery's on-site tap-room at its headquarters in Ellon. General Manager Sara Jastrzebski related "Shortly after we moved to Ellon in 2011, we realised we needed to expand production rapidly to meet spiralling demand, hence the shiny new fermentation plant attached to the original factory building." Global domination is the companies stated aim and to that end BrewDog now exports beers such as 'Sink the Bismarck' and 'Punk IPA' to markets right across the globe.

Ellon has strong connections with a good many famous folk, many of whom would have attended Ellon Academy. A Queen's Scout, Bill Spence (1943-2020) began his career as a farm labourer after leaving school at fifteen with little in the way of academic qualifications. Son of a van driver he ended up as Deputy Chief Constable of Tayside and is remembered for his early support for the use of DNA testing in police work. Instrumental in the setting up of the Police Forensic Science Laboratory in 1989, he was perhaps unfairly vilified in the press when he allegedly ordered officers to ban the Dons victory lap at Hamden following their 1982 Scottish Cup win in a bid to avoid unrest.

Percussionist Dame Evelyn Glennie was also educated at Ellon Academy. Another Ellon worthy was Alexander Mitchell who emigrated from Scotland to the US at age twenty-two to eventually become the Congressional Representative for Wisconsin; and then there was Tom Pirie. Better known perhaps as Boatie Tam, he was well known in the town and famously ferried folk across the Ythan just as his forbears had done for well over a century. In days past, passenger ferries lined the Scottish waterways and Deeside alone boasted as many as nineteen along the length of the River Dee at one time.

Boatie Tam died in 1992 and there the tradition ended. His family had operated the passenger ferry over the Ythan since the middle of the Nineteenth century. They were essentially crofters and had several other income streams. But maybe the ferry service paid most of the rent. In the early years of the Twentieth century, you could cross for a penny although poorer folk might pay with a snared rabbit or an empty jam jar which could be swapped for a few half-pennies at the local store. Local lore insists that the postie and the minister travelled free of charge. Even the laird is rumoured to have gotten a free ride on occasion although why he would want to cross his own river in a coble is baffling. The river crossing where Tam plied his trade sports a footbridge nowadays and the family croft house is all done up and modernised. In fact, I doubt if Tam, if he were alive today, would even recognise the place.

James Boswell and Samuel Johnson stopped in the town for an extended breakfast whilst en route to the Western Isles in the late August of 1773. Robert Burns seems to have been less fortunate however as this diary entry regarding his September 1787 proposal to dine with George Gordon, Third Earl of Aberdeen illustrates: "Entrance denied to everyone owing to the jealousy of Threescore over a kept country wench!" He writes acidly. The bard's reputation with the ladies had likely forewarned the old Earl who seemingly kept several mistresses in various local country retreats including Ellon Castle. Known widely as the Wicked Earl, the scandal ridden peer sired children by at least three of his mistresses in addition to the six borne by his long suffering wife, Catherine Hanson, a cook from Wakefield who had allegedly forced him into marriage at gunpoint in 1759 following an affair. Ellon Castle nowadays is in ruins and the Wicked Earl's mistresses are long gone. The town of Ellon however continues to adapt according to the needs of the times just as it has always done. As Burns once said "There is no such uncertainty as a sure thing."

An infrequent but notorious visitor to Ellon was the safe cracker and prison escapologist extraordinaire, Johnny Ramensky. Having drifted into organised crime at an early age Gentle Johnny as he was often called, due his frequent habit of surrendering to the police without much of a struggle, was to spend much of his adult life in prison and much of his prison life escaping from behind bars. In 1934 he escaped from Peterhead Prison and in scenes reminiscent of the manhunt in John Buchan's famous novel *The 39 Steps*, police set up roadblocks throughout Scotland. Crofts and farms were searched and vehicles were stopped to check for suspicious looking passengers wearing prison issue garb. Quite which bridge Johnny used to cross the River Ythan is not certain although most accounts point to the road bridge at the foot of Bridge Street as being the likely culprit. What is however fairly certain is that the escapee evaded the police road block on the bridge by edging hand over hand along the stonework underneath the structure before slipping quietly away south only to be recaptured in a tattie field near Balmedie.

Johnny Ramensky was to repeat his trick of sneaking over the Ythan unseen some eighteen years later before yet again being caught near Balmedie. In the intervening period he had gained a certain notoriety when he broke into an Aberdeen laundry and blew one of the two safes inside. In a letter dated October thirteenth 1938 intended for the prison review board he writes

> "I want to inform the proper authorities to remove a charge of gelignite which is inside the lock of the small safe. The police think that the explosive was used up but it was not ... I had both safes ready for firing. I blew the big safe first and on searching it found the key for the small safe. So, I put the key in the lock of the small safe and opened it. I could not get the gelignite out again because once in and round the lock it was out of sight."

The Aberdeen police were not at all amused since the gelignite rigged second safe was at the time locked securely up in a police department strong room awaiting return to the laundry head office. Ramensky went on to serve as a demolition engineer during WW2 after which he returned to his old ways. A popular song about him titled *The Ballad of Johnny Ramensky* was composed by Labour MP Norman Buchan and recorded for posterity by the Scottish folk singer Hamish Imlach. Gentle Johnny died aged 67, in Perth Royal Infirmary in November 1972. He was in the midst of serving yet another sentence, this time at Perth Prison, having passed through Ellon during the course of at least two further escape attempts. Like many before him, including the ancient Romans, he simply couldn't resist crossing the Ythan at Ellon on the long road south.

15
FOCHABERS – SOUP, JAM AND ZULUS

Typical of the many planned villages of the North East, the Speyside village of Fochabers was largely demolished then rebuilt on the present-day site by a past Duke of Gordon to make way for his new castle. Nowadays the castle is largely diminished but Fochabers still flourishes, not least because of its strong connection with Cock-a-Leekie Soup and jam. In fact, the village is in a way a sort of Dundee but without the journalism or the jute. The soup and jam story runs along the following lines according to Baxters of Speyside's marketing blurb: "George Baxter had been working as a gardener for the Duke of Richmond and Gordon on the Gordon Estate, when he decided, with encouragement from friends and family, to start his own grocery business. The story goes that George Baxter borrowed £100 from family members to open a small grocery shop in the village of Fochabers. Here, in the back shop, his wife Margaret began making jams and jellies with fruits from the local area."

Gordon Castle entrance, Fochabers

Seemingly the Baxter products were an instant hit with the duke and soon found their way onto the table at Gordon Castle. Land for a jam factory was soon purchased from the Duke of Richmond and Gordon and - to cut a long story short - the family firm grew from strength to strength. In modern times the factory employs some 1600 workers, exports produce worldwide and turns over (in 2016) £248 million. And all on the back of a few jars of jam and a few saucepans full of Cock-a-Leekie Soup! Then of course there are the fountains of which Fochabers boasts two. The first, and most obvious is the fountain in the main square and bears the inscription:

"Erected by the inhabitants of Fochabers in acknowledgement of the liberality of the Sixth Duke of Richmond and Gordon in supplying water to the town – 1878."

Recently restored, this extravagantly decorated Victorian cast-iron fountain boasts two circular basins atop a decorative base replete with acanthus leaves and attendant cherubs. Listed Grade B, the impressive structure sits alongside a fine Georgian church complete with clock tower and dated 1798.

Meanwhile down at the local cricket field Fochabers boasts a much less grand fountain but with perhaps a much more interesting history. Hollywood hero Michael Caine may have successfully defended Rorke's Drift against the Zulu armies on the big screen, however the truth about the Zulu war turns out to be slightly different from the studio version. Travellers often drive past this fountain, never thinking to stop and read the inscription. The curious however will discover that it commemorates none other than Major Allan Wilson, late bank clerk of the Fochabers Savings Bank.

In December 1878 a colonial government headed by Sir Henry Bartle Edward Frere, a British colonial administrator, had invaded the Kingdom of Zululand. He did so without the prior permission or indeed prior knowledge of the British Government and in the hope that he could capture Cetshwayo, the politically troublesome Zulu King, before his London masters had even discovered that hostilities had begun. Communications in the 1890s were slow and news of the invasion would he hoped reach London long after hostilities had ceased. Things however did not go smoothly and the war was to last until 1881. The bloodshed and political upheaval resulted in Bartle Frere's recall to London where he faced charges of misconduct and was disgraced. This small monument on the path to the cricket field provides a solid link to those sombre events.

The Wilson Fountain at Fochabers

The Wilson Fountain was commissioned by the Duke of Richmond and Gordon in 1895 and is inscribed:

"Erected by the natives of Fochabers to commemorate the heroic stand made against the forces of the King of Matabeleland by Major Allan Wilson of this town who with a small band of comrades fell bravely fighting against overwhelming odds near the Shangani River in South Africa on the fourth of December 1893."

Major Wilson (1856-1893) was born in Glen Urquhart and is perhaps best remembered locally for his leadership of the Shangani Patrol. His death in battle against the Zulu army made him a national hero. Upon completion of his apprenticeship at the Fochabers bank, he sailed to the Cape Colony to join a locally recruited paramilitary outfit named The Cape Mounted Rifles. He then fought in the first Anglo-Zulu War (1879) and the First Boer War (1880-1881) and was promoted to Sergeant. After taking his discharge he became a trader and gold prospector and he took up a commission in the Basuto Police. Later he served in the Bechuanaland Exploration Company as Chief Inspector and was sent as their representative to Fort Victoria (now Masvingo) in Matabeleland, serving as the senior officer in the Victoria Volunteers. He quickly rose to the rank of Major and commanded the Shangani Patrol during the First Matabele War. On the fourth of December 1893, he and thirty-four of his men were completely cut off from the main column and killed by Ndebele warriors in what newspapers of the time portrayed as the British equivalent of Custer's Fifth Cavalry last stand at the Little Bighorn. In desperation and only hours before his death, Wilson sent Frederick Russell Burnham, an American adventurer and close friend of Baden-Powell, and two other scouts to seek reinforcements from the main column commanded by Major Patrick Forbes.

Unfortunately, the battle raging around the main column was just as intense and there was never any realistic hope of anyone reaching Wilson and his men in time to avert disaster. Wilson is buried, along with most of his patrol alongside Cecil Rhodes in the Matabo Hills in modern day Zimbabwe. Rhodes was to continue the colonial exploitation of that part of Africa and even today the ramifications of his misrule rumble on. In a modern day Zimbabwe suffering economic ruin and hyperinflation a post Mugabe regime seeks the return of the severed heads of "Freedom Fighters from the First Revolutionary War". Better known nowadays as Chimurenga, the skulls include patriots hanged by British colonialists and are nowadays stored at the British Museum. The modern-day narrative echoes both that of the Elgin Marbles and the desecration of the graves of indigenous people in Australia and other lands.

There is no suggestion of Wilson having either oversight or even knowledge of such sacrilege. Wilson's death made the London headlines and alongside achieving a lasting and prominent place in Rhodesian colonial history, led to a run in of all places Covent Garden. A patriotic play titled *Cheer, Boys, Cheer!* was produced and ran in London for just over two years. In the play it was claimed that in the killing of Wilson and his small band of heroes, Lobengula lost at least eighty of his Royal Guard plus around five hundred Ndebele warriors. Wilson was portrayed on stage as the very last to fall with the wounded men of the Shangani Patrol loading rifles to pass to him during the final stages of the heroic action.

When the ammunition ran out, the wounded men of the patrol are said to have risen to their feet to sing a patriotic rendering of *God Save the Queen* before succumbing to their attackers. Finally, unable to fight on and with both arms shattered, the bloodstained Fochabers bank clerk stepped out from behind a barricade of dead and dying horses, staggered toward the enemy, and was promptly speared to death by a young Ndebele warrior. The truth of the matter may have been slightly different, but that's showbusiness! Maybe the Major would have approved. But then again, maybe he should have stuck to banking.

16
FRASERBURGH – THE BROCH

Local author Stanley Bruce, sometimes known as The Bard o' The Broch, records that "The Fraser family is thought to have originated in Anjou or maybe Normandy in France." He goes on to say that "The French word for strawberry is Fraise" and that the town name derives from the silver strawberry flowers of the Fraser coat of arms. It's a useful theory. A prolific poet and local historian, Stanley's flowing pen covers a multitude of places, people and events relating to Fraserburgh and the land around the fisher town. From the Marconi wireless shack which once broadcast to America from Broadsea, to connections with Scottish Samurai Thomas Blake Glover, to the fisher-folk and the lifeboat volunteers his body of work rarely misses a beat when it comes to his home town. Alongside the likes of Christian Watt, the fish wife who lost her man at sea and his eloquent piece about First Footing in the Broch, he even finds beauty in the *Shearwater*, the local dredger tasked with keeping the harbour entrance clear of silt:

> "Without her services where would we be?
> We widnae get ony fishing boats,
> Oot tae the North Sea.
> The harbours wid a' be silted up
> and that's a guarantee,
> If it wisnae for the work,
> O' this dredger."

But even Stanley failed to record that big event in 1904 when the streets of Fraserburgh were filled with the whoops of Red Indians and the sharp bugles of US Cavalry advancing on the links in an early Twentieth century American invasion of Fraserburgh. Shortly after dawn on Tuesday August the thirtieth 1904, several hundred curious onlookers looked on as three special trains from Peterhead pulled in to Fraserburgh railway station. The assembled crowd must have been agog as an army of strangely clad men and women began to unload the contents of the boxcars before proceeding down Dalrymple Street towards the Links. Dozens of horse-drawn wagons piled high with circus tents, eighty mounted Lakota Indians in traditional dress and a contingent of blue liveried US Cavalry led the way, closely followed by Cuban Patriots, South American Gauchos and Mexican Vaqueros. On arrival at the Links, the cortege set about assembling a vast tented village complete with side shows, stables, carpenter's shop and even a smithy. The Fraserburgh Herald reported on the "marvellously quick way that the greater part of the Links was transformed into a canvas village" and commented on the "enormous number of visitors" who had arrived from nearby towns such as St Combs, New Aberlour and Strichen.

Widely billed in the local newspapers as "POSITIVELY THE FINAL VISIT TO GREAT BRITAIN" and "AN INTERNATIONAL CONGRESS OF THE WORLDS ROUGH RIDERS", the eight hundred performers and five hundred or so horses of Buffalo Bill's Wild West Show had arrived in town. At 2 pm on the dot a bugle note signalled the start of the show of the century. The Cowboy Band marched into the arena playing the *The Star-Spangled Banner* to an audience of perhaps as many as ten thousand and the event of the century began with a series of stirring pageants which, although distinctly lacking in historical authenticity, must have represented something of a culture shock to the assembled audience of country folk and fishers. With Colonel William F. Cody atop his white charger directing proceedings, a litany of sanitised US history was re-enacted for the benefit of the folk of the Broch. The Deadwood Stagecoach was ambushed, Custer's Last Stand was re-enacted and, as was his habit, Buffalo Bill demonstrated his marksmanship and horsemanship to an

Buffalo Bill and 'The Greatest Show on Earth' on the pier at Fraserburgh - 1904

admiring crowd. No spectators were reported shot but Native Americans were apparently slaughtered by the dozen. Somewhat oddly perhaps, one of the biggest draws of the show was billed as "The Intrepid Cowboy Cyclist in his Wonderful Bicycle Leap through Space." A precursor perhaps of those daredevil motorcycle stunt riders so beloved of folk at the likes of Keith and 'Turra' Show. Following the evening performance, the show village was dismantled and loaded onto the waiting trains for the short journey south to Huntly before heading off to Perth.

The same railway which brought the Intrepid Cowboy Cyclist to Fraserburgh had been instrumental in the increasingly rapid growth of the town in the years following the extension of the Great North of Scotland Railway to the town in 1865. When the very first passenger steam train was run on the line in the April of that year, thousands of folks who had maybe never even seen a train before descended on the Broch to see the opening ceremony and indulge in the cheap introductory fares offered by the railway company. The railways soon caught on and although they must have had a detrimental effect on the coastal shipping trade to and from the harbour, the speed and efficiency of rail transport brought many benefits to the town. In the boom fishing years of the nineteenth and early twentieth centuries the railways provided both transport of goods out of Fraserburgh to markets all over the UK and beyond and also brought in the workforce needed to process the annual herring harvest. David Toulmin in his short story *The Last Journey* provides a first-class account of the boom and bust of the Buchan railway system. He writes eloquently that "At the height of the herring season upwards of twenty-one fish trains left Fraserburgh daily ... but by 1928 the engines on the Buchan line were having an easier time." By the 1960s demand had fallen off again despite a boom during WW2 and in 1965 passenger services were withdrawn with freight traffic continuing until 1979. Nowadays the Buchan Line is better known to walkers as the Formartine and Buchan Way linking Dyce to Peterhead and Fraserburgh.

The fortunes of the town have waxed and waned over the centuries. At one time a university town, briefly rivalling even Aberdeen perhaps, the population of the parish in 1840 was recorded as 3,080 and by 1901 this had increased to 9,715. The short-lived university (1595-1605) is long gone and only remembered in print although a few scattered stones are allegedly built into houses around the town. In around 1880, following significant harbour investment including the construction of a new breakwater, Fraserburgh emerged as the Scottish herring capital; overtaking even the mighty Wick and nearby Peterhead in status. Period photographs show the harbour basin filled with literally hundreds of fishing boats.

Fraserburgh Harbour in 2014

Economic progress does not always come cheap however and the social effects of the annual seasonal influx of fishermen and their families from all over the Scotland plus a few thousand 'Heilanmen' could on occasion lead to law-and-order problems. Billed in some circles as the 'Great Riot of 1874', the events of August that year stemmed, at least partly, from the fish curers' practise of the time of paying not by the day but by the engagement. One such pay day fell on August the first 1874 when the seasonal workers collected a full two months' wages which many began to invest in the local brewing industry.

    The Saturday evening started out well. However, as closing time approached tempers frayed and a Lewis man by the name of Buchanan began attacking passing locals. A riot grew and when local police retreated back to the Town House, they were repeatedly rushed by the drunken mob who had wrongly assumed their ringleader to be under arrest within the building. After much breaking of heads by the police plus an abortive and completely illegal attempt by newly armed local civilian volunteers to open fire on the mob it began to rain heavily and the rioters gradually drifted off in small groups and dispersed into the night. Backed by armed Gordon Highlanders from Aberdeen, the police next day began stopping and searching the 'Heilanmen'. In particular they examined heads for signs of baton wounds, leading local wags to nickname the

Fraserburgh Police 'The Phrenologists of the Bobby Brigade'. Several convictions resulted from what may have been the last North East riot in which the military took to the streets.

With a population nowadays hovering around the 12,500 mark there have been recent moves to attract new business to the town. Modern day Fraserburgh lays claim to being the largest shellfish port in Europe and is also a major white fish port with a busy commercial harbour. Alongside the landing of fish, the town is home to a number of large fish processing factories and a busy fish market. However recent contraction within the fishing industry has led the Harbour Board to seek out new markets. In March 2014, Moray Offshore Renewables Ltd (MORL) gained planning consent from the Scottish Government to construct and operate a 1.116MW offshore wind generation farm 13 miles offshore in the outer Moray Firth. To be known as the Telford, Stevenson and MacColl Offshore Windfarms the project's sixty giant turbines will require significant onshore facilities for operation and maintenance for decades to come. With around 330 jobs in prospect, the Harbour Board and MORL plan to build berthing, dry dock and ship lift repair facilities to service the project. With the town's Kinnaird Head holding the record for the highest low-level wind speed ever recorded on the UK mainland, 142mph on February.

Kinnaird Head Lighthouse

thirteenth 1989, the success of the offshore generating project seems pretty much guaranteed The Kinnaird Head Lighthouse on the town's Castle Terrace is seemingly the oldest mainland light in the whole of Scotland. Completed by the Northern Lighthouse Board in December 1787 and initially lit using whale oil, the beam could be seen some fourteen miles out to sea. Rebuilt between 1821 and 1830 it has withstood both weather and attack by German bomber crews during the Hitler War. Fraserburgh Lifeboat Station was the first official RNLI station opened in Scotland and when opened in 1858 it superseded the privately operated local lifeboat which had been in operation since 1806. Despite three tragic Twentieth century lifeboat disasters resulting in the deaths of thirteen crew members the Fraserburgh Lifeboat continues to attract local volunteers. In 2010 Lady Saltoun unveiled a memorial statue to those lost men at Fraserburgh Lifeboat Station. Paid for by public subscription, the life-size Lifeboatman sculpture was created by Orkney sculptor Ian Scott.

Golf is first documented as having been played at Fraserburgh in 1613 when Kirk Session records record the case of John Burnett who was chastised for "playing at the gouff" on a Sunday instead of going to church. As punishment he was sent to the "maister's stool for correction". Fraserburgh Golf Club is possibly the fifth oldest club in Scotland and lays claim to be the seventh oldest in the World. The club may even be the oldest golf club in the world still operating under its original name. A notice on the club's digital notice board invites visitors to the clubs forthcoming golfing anniversary. Seemingly on April fourteenth 2027 club members plus invited guests will celebrate the Fraserburgh Golf Club's Sestercentennial (250th Anniversary). Only a true Brocher could have thought that one up!

Then there is the local connection with Bill Gibb "The man who put the Bee in Fraserburgh". Described by fashion model Twiggy as her "knight in shining armour" and by journalist Jack Webster as "quite simply one of the most gentle, kindly and considerate human beings I have ever known, a big, bearded, gangling Buchan loon", fashion designer Bill Gibb's creations are represented in the permanent collections of many museums and art galleries throughout the world. London's Victoria and Albert Museum, New York's Metropolitan, Aberdeen Art Gallery and Zandra Rhodes's Fashion and Textiles Museum in Bermondsey - to name but a few - have hosted retrospectives of his designs. Born near New Pitsligo and schooled at Fraserburgh Academy, Bill showed a talent for design from an early age. Encouraged by his maternal grandmother, herself an accomplished landscape painter, and his art teachers at the academy he went on to study at London's St Martin's School of Art and the Royal College of Art. Fellow fashion students included Ossie Clark and Zandra

Rhodes, with whom he shared an unbridled vision of what the Urban Dictionary likes to term "fabulosity."

Indeed, years prior to the deconstructing of the kilt by the likes of Vivienne Westwood, Bill and fellow celebrity fashion designer Kaffe Fassett were creating the bold chequerboard tartans and those wildly eccentric richly mismatched knitted tartan and floral layers that came to symbolize the high fashion of the 1970s. Bill's audacious and often wildly theatrical designs replete with colour combinations such as lime green, purple, mustard and navy soon caught on and by the early 1970s he found himself designing individual creations for the rich and famous. Novelist Roald Dahl's daughters wore his wedding dresses. Elizabeth Taylor, Bianca Jagger and Twiggy collected wardrobes full of his designs. Currently, Fraserburgh Heritage Museum hosts the only permanent display of Bill's work in the UK outside of the Victoria and Albert Museum.

Previously a foundry for the Consolidated Pneumatic Tool Company Ltd, known locally as the 'Toolies', Fraserburgh Heritage Museum is a must for those interested in the history of Fraserburgh and its folk. Bill's creations plus his signature 'Bumble Bee' motif share museum space with extensive displays illustrating the life of Scottish Samurai Thomas Blake Glover, the history of the local Marconi Wireless Shack plus the varied career of local musician, Charlie Chaplin look-alike and chicken hypnotist Steve Fairnie (1951-1993). A man best known perhaps as front man of the post-punk band Writz, Fairnie's main claim to fame was his partnership with singer songwriter Bev Sage. Together they took the charts by storm with a remake of Frederick Hollander's 1930s hit 'Ich bin von Kopf bis Fuß auf Liebe eingestellt', better known perhaps as 'Falling in Love Again (Can't Help It)'.

Both Billie Holiday and the Beatles recorded cover versions of the song, but somehow the Sage/Fairnie Techno Twins version stands out. Fame however does not come 'cheep' and in what was most probably a PR stunt, he made the front pages when he publicly mesmerised a chicken in a Cornwall cafe. It was summer 1983 and obviously a short news day. He and Bev had been out dining in a local café when inexplicably in walked a feathered hen. The rest is history. The lad from Fraserburgh was about to release a new single titled *Foreign Land* and in the true spirit of 'Freddie Starr Ate My Hamster' the Techno Twins scored a few headlines in the national press.

In the Hitler war, the Toolies manufactured and assembled parts for Bofors guns and was targeted by German bombers on several occasions. The factory survived the war intact but many parts of the town were much less fortunate. Alongside the local deaths, and there were many of these, the birthplace of the

Scottish Samurai - Thomas Blake Glover - was reduced to dust and rubble. Glover died in Tokyo in 1911 aged 73 leaving behind a legacy of strong links between Scotland and Japan. Even today occasional Japanese tourists turn up in Fraserburgh to search out the man's bombed birthplace and follow the Glover tourist trail around the North East.

But back to the man who put the Bee in Fraserburgh. Bill Gibb's younger sister, Patsy Davidson, recently commented that "The family are keen to keep Billy's memory very much alive." Posing for a photograph alongside a montage of her brother's life created by the pupils of Tyrie Primary School she became concerned that her choice of shoes clashed with her outfit. The attendant photographer promised to crop the image but on balance decided that a clash of colours seemed completely appropriate given Bill Gibb's history of artistic licence in that department. With a design legacy which continues to inspire international fashion designers a quarter of a century after his untimely death, Bill would hopefully have approved. Mind you, according to the Bard of the Broch - Stanley Bruce - it's not uncommon for Fraserburgh to experience a Vivaldi of clashing colours. He records in his poem *Four Seasons* that "In the Broch, or down at Broadsea Bay, it's not uncommon to experience four seasons in one day".

17
HUNTLY – ANCIENT CAPITAL OF STRATHBOGIE

Prior to the COVID-19 pandemic few folk thought twice about air travel. Apart from the hassles of going through security, flying was generally both safe and affordable. A journey to Australia, which once upon a time took 100 days by sailing ship, took perhaps twenty hours by airliner. Per passenger mile, flying, at least according to the airlines, is amongst the safest forms of travel. In the very early part of the Twentieth century however, air travel was a novelty afforded only by the very wealthy and perhaps the very brave.

Louis Charles Joseph Blériot flew the channel in 1909. He had been a car parts manufacturer and is credited with a design for a 'practical headlamp for cars' and using capital from his automotive business he moved into the new industry of aviation. Huntly was not far behind the trend. The town's earliest recorded brush with aviation came as early as 1910, just a year after that first channel crossing, when an advert in the *Huntly Express* announced that aviator Douglas Gilmour was planning to take off from the town's Castle Park on Thursday fourth of August. Seemingly around two thousand people turned out on the appointed day to marvel at the spectacle. Owner of an early Bleriot monoplane, Gilmour had a keen nose for publicity and was a favourite with the press having gained notoriety by bombing the Submarine Depot at Portsmouth with oranges. Although his Huntly flight ended safely, the plane landing in a field near East Park Street, Gilmour was killed in 1912 when his aircraft suffered structural failure over Richmond.

During the interwar years there are many instances of individual aircraft offering sightseeing flights over North East towns including Huntly. For the most these were short trips in tiny biplanes typically at a cost of five shillings which was a hefty sum in those days. By the 1930s however air travel was beginning to literally take off. Pioneers such as Captain Ernest Fresson had, by 1934, begun regular passenger flights from Aberdeen's Seaton Park to Orkney and all over the UK similar routes were being developed. Public interest in aviation had never been higher and the phenomenon of the air circus had much to do with this. The folk of Huntly were quite used to circuses. To this day the likes of Zippos and The Netherlands National Circus regularly perform on the Market Muir. In the August of 1904 the town's Market Muir had played host to Buffalo Bill's Wild West Show. On performance day, an estimated twenty thousand spectators from as far afield as Strathdon arrived at Huntly eager, despite horizontal rain, to see both the cowboys and the native Americans battle it out in the heart of Strathbogie. The local paper covered the event commenting that the Native Americans had "a pleasant smile for the white-faced stranger, whose scalp under other conditions might have been a trophy for the dusky warriors." Following the Huntly performance, a Native American Indian performer by the name of Little Bear had to be left behind for treatment at the local cottage hospital due to a foot infection. He was to re-join Buffalo Bill's Greatest Show on Earth at Perth a week later; but not before he had taken Huntly by storm when he attended Sunday Service at St Margaret's Roman Catholic Church on Chapel Street dressed in full costume and war paint.

The Wild West town of 'Tranquility' near Forgue

Mind you, even today there are cowboys on the edge of town. Built and manned by re-enactors, the Wild West town of [sic] Tranquility near Forgue boasts a saloon, a barber shop, a telegraph office and even a town jail. There's also a modest graveyard appropriately named Boot Hill which is the last resting place of bad guys and of those innocents variously 'hung by mistake' or 'shot at noon because they stole a horse'. The carved grave markers speak of bank robbers and cattle rustlers who suffered the indignity of neck stretching after trying to shoot the Sheriff of Tranquility, local man Alistair Baranowski. In a 2017 Scotsman article Alistair is quoted as saying "It's basically a big game of hide and seek, the good guys hunting down the bad with blank firing guns. If you get within ten feet of your target they are 'shot'. But sometimes a little light hearted argument might break out ... it is a great way to spend your time." Aside from making their own Western movies - you can view these on YouTube - the thirty or so townsfolk of Tranquility have on occasion featured in the mainstream media. The BBC has filmed on site and a series of films based on the computer game *Red Dead Redemption* have also featured Tranquility as a digital film set. That great showman Buffalo Bill Cody would have wholeheartedly approved of the venture.

In 1933 Sir Alan Cobham's Air Circus came to town. Cobham was a popular advocate for the building of airports across the UK and his public air displays fired the imagination of many a wartime RAF recruit; but in essence the name of the game was just as it had been for Buffalo Bill Cody back in 1904, bums on seats. Friday the fourteenth of July 1933 was show day. Despite rain, crowds filled the showground near the Huntly Lodge Hotel, to await the arrival of the flying circus. As the fourteen strong air fleet swept in over Huntly, few spectators would have realised the extent of the preparations made prior to the event. The complex nature of Cobham's Air Circus required meticulous pre-performance planning. The town council, local landowners and local newspapers all had to be brought, and in some cases bought, onside. Permissions, suppliers and publicity had to be in place well before the event. To facilitate this an advance crew visited the town led by a manager, whose job it was to arrange everything from hotel accommodation for the pilots to the selling of catering concessions to local companies. Crucially he had to gain the cooperation of landowners who could provide crop free and level landing areas, often with the promise that they would make an absolute fortune after the show by selling off land for a proposed Huntly International Airport. Local business owners were offered sponsorship deals and the likes of the Huntly Palace Cinema ran a raffle for patrons with a flight worth five shillings as the prize. On show day, Provost Christie welcomed the fliers and, after a brief speech in which he enthused about the bright future of air travel, he encouraged the crowd to purchase tickets for "a flight, if not two". He was then treated to a complimentary joyride. The performance then began in earnest.

Accompanied by a blaring commentary from the loudspeaker van, displays of Really Crazy Flying, Formation Aerobatics and Dancing in the Air wowed the crowd. Wing walkers, a solo parachute descent and a scaled down Schneider Cup Trophy Race quickly followed. Aircraft flew through hoops, looped-the-loop and performed a manoeuvre mysteriously billed as Aerial Pig Sticking. A highlight, described in the programme as a 'Surprise Item', involved a Cobham pilot disguised as a member of the crowd running onto the flying arena accompanied by shouts of "Stop that Man!" before taking off in a stolen biplane. Once airborne, the thief performed several wobbly low-level circuits while waving excitedly to the crowd below and making a great show of lighting his pipe in mid-air. He then climbed out onto the wing leaving the aircraft pilot-less. Perhaps unsurprisingly a Cobham flyer was killed a year or so later performing this very same stunt.

In truth though, such dangerous behaviour was a frequent feature of public air displays and often with catastrophic results. In the early days of the Hendon Air Display for example, crashes were common and dangerous stunts included the shooting down in flames of captive observation balloons (known to the initiated as Ruperts) following the escape of the crew via parachute. Then there was the dubious practice of strafing and bombing mock infantry trenches in the centre of the show arena. At Huntly however, the displays did not involve either bombs or machine guns and after the evening performance the Air Circus flew on to Macduff to repeat the performance in front of fisherfolk the very next day.

Visitors to Huntly often wonder about the ancient history of the town and a popular circular walk around Battle Hill leads the walker through several thousand years of local history. Battle Hill takes its name from a skirmish which took place in December 1307 during the Scottish Wars of Independence. Often called the Battle of Slioch, details are sketchy with one account asserting that the skirmishing lasted all of three days. Whatever the truth of the matter the outcome saw Robert the Bruce's army proclaim over John Comyn, Earl of Buchan's troops although it seems likely that neither side gained much advantage and that Buchan's troops simply made a strategic withdrawal to regroup prior to the more decisive Battle of Barra at Oldmeldrum in May 1308. Nowadays though, a series of way-marked paths run through the woodland and excavations reveal archaeology dating back some three thousand years. Recent archaeological digs have exposed previously unmapped signs of human habitation dating from the Mesolithic, Neolithic and Bronze Age including an Iron Age fort and the remains of an ancient hut circle. Nowadays the hill is mainly in woodland and the archaeology is largely hidden from view although recent felling of parcels of timber using horse logging has allowed investigators temporary access to the higher ground.

With a population fast approaching 4,500 Huntly comes high on the Lonely Planet list of places to visit in Scotland. The guidebook - a sort of modern-day Bradshaw's Guide for the inquisitive tourist - suggests that the town is worth a stopover due to its "attractive main square and impressive ruined castle" Situated a mere forty miles from Aberdeen, Huntly boasts both traditional owner-operated shops plus a couple of branded nationals. Local businesses such as Sinclair's Bakery and Watt the Ironmonger happily trade alongside national superstores. Also, there is an ice cream parlour in the centre of town boasting the infamous strapline "You can't lick a Rizza's Ice Cream".

With the Bin Forest on the doorstep and Clashindarroch Forest a few miles to the south, both visitors and locals seeking outdoor adventure don't have far to travel. Walkers, skiers, riders and off-road bikers are spoiled for choice. A two-hundred mile trans-Scotland equestrian trail links the town with Shiel Bridge in Lochalsh; and the town's Nordic Ski Centre, a joint venture between Aberdeenshire Council and Huntly Nordic Ski Club, offers year round skiing on an all-weather track at Hill of Haugh.

Magnificent even in decay, and in the care of Historic Scotland, Huntly Castle occupies the site of a much earlier fortified building. The First Marquis of Huntly completed the castle in around 1606 and over the ensuing years it has sheltered, amongst many others, Robert the Bruce and Mary of Guise, mother of Mary Queen of Scots. Unusually, there appears to be no claim that Mary herself slept within its walls, although the place was pillaged on her orders following the Battle of Corrichie at Hill of Fare in 1562. Famed for possessing the most unpleasant dungeon in Scotland, the fortress became a garrison for government troops during the 1745 Jacobite rebellion when Huntly, like many Scottish towns was a hotbed of pro-Jacobite sentiment.

More recently, author and artist Peter Anson records that he grazed his two horses, Jack and Bill, in the Huntly Castle grounds during his epic Caravan Pilgrimage around Britain. The purpose of his 1938 visit was to sketch the town's St Margaret's Roman Catholic Church in Chapel Street which he described as "a curious octagonal shaped building unlike any church I have ever seen … it was the first Catholic chapel in Scotland to be provided with a bell since the Reformation. What a sensation it must have caused when that bell rang out for the first Mass." Funds for construction were provided by John Gordon of Wardhouse, then living in Cadiz which undoubtedly influenced the distinctly Spanish styled structure with its magnificent baroque tower. Completed in 1834 St Margaret's underwent complete restoration in 1990 with funding from the Scottish Heritage Trust. Main contractor, Doric Construction, was awarded the prestigious 'Plasterer's Trophy' in recognition of their high-quality input to the project.

Christ Church, an Episcopal church on Provost Street, has more recently been renovated and substantially upgraded. Originally completed around 1849 by Thomas Mackenzie and known as the 'Little Cathedral in the East' the recent project, undertaken by local conservation architects Acanthus Architects, attracted funding from sources including Heritage Lottery and Historic Scotland.

Huntly Town Centre and Duke of Gordon Statue

Visitors to the town are sometimes puzzled by signs on the outskirts which read "Huntly Room to Roam." Orb's Community Bookshop in the town's Deveron Street has an answer. Formerly a retail grocer shop, the building now houses several thousand pre-loved books alongside a smattering of new titles. Pride of place though goes to the writing of George MacDonald (1824 - 1905). MacDonald's writing appealed to a worldwide audience. He published some sixty works, including twenty novels, many with settings in and around his home town of Huntly. His popularity eventually extended to all levels of society. When he was suffering from a lung complaint, Lady Byron gifted him an expense paid trip to recuperate in Algiers. Some years later Queen Victoria presented her grandsons with copies of his books for children.

Born in the town's Bogie Street, where a plaque commemorates him, he is perhaps best known as the author of books such as *The Princess and the Goblin* and fantasy novels such as *Lilith and Phantastes*, subtitled a *Faerie Romance for Men*. Cited as inspiration for the likes of C.S. Lewis and T.S. Elliot, MacDonald's writings had an enormous impact on the literature of the day. A poem from Phantastes, entitled 'Room to Roam', was set to music in 1990 by the Celtic folk-rock group The Waterboys and in 2005 a line from the poem was adopted as part of Huntly's branding. In a collaboration between Mike Scott, lead singer of The Waterboys, and South African Artist Jacques Coetzer, co-ordinated by Aberdeen Towns Partnership, Aberdeenshire Council Arts Development and Deveron Arts, MacDonald's poem was also developed into a town anthem with a chorus reflecting MacDonald's work:

"Room to roam but only one home for all the world to win
So you go yours and I'll go mine and the many many ways we'll wend
Many days and many ways ending in one end
Room to roam but only one home ending in one end."

Alongside an Architectural Trail around the town centre, Huntly boasts a George MacDonald Trail featuring many of the locations described in the novels. The Gordon Arms Hotel on The Square became The Boar's Head in *Robert Falconer* and The Castle Hotel is Glassford's House in his *David Elginbrod*. Huntly town is variously portrayed throughout his works as either Rothieden or Howglen.

The literary connections do not stop with MacDonald however and writer and art critic Paul Shepherd's take on Huntly town is quoted on the Deveron Arts website: "There is a central square with a maze of little streets leading off towards the open landscape beyond, a big castle in the style of King George, and a plunging river full of fish and stones and clear water." The town at the confluence of the River Deveron and the River Bogie has perhaps never been described more eloquently.

18
INSCH – CLOSE TO WHICH IS CRAIGIEVAR

Perhaps oddly, *Bradshaw's Railway Guide* makes scant reference to the Garioch village of Insch commenting only that "Insch, close to which is Craigievar, is the seat of Sir W. Forbes, Bart; here fairs are held on Friday." Writing in around 1863, Bradshaw obviously was completely unaware that the very first section of the Great North of Scotland Railway linking Aberdeen to Inverness was laid just two miles down the line at Westhall Estate following the cutting of the first sod by Lady Elphinstone in the November of 1852. The railway became a key factor in the village's prosperity, enabling easy movement of agricultural and heavy goods including slate from nearby Culsalmond and fertiliser from the south. Over the past fifty years however goods traffic has given way to commuter traffic and nowadays the station is currently unmanned save for a single robotic ticket machine. Despite this the rail link remains vital to the growth of the settlement offering fast connections to Aberdeen and Inverness.

At the last census, in 2011, enumerators recorded that the village had a population of 2,280 living in 976 distinct households. Alongside the traditional granite builds in the village centre, recent and extensive housing development along the arterial roads leading into Insch have probably boosted the population beyond the three thousand mark. While Aberdeenshire house prices dip due to concerns about North Sea oil reserves, Insch already suffers from lower than average house prices which in combination with good transport links adds greatly to the appeal of the place for the commuting class. The village centre boasts convenience stores, a bank, pub, Post Office, chemist and butcher while in the surrounding countryside visitor attractions such as Kellockbank Country Emporium and new kid on the block 'Lil' C's BBQ' offer a choice of either traditional Scottish or American Diner style eating. With the Bennachie hill range on the doorstep, the iconic hill of Dunnideer dominating the village skyline and the Cairngorms just an hour or so away, outdoor enthusiasts are spoiled for choice. Nearby sporting facilities include the Bennachie Leisure Centre, the 18-hole Insch Golf Club and the Loch Insch Fishery.

Insch Connection Museum, a Registered Scottish Charity, holds an extensive archive relating to Insch's past. Housed within the Railway Station the museum hosts exhibitions celebrating various aspects of village life. The focus for 2016 for example was Souters of Insch, a family business once central to the local economy. Trading in everything from fencing supplies and chainsaws to wedding presents and outdoor gear, the Souter brand was instrumental in bringing both electricity and employment to the village and for over 90 years operated a popular general goods store on Commercial Road. Insch nowadays boasts an aerodrome, a manufacturer of landmine clearance machines plus a good selection of archaeology. It can also claim the distinction of being one of only a very few parishes in Scotland bombed by the Germans in the First War.

Insch War Memorial Hospital

The Twentieth century conflicts were unkind to all of Scotland and Insch suffered as much as most communities across the land. Alongside the cruelty and the slaughter in the trenches and at sea, there were long-lasting social effects brought about by the conflict including a post WW1 imbalance of males to females prompting the *Daily Mail* to proclaim in 1920 that, UK wide, there were "A million women too many" involved in what they termed "A desperate husband hunt". The 2014 Registrar General's Annual Review of Demographic Trends highlighted wartime impacts on the Scottish population. Birth rates and marriage rates fell markedly during the conflict. The 1917 statistics for instance recorded just 97,441 births, the lowest number since records began in 1855. By 1920 a post-war baby boom emerged with 136,546 births recorded nationwide. Marriage rates similarly bottomed at 30,421 in 1917 rising to a 1920 high of 46,754. In short, old men, old women, widows and fatherless children were left to make the best of it. Clearly the conflict was important for woman's rights though. Male roles were delegated to females due to the necessities of war production and returning heroes faced the reality of a changed industrial and social landscape. The genie was out of the bottle!

The war dead of Insch and the surrounding parishes of Old Rayne and Colpy are recorded at Insch War Memorial Hospital. Instead of building a simple granite monument, the village raised funds via public subscription to build a cottage hospital. A plaque in the entrance hallway records the donors by name and amount given. The roll of honour at the hospital entrance is particularly poignant since the casualty list records both name and parish, providing a stark picture of the localised impact of the conflict. While initially the farming community undoubtably profited from the war economy in terms of a greater demand for agricultural produce, the reality of men going off the land to fight and die in a patriotic war soon negated any gains. Local GP Stephen Teale commented that birth records reflected the devastating effect of the war on the rural community. "The social effects were immense, the lack of available men meant that many women never married and were left to run farms single-handed. The war had a tremendous impact … there were also many men who returned injured and unable to work." Additionally, inheritance became problematic with farms changing hands simply because families had no young folk to take over when the incumbents grew old or died. The hospital opened in 1922 and has been variously extended in the intervening years. Currently the fifteen bedded facility faces the prospect of major modernisation to meet modern needs and Friends of Insch Hospital are working alongside NHS Grampian with a view to replacing the current building with a modern Insch and District War Memorial Hospital.

Parish boundaries can be a complete nightmare for both travellers and historians. Inverurie's Port Elphinstone, the Port in the shire, was once part of the parish of Kintore and travellers seeking the Garioch village of Auchleven are often directed to the parish of Premnay, or is it the other way around? Insch may be no exception to the likelihood of visitor confusion since it straddles the adjoining parishes of Insch and Rothney but fortunately the boundary signs clearly identify the village as Insch. Road signs however would have made little difference to the events of early May 1916.

An estimated 4,800 British civilians were killed or wounded as a result of German air raids from 1914 to 1918. Many of those were killed in the course of air raids by Zeppelins. Zeppelin raids were fairly common over parts of England and the continent, but it had been assumed that North East Scotland was out of range of raiders whose bases were in northern Europe and around six hours flying time away from military targets at Rosyth, Scapa Flow and Invergordon. Although the usual targets for the German crews were naval and military bases, in 1916 the art of night time aerial bombing was uncertain at best with most bombs falling wildly off target. The raiders relied on navigation based on ground observation. There was no radar and bombs were often dropped by hand.

There had been a raid on Scotland on April second 1916 when German airships bombarded Edinburgh's Grassmarket and destroyed a bonded warehouse at Leith killing thirteen civilians; a plaque at the Grassmarket at the foot of Edinburgh Castle records the event. Exactly one month later the raiders returned. The targets this time were the Forth Rail Bridge and the Naval Base at Rosyth but the navigation was faulty and only two of the eight hydrogen filled airships, the L14 and the L20, even managed to locate Scotland. Such navigational errors were not uncommon and the L20 had previously been involved in the accidental bombing of civilian areas at Loughborough in January 1916 having mistaken the town for Liverpool, some ninety miles distant. In the Scottish raid however weather and poor navigation led Zeppelin L14 to mistake the Firth of Tay for the Firth of Forth and eventually the huge machine dumped its bombs over Lunan Bay near Montrose injuring a horse. The 585ft long L20 however lumbered confidently north at a steady 45mph, possibly intending to bomb a secondary target of Royal Navy warships in the Cromarty Firth, before fixing its position over Buchan's Rattray Head Lighthouse and heading east over to Norway. However, things became even more farcical. Wildly off course and completely disorientated, the sixteen strong crew of the L20 flew inland bombing the newly floodlit Craig Castle at Lumsden before over-flying Kintore, Pitcaple, Old Rayne and Insch where they dropped bombs and a flare in a field at Hill of Flinder. Mill of Knockenbaird and nearby Freefield House were also targeted but escaped with minor damage. Amazingly there were no casualties and next day, excited locals went in search of souvenirs in the form of bomb fragments.

In the aftermath *The Aberdeen Free Press* ran a heavily censored account of "Bombs Dropped in Fields … some windows in a mansion house and a cotter house broken by the concussion … no person sustained the slightest injury". The L20 eventually headed out over the North Sea to ask directions via loudhailer from the startled crew of a passing trawler before reaching the coastline of neutral Norway at Hafrsfjord near Stavanger. where it finally ran out of fuel and crashed into the sea some hundred yards offshore. Thanks to the efforts of local fishermen the zeppelin crew survived to fight another day however a Norwegian Army officer reportedly set the airship wreck aflame with a well-placed shot from a flare pistol ending this truly bizarre episode in the history of aerial warfare. A bomb fragment from the raid was displayed at

Alford Transport Museum in 2016 as part of The National Museums Scotland 'Next of Kin Exhibition' and a full account of the raid appeared in the January 1999 edition of *Leopard Magazine*.

The Zeppelin's visit was both unexpected and unwelcome however modern day Insch aerodrome, more correctly known as Grampian Microlight & Flying Club, welcomes visitors with open arms. Situated two miles south of Insch at Auchleven and operational since 1985, the club is home to a wide range of microlights and light planes including a 1943 vintage L-4H two-seater Tiger Cub spotter plane undergoing restoration. Owned jointly by airstrip owner Ken Wood and colleague Forrest Watson, the aircraft is a rare survivor of the 1944 battle for Europe. "It was used for artillery spotting" says Ken. "Those aircrew must have been very brave indeed. They flew over the battlefield at about 500ft with friendly shells flying almost alongside and the Germans shooting at them from the ground … around 5,500 were built and less than 1,000 remain worldwide."

The area around Insch is particularly rich in archaeological remains including stone circles, vitrified forts and other megalithic structures. The Picardy Stone at Inschfield and the Stonehead Recumbent Stone at Aulton are just two examples, but perhaps the jewel in the crown is the stone circle at Dunnideer. Sited on the western slopes of the hill, the site is nowadays overgrown and partially hidden from view. It consists of a recumbent stone plus two upright flanking stones formed in the style of the Loanhead of Daviot stone circle. The ancient site, with the Hill Fort of Dunnideer in the background, is simply stunning. Visible from all points of the compass, a ruined mediaeval castle on the summit of the 879 foot Dunnideer Hill dominates the landscape around Insch. Information published by Historic Environment Scotland indicates that the castle, although traditionally thought to have been erected by Gregory the Great in AD 890, was more likely constructed by David Earl of Huntingdon and Garioch in 1178 and built largely using recycled material from an earlier vitrified fort. It may in fact represent the earliest authenticated example of a tower house in Scotland. Around the ancient structure there are clearly defined earlier turf ramparts and obvious remains of vitrified stone fortifications.

No take on Insch would be complete without an aardvark. Technically, the aardvark is a small burrowing mammal native to Africa which uses its long snout to sniff out food. The nearby Shevock Estate is home to a mechanical version of the animal. The rail line north from Insch Station to Inverness runs past Aardvark Clear Mine Limited, perhaps Scotland's most unusual industrial equipment supplier. Specialising in de-mining technology and exporting worldwide, Aardvark manufacture a range of dual role anti-tank and anti-personnel landmine clearance vehicles.

Insch Railway Station with the Hill of Dunnideer in the background

Mammals of a quite different kind feature in the old tradition that the teeth of sheep grazed on the Hill of Dunnideer turn to gold because the hill has gold ore hidden deep underground. Some sources point to grass borne iron pyrites as being the likely culprit. Others assert that the golden discoloration is down to dental encrustation caused by a chemical reaction between ovine saliva, lime and phosphoric oxide. Seemingly the phenomenon is not confined to the sheep of Dunnideer since many other mammals worldwide including camels, hippopotamus and even Cretan goats have exhibited similar symptoms. Whatever the truth of the matter visitors to the area are often fascinated by the tale and it is surprising that alongside being one of the most delightful villages in Aberdeenshire, Insch has not, to date at least, become the focus of a Garioch Gold Rush.

19
INVERURIE – LANG TOON O' THE GARIOCH

Sheriff Court circulars and newspaper archives are full of reports of theft from buses. Often the crimes are petty in nature and involve offences such as pickpocketing or theft of items of baggage from the luggage rack. Annoying in the extreme for the unfortunate victim, but not by any stretch of the imagination grand theft. But, back in 1997, folk in Inverurie choked on their porridge when the morning paper reported that thieves had stolen an entire single decker bus.

Locals choked on their porridge at the sheer audacity of the theft!

Dubbed a 'Professional job' by the local constabulary, overnight raiders had made off with a Bluebird Leyland single decker worth in the region of £10,000. Ian Smart, the Bluebird Bus Company general manager offered a substantial reward for information leading to the recovery of the vehicle and commented "It's one of our older vehicles" he told reporters "but it would cost in the region of £100,000 to buy it new." The two thieves had however been caught on security camera as they smashed through the gates at the Harlaw Depot during the getaway and that, plus the reward, led the police to a farm over at Rothienorman where the remains of the vehicle were discovered in a shallow grave. Stripped of everything saleable, the Bluebird had been buried in a field. Thankfully, such anti-social behaviour is not typical of the behaviour of the inhabitants of the Lang Toon o' the Garioch.

In the late May of 1940 heavily censored news of the military disaster in France began appearing in newspapers across the UK. Newspaper headlines proclaiming "Defence lines hold firm" very soon gave way to "Evacuation under bombs, BEF men arriving home in thousands" as the retreat of the British Expeditionary Force, officially titled Operation Dynamo, from the beaches of Dunkirk began in earnest. The retreat was soon propagandised as a victory in defeat and the strapline "The Miracle of Dunkirk" became common currency. In defeat the politicians and the kings have always worked to turn defeat into victory. Both Romans and Nazis claimed victory when none existed. An Antonine Wall did much to bolster the reputation of the Romans despite the fact that its very existence was an admission of the Roman failure to subdue the Picts. An Atlantic Wall did much the same for the Fascists. Neither worked particularly well despite the propaganda. In the summer of 1940 however, the trickery of turning defeat into victory paid dividends. A beleaguered Britain was persuaded by a similarly beleaguered Churchill that the defeat in France was in fact a victory for the allies.

Despite continual German attack some 338,000 allied troops were ferried across the English Channel and disembarked at channel ports between the twenty seventh of May and the fourth of June. In the space of just eight days a total of six hundred and twenty passenger trains transported the exhausted and demoralised troops from the Channel ports north to garrison towns throughout the UK for rest and re-equipping. And so it was that on June sixth 1940, the citizens of Inverurie awoke to find that the town had been invaded, not by the victorious Germans but by the scattered remnants of a defeated British Army. In the early hours a train from Dover had disembarked several hundred hungry and demoralised soldiers who now sat in little groups all around the town centre, awaiting orders.

Small groups of soldiers had in fact been arriving piecemeal at the local railway station since late May and billeting officers had been busy liaising with the Inverurie Church Council who had set up a canteen in the West Church Hall. However, the scale of the invasion overwhelmed even the best laid plans. As further trains arrived with even more troops the locals rallied to feed and house the bedraggled army. The invasion of Inverurie lasted about a week and as many of the now reformed units moved on to outlying towns such as Huntly and Turriff, the crisis abated. However, Inverurie had become a garrison town almost overnight and throughout the rest of the war years the inhabitants would share their lives with a succession of British and Polish troops plus an assortment of Italian and German POWs.

Another wartime link concerns an RAF pilot named William Reid. There's a drill hall in Inverurie called The Reid VC Cadet Centre named in honour of the man. Bomber pilot William Reid was invested with his Victoria Cross by King George VI at Buckingham Palace in June 1944. Born in Baillieston in 1921, he moved to Perthshire after the Second World War and died in Crieff at the age of 79 in 2001. A few years after his death his VC medal was auctioned off and sold to a medal collector for £348,000, at the time a record sum. So what did Flight Lieutenant William Reid do to get his gong?

The London Gazette for the fourteenth of December 1943 has a decent write up of the episode and records that he was wounded in the head, shoulder and both hands in the course of a bombing mission over Europe. The objective was Dusseldorf and despite his injuries, he continued with the mission. It took a further hour to fly the 200 miles to the target and drop his bombs. Mission accomplished, he now had to get himself and his crew home in one piece. Navigating by the moon and the pole star - his navigator had been killed in a second attack during the outward trip - Reid brought his Lancaster bomber back to England despite the fact that his windscreen had been shattered and the oxygen supply had given out. Worse was to come. Partially blinded by his own frozen blood, he made an emergency landing on a fog bound RAF airfield. The undercarriage collapsed and as the plane slithered to a halt, he realised that the wireless operator had also been badly wounded.

Interviewed by the BBC many years later he was reluctant to brand himself a hero. "I think it was the fact that we carried on to the target that made them make all the fuss. But if you bear in mind that we were in the bomber stream and there were maybe around seven hundred aircraft at different altitudes all around us over a ten mile broad flightpath, it would have made no sense whatsoever to turn around and risk flying back through them all." After a spell in hospital, Reid returned to active duties in July 1944 only to have his aircraft destroyed by friendly fire. Over France, his aircraft was struck by a bomb dropped from another Lancaster flying above him. He and his crew bailed out and Reid, who broke his arm when landing, ended up as a prisoner of war. Demobilised in 1946, he went on to work in agriculture.

A resourceful and resilient lot, the folk of Inverurie have often faced adversity. In May 1308 for example the townsfolk witnessed the forces of Robert the Bruce fording the Don and trudging the five miles north to fight the bloody Battle of Barra. The 1411 Battle of Harlaw was fought just a mile north west of the town with one local laird, Sir Andrew Leslie, losing all six of his sons in one day. The 1745 Jacobite rising saw further local bloodshed when government troops including a contingent of French mercenaries clashed with rebels on the south west boundary of the town. Perhaps as many as forty men were killed in the running battle.

Inverurie Locomotive and Carriage Works

In more recent times events such as the closures of the Loco Works in 1969 and Tait's Paper Mill in 2009 led many to despair over the town's economic future. Retired railway engineer Joe Strachan recently commented "When those major employers quit the town everyone thought it would be the end of Inverurie, but look at it now. Saved by the oil!" Occupying a twenty-acre site on Harlaw Road, the Inverurie Loco Works had been constructed over the period 1898-1905 to replace the outdated Great North of Scotland Railway Kittybrewster railway workshops in Aberdeen. To accommodate the influx of labour, railway worker's housing was built at what became known locally as the Colony. In those class ridden times the 'gaffer's houses' were built to a superior standard in comparison to the more functional tenements provided for the manual workers. However, and unusually for the time, all of the Colony houses boasted electric lighting courtesy of the works generating plant at a time when most Garioch folk would have relied on gas or even whale oil for lighting and cooking. Concentrating mainly on steam locomotive and rolling stock repairs, with only some ten steam locomotives actually being built from scratch on site, the facility very quickly became the major employer in the town with employee numbers peaking at 847 in 1946 out of a total Inverurie Burgh population of 3960.

Alongside the repair of rolling stock, the Loco Works also became involved in the construction of the early motor buses which were to oust the competition of horse drawn coaches. At first, the GNSR bought in ready built vehicles from Daimler but this practice soon gave way to the buying in of chassis from various suppliers including Maudsley and the German company Durkopp. Coachwork and seats were added locally and some vehicles were even equipped with demountable bodies for dual use as charabancs in summer and as flat-bed trucks in the off season. Most of the buses were single-deckers but at least four double decker examples were constructed between 1905 and 1907. The railway works eventually closed in December 1969 with over five hundred job losses. Some of the buildings remain in repurposed form as residential accommodation and one of the old repair sheds now functions as a local heritage centre. But memories dim and much of the original site is now occupied by retail units full of shoppers who possibly have no idea that they are treading ground where once upon a time steam trains belched fire and furnaces roared.

The legacy of the Inverurie Loco Works however lives on in the form of clubs such as the Hopeville Social Club and Inverurie Loco Works F.C. The social club building was originally the family home of the manager of the British Railways Locomotive Works. Built in 1904, and complete with servant quarters the rather grand building nowadays boasts some 2,200 members and hosts functions and live music. Founded in 1902 and nowadays elevated to the Highland Football League, Inverurie Loco Works F.C. has played continuously throughout its long history. Indeed, club historian David Fasken has uncovered evidence that the Locos were probably one of only two Scottish Junior clubs to play without interruption throughout WW2. "Mind you" he relates, "due to wartime conscription, there were occasions when the team manager was forced to borrow a couple of Italian POWs from the camp next door to make up a shortfall in the team." Whether armed guards were in place during such matches is not recorded however the club ground to this day sports a fine example of a 'Type 24' concrete pillbox, on a site formerly occupied by a WW2 Royal Engineers supply depot. The Loco pillbox is one of only two still surviving above ground in the town.

Sometimes described as the Lang Toon o' the Garioch, Inverurie nestles between the Rivers Don and Ury along the line of the old Aberdeen to Huntly road. In modern times the old ribbon development town layout has given way to a much more rounded shape due to continual expansion of residential housing and industrial development on all points of the compass. The Twenty-first century has even seen new-build housing creeping along the flood plain of the River Don leading to local speculation that council planners are maybe intent on fostering a Venice of the North in the Garioch.

Historical sites in and around the town include the Bass of Inverurie, a natural mound about fifty feet high, which towers above the gravestones of the Old Cemetery. Although reportedly 'landscaped' by enthusiastic Victorian archaeologists it is still possible to interpret the site as a classic Motte-and-Bailey Castle. Until perhaps 1775 a small chapel stood at the foot of the Bass but according to McConnachie's 1900 Donside travelogue it was levelled and the stone re-used in the kirkyard dyke which surrounds the fortification. The Bass Cemetery sports a few interesting inhabitants. Two of the so called 'Inverurie Poet' William Thom's wives lie buried in unmarked graves somewhere in the grounds and the graveyard also holds the remains of Mary Elphinstone, known locally as Mary 'Eerie-Orie' Elphinstone. The unfortunate Mary Eerie-Orie was seemingly buried alive in around 1600 after being mistakenly pronounced dead following a short illness.

The story is told in many versions and many towns across Scotland have their own distinctive rendering of the folk-tale. In the case of Inverurie's Mary, her distraught second husband rescues her when he hears her desperate cries for help coming from the freshly filled grave. In another version of the tale, the gravedigger spies a gold ring on the corpse's finger and returns after dark to retrieve the booty. He tries and fails to remove it by hand and finally resorts to cutting off the unfortunate corpse's finger at which point the 'deceased' wakes up howling in pain. She then leaps from the grave and runs home to Ardtannes where she lives on until 1622. A third version of the tale has her running home to the house of a former husband. Whichever version you adhere to, it seems that Mary Elphinstone was one of those rarities to have had the privilege of being buried twice.

To the north of the town and on a ridge above the River Ury sits the imposing Battle of Harlaw Monument. Designed by William Kelly of 'Kelly's Cats' fame and completed by local mason John Smith in 1914, the hexagonal red granite column commemorates the 1411 clash between the forces of Alexander Earl of Mar and Donald Lord of the Isles. Perhaps as many as two thousand soldiers and camp followers perished in a bloody clash widely seen as having saved Aberdeen from sacking. Despite this, both sides claimed victory although Donald's ambitions to expand his kingdom eastward were thwarted; so, on balance, it may be said that Mar alone triumphed. There is a chapter on the battle in my previous book *The Little History of Aberdeenshire*. But suffice it to say that despite the wildly differing accounts of the bloodletting and the oddly skewed politics which surround the construction of the memorial, the Battle of Harlaw remains in popular imagination a hard won victory by the righteous citizens of Aberdeen over the kilted savages of Donald Lord of the Isles.

Aberdeenshire boasts around ten percent of the total number of stone circles recorded in Britain and Inverurie's Easter Aquhorthies site must rank as one of the most complete. Dating from Third Millennium BC the site pre-dates the Egyptian pyramids at Saqqara. Lesser known is Conyng Hillock which nowadays sits partially hidden within a residential area behind Kellands Park. Local lore suggests that the mound is the resting place of Eth the Swift Foot, a Pictish king slain in battle nearby and buried at Inverurie in AD 878. Eth was seemingly named for his "abnormal nimbleness of limb" enabling him to "outstrip all his fellows in a running match." The jury is still out on the burial claim however since King Eth is also said to be interred on the island of Iona amidst a graveyard full of Scottish kings.

Famous folk associated with Inverurie include Andy Beattie the Inverurie Loco FC player who went on to become the first Scotland team manager in 1954. Aberdeen-born Scots language poet and hand loom weaver William Thom (1798-1848) resided in the town during the 1840s. His workshop in North Street is long demolished but his reputation as the 'Inverurie Poet' lives on in the form of works such as *Blind Boy's Pranks* and *Rhymes and Recollections of a Handloom Weaver*. *Blind Boy's Pranks* was his first public piece. The epic poem was first published in the January 1841 edition of the *Aberdeen Herald* alongside editorial comment praising his "natural genius and cultivated taste". Born shortly after the death of Robert Burns, Thom in reality spent just four years living in Inverurie having moved there with his second wife Jean Whitecross in 1840. He had spent much of his early life working as a weaver in both Aberdeen and then Dundee and although poverty and near starvation were to follow him to Inverurie, it was here in the Garioch town that he produced his finest written work.

Nowadays the Inverurie Poet' is perhaps best remembered for *The Mitherless Bairn*, a poem inspired on overhearing the "greetin' o' a wean" in an Aberdeen street. Seemingly "a lassie was thumpin' a bairn, when out cam a big dame, bellowin', Ye hussie, will ye lick a mitherless bairn!" However, it was the publication of *Blind Boy's Pranks* in first local then national newspapers which lifted him from penniless obscurity and launched him into polite London society where, for a year or so at least, he associated with the literary and political giants of the day including Dickens and Thomas Carlyle. He was, he records, "soon dashing it in a gilded carriage through the streets of London." Patronage and profits from book sales followed. But, as is often the case with new found fame, success attracted fair-weather cronies who took full advantage of his good natured and freely given hospitality until such time as both the money and the gin ran out. Thom's fortunes then declined rapidly and, now heavily in debt, he journeyed north to die virtually penniless in Dundee. His tombstone in Dundee's Western Cemetery erected in 1857, long after his 1848 death, by admirers of his work, confusingly records his year of birth as 1788 rather than the more generally accepted 1798. Fortunately, his fame had outlived him and a benevolent fund was set up to provide for his widow and third wife Jean Stephen, attracting donations from both Charles Dickens and Queen Victoria. Thom's second wife Jean Whitecross died in childbirth shortly after the move to Inverurie and is buried in an unmarked grave at the foot of the Bass at Inverurie. A plaque at the cemetery gate, erected by the Rotary Club of Inverurie in 1991, records her interment. Thom for his part, despite the difficulty of the unmarked common grave, was to sing Jean's praises in verse:

"Move noiseless, gentle Ury around my Jeanie's bed,
And I'll love thee gentle Ury where'er my footsteps tread,
For sooner than my fairy wave return from yonder sea,
Than I forget yon lonely grave and all it hides from me."

As previously mentioned, the Motte-and-Bailey Castle site locally known as the Bass of Inverurie, consists of two conical hillocks the largest of which towers above the surrounding graveyard. Such castles were once common throughout Scotland, although many have been overlaid by later stone built fortifications. Nowadays recognised as a naturally occurring geological feature created by the actions of the Rivers Don and Ury, legends and fantastical theories abound regarding the origins of the Bass. A burial mound containing the remains of plague victims, a place of hidden buried treasure or a fire signal station dating from the times of the Danish invaders are just a few of the more adventurous suggestions. In June 1944, on the very eve of D-Day, the Bass was subjected to intensive study by a paranormal investigator who concluded that the site was the dwelling place of a range of monstrous spirits buried by Druids so as to frustrate the "Evil Earth Magnetism of the Mound of Death!" Whatever the truth of the matter, the Bass probably hosted the administrative centre of the Earldom of the Garioch during the Twelfth century. Nowadays it presides over the residents of the towns Old Cemetery.

West High Street Inverurie

Spirits of a different kind feature in a 1902 publication titled *The Royal Burgh of Inverurie in the Coronation Year*. Following a reign of almost sixty-four years, Queen Victoria had died in January 1901 and for the next nine years her eldest son Edward was to rule the Empire. The book records the construction of the new locomotive works and the newly completed railway station - the original having been opposite the Kintore Arms Hotel - plus the School Board's plan for a newbuild £7,000 primary school in Market Place. The book also featured several paid adverts which provide a unique flavour of the commercial status of the town at the very beginning of the Twentieth century. Thus we learn that trading from the West High Street premises until recently occupied by the Yangtse European and Chinese Takeaway, a Mr Robert Brown operated a photographic studio offering both "Portraiture and Commercial and Scientific Photography". The newly built Gordon Arms Hotel on Station Road, nowadays Edwards Bar and Nightclub, offered family accommodation complete with "All the latest sanitary improvements" and The North of Scotland Milling Company on Harlaw Road advertised "Scotch Oatmeal, Pearl Barley and White Groats in bags for home trade and kegs of all sizes to suit the export trade." Alongside adverts for the Commercial Hotel and the Black Bull Inn - both sited on North Street alongside the Market Green and both still trading - specialist family grocer George Jackson advertised his whiskies as "Pure, unblended Malt Whiskies from the best Highland Distilleries" and went on to claim somewhat oddly that "The public, by dealing with me are safeguarded from the evil effects of using those poisonous compounds called Blends."

George Jackson's grocery business is long gone but interest in fine Malt Whisky continues unabated. Local businessman Michael Stuart, joint proprietor of the town's Black Bull Inn on North Street recently opened the Garioch town's first dedicated whisky shop. Co-owned with Garioch Blinds director Claire Hawkins, the shop stocks some three hundred malts ranging from a Glen Garioch Founder's Reserve to a £1200 1974 Speyside Benromach. "The idea for the Inverurie Whisky Shop came from our experience at the Black Bull" says Mike. "I've always been a whisky connoisseur and when tourists asked us where they could buy quality Scottish Malt, we usually sent them all the way to Dufftown to buy from an established specialist outlet … one German couple returned with twenty-six bottles of Malt and it occurred to me that the local economy could have easily benefited from the purchase." Alongside whisky taster sessions the shop runs guided distillery tours. As Michael says "There are at least seven distilleries including Ardmore, GlenDronach, Glen Garioch and Knockdhu within easy distance of Inverurie which makes the town a potential Whisky Hub." In the COVID-19 lockdown days of 2020, The Inverurie Whisky Shop began offering innovative virtual tasting sessions over the internet. George Jackson would no doubt have been amazed! Alongside the Whisky Shop, Inverurie boasts over thirty cafés and eateries ranging from the 'Kilted Frog Deli' on West High Street to 'Fly Cup Catering', a Scottish charity located on the towns Blackhall Industrial Estate which enables adults with learning issues to access training within the catering sector. That's around one caffeine outlet per 449 of the local population, easily beating Edinburgh's record of just one for every 2,082 people. No wonder Inverurie is buzzing with activity.

Although not blessed with much in the way of traditional statuary, unless of course you count the carved figure of the First War soldier atop his plinth outside the town hall, the town does sport a few modern pieces of public art. Most obvious perhaps is 'Flying Visit' by Deeside artist Helen Denerley. Commissioned in 1997 by Safeway PLC this piece consists of a group of giant crows crafted from ploughshares and sits opposite the Police Station. Port Elphinstone also boasts two public art pieces in the form of Gordon Lochhead's 'Port Arch' and the granite built 'Memorial to the Aberdeenshire Canal' on the southern approach to the Don Bridge. 2016 saw the installation of a new and exciting artwork on parkland just off George Square courtesy of Huntly artist Gary Shand, a chainsaw carver. When Aberdeenshire Council Landscape Services Officer Ken Regan realised that he had a dead elm tree on his hands he decided to approach Gary in the hope of commissioning him to transform the 25ft high stump into a piece of public art. "I had seen carved tree stumps in the parks of Barcelona ... the notion that folk could almost randomly stumble upon them appealed and when this opportunity arose it seemed appropriate to create one for Inverurie" said Ken.

Sited in public parkland just off George Square outside Inverurie's St Andrew's School, the sculpting process immediately drew comments from local residents. Carving a tree trunk with a power-saw is after all a very public process. Says Gary, "It was really interesting overhearing the various comments. At the beginning folk were mainly asking what it was for and what did it mean. Towards the end of the week, I detected what I can only call a sense of ownership. Folk had literally adopted the piece as a part of their local environment." The design stage involved consultation with St Andrew's School pupils. Drawings were produced in class and, as Gary puts it "all of the ideas were put into the blender." The image of children with arms around each other, lifting each other up and reaching for the sky was the result and 'Aspire' was born. With a background in forestry and a lifelong interest in the creative arts, Gary was an obvious choice for the project. "In fact, we were fortunate that he was able to commit to the artwork" said Ken Regan. Alongside what he terms his Stump Sculptures Gary creates bespoke pieces, often from elm, suited to the average size home. "Dutch Elm disease has been a mixed blessing" he says. "it's not quite so good for forests but is useful if you are a carver ... Elm is an ideal timber for outdoor sculpture and providing you keep it moist, which is easy in Scotland, it will last forever."

The town also boasts a fine collection of Pictish sculpture. Port Elphinstone's Broomend of Crichie Stone Circle is little known but quite impressive. Partially destroyed and allegedly dynamited in Victorian times, this monument sits neglected on rough ground alongside a petrol station at the

Kemnay roundabout. Less neglected is the Brandsbutt Stone in the north of the town at the corner of Brankie Road and Garden Terrace. Found in shattered pieces in amongst a farm dyke and painstakingly restored by a local resident, the monument dates from around AD 600 and is highly decorated. An Ogham inscription on one face reads IRATADDOARENS which seemingly translates from Ogham to English as the modern-day forename Adrian.

More modern times saw the birth in Port Elphinstone of sculptor James Pittendrigh Macgillivray who must surely be one of Inverurie's best kept secrets. Born in a riverside cottage at Port Elphinstone in 1856, Pittendrigh studied sculpture in Glasgow under, amongst others, William Brodie from Banff and early on in his career produced exquisite busts of the Glasgow painter Joseph Crawhall and philosopher Thomas Carlyle. His later work achieved national fame and includes Edinburgh's ornate Gladstone Monument, the David Livingstone statue in Glasgow and the Lord Byron statue which stands in the grounds of Aberdeen Grammar School. Alongside the sculpture Macgillivray painted and wrote poetry. He may also have taught briefly at Inverurie's Port School just up the road from his birthplace next to the Don Bridge. Buried in Edinburgh's Gogar Churchyard his tombstone, which he carved in 1910 in memory of his wife Frieda, closely resembles in form the Pictish Maiden Stone just north of Inverurie. Aberdeen Art Gallery hold a collection of his work including a bust of William Alexander, author of the 1881 classic *Johnny Gibb Of Gushetneuk*. This novel reveals, for all to see, the parish politics in the fictitious parish of Pyketillim, a thinly disguised amalgam of the various towns and villages of his native Aberdeenshire.

Johnny Gibb was the tacksman of Gushetneuk, "a two-horse haudin on the property of Sir Simon Frissal of Glen Snicker". Penned in part in an unforgiving Doric the novel begins with the immortal lines:

"HEELY, heely, Tarn, ye glaiket stirk ye hinna on the hin shelvin o' the cairt. Fat hae ye been haiverin at, min? That cauff saick be tint owre the back door afore we win a mile fae hame. See 't yer belly-ban' be ticht aneuch noo. Woo, lassie! Man, ye been makin' a hantle mair adee aboot blaikin that graith o' yours, an kaimin the mear's tail, nor balancin' yer cairt, an' gettin' the things packit in till 't.
Sang, that's nae vera easy deen, I can tell ye, wi' sic a mengyie o' them. aw pit puckle girss to the mear?
Ou, fat 's the eese o' that lang stoups ahin, aw wud like tae ken? Lay that bit bauk across, an' syne tak' the aul' pleuch ryn there, an' wup it ticht atween the stays; we canna hae the beast's maet trachel't amo' their feet.

Foo muckle corn pat ye in?
Four lippies gweed mizzour will that dee?
We 'se lat it be deein. Is their trock a' in noo, aw won'er?
Nyod, seerly it is."

The above conversation occurs between Johnny Gibb and his servant Tarn Meerison in the June of 1839 as they harness the horse and cart in preparation for their annual trip to the curative wells at Tarlair just outside of Macduff. Originally published as a series of short stories in the *Aberdeen Free Press* in about 1870, the book is still read today by those interested in the politics of Victorian Aberdeenshire. Prospective readers will be pleased to learn that later chapters include quite a bit of standard English in amongst the Doric which makes for a much wider understanding of the tales.

The original Don Bridge at Inverurie was completed by Banff mason James Robertson in 1791 and despite powerful floods and the ravages of time remained sound until the needs of modern day transport forced its demolition to make way for the new crossing. The narrowness of the roadway plus the hump backed central arch had rendered it quite obsolete. The contract for the new bridge was awarded to William Tawse and Son, a respected civil engineering contractor, and following the building of a temporary wooden crossing and demolition of the old bridge, construction of the new re-enforced concrete bridge began in the April of 1924. Remnants of the original 1791 bridge however remain at the south end where granite abutments can be seen near the car park at Davidson Park. The project took just over a year to complete and on the morning of the thirtieth of May 1925 an excited crowd of onlookers gathered at both ends of the newly completed bridge to witness the official opening by none other than His Lordship the Rt Hon Earl of Kintore.

At 10 am, a signal was given and with a mighty roar, two massive steam driven road trains, each consisting of a road roller towing two eight-ton trailers plus a smaller twelve-ton steam road roller, moved slowly in tandem on to the bridge. As the engineers watched the road trains slow progress towards the north span they must have wondered, at least briefly, if the design calculations and indeed the standard of construction would withstand the combined weight of the ninety-two tons of fire breathing metal now heading straight towards them.

This was however not the official opening ceremony, that would come three hours later. In a somewhat confident move, the load testing of the bridge, as required by the Ministry of Transport, was being carried out in confident anticipation of a successful test. Indeed, the silver scissors and blue ribbon which His Lordship would use during the official opening ceremony were already to hand, as were the carefully prepared opening speeches and the local brass band. The actual loads used were however somewhat less than those specified under the official testing specification being 26 tons short of the recommended loading which may perhaps have inspired the somewhat ambitious plan to test and also open the bridge on the same day. Seemingly the required heavier road rollers could not be obtained and two lighter machines were employed. One of these was an eighteen-ton French built steam roller captured from the Germans during the 1914-18 war and bought by Tawse from the Disposals Board of HM Government. This leviathan had earlier proved its worth in the construction of the approach roads to the new bridge and had also been used to load test the temporary wooden bridge constructed to allow passage of traffic, gas and water pipes during the period June 1924 to May 1925. As the bridge engineers stood grouped around a wooden gauge designed to measure the deflection of the roadway while under load, they must have been relieved to record a mere sixteenth of an inch lowering of the road surface which increased to twice that when both road trains were later run across the bridge at full tilt. Seemingly a full half inch of compression would have been more than acceptable but they must nevertheless have breathed a sigh of relief at the result. The structure had passed the trials with flying colours and the official opening could now proceed as planned.

    Accordingly, at just after 1 pm that same day and to the rousing sound of the Inverurie Brass Band the Earl of Kintore rose to make the opening ceremony speech. "May this bridge stand for generations as a memorial to all concerned with its erection … I have now the pleasure of declaring this new bridge open for traffic." On being presented by head engineer William Tawse with a gold engraved cigarette case to mark the occasion, the Earl warmly thanked the contractor "It is all the more appropriate since, just a few weeks ago my rooms in London were burgled and amongst the things I lost was a gold cigarette case." Despite the slightly dodgy testing procedure, the road bridge over the Don at Inverurie continues to give good service and is a credit to both the engineers and the town. As for the Earl of Kintore's stolen cigarette case, the crime remains unsolved.

    There can't be that many towns in Scotland which can lay claim to both a Magic Roundabout AND a Bridge to Narnia. The Magic Roundabout in question sits on the A96 bypass at the Morrisons' junction and is locally hated due to confusing road markings. "If you try to turn right to head north on the A96 towards Huntly" commented one resident "the chances are you'll end up back where you came from." When the road markings around the interchange were recently repainted, everyone breathed a sigh of relief, only to find that the original lane markings had simply been refreshed! The Bridge to Narnia however, officially named the Osprey Bridge, nowadays has a destination. A source of local speculation for several years and constructed as part of the Osprey Village residential development at Souterford, the pedestrian bridge literally led to absolutely nowhere and during the spring when the River Ury floods at Souterford, the decking of the bridge would vanish from view beneath the river. In recent years though a footpath has been built across the flood plain to link Osprey Village with the nearby retail park and, subject to spring floods, the curious footbridge has finally been re-purposed for its intended use. No doubt both C.S. Lewis and King Canute would approve.

Inverurie town centre - 2014

On a more serious note, Inverurie's population growth has led to a number of planning initiatives designed to cater for the changing needs of this fast-growing town. Aberdeenshire has over 3,300 miles of tarmac roads, most of them rural and uncongested, but the existing two-lane A96 Inverurie bypass is currently congested to the point of choking and with the Scottish Government committed to dualling the entire Aberdeen to Inverness route, Transport Scotland is investigating options. Sideways expansion of the current Inverurie bypass is constrained by both old and new developments running tightly alongside the carriageway, so a new bypass, bypassing the current bypass looks to be a likely solution. Garioch medical services and education are also under severe pressure. The old medical centre on Constitution Street provided health services for over 20,000 patients from the town and the surrounding area and was structurally outdated without room to expand. In 2012, following ten years of consultations, plans were finally approved for a £14.7 million replacement multidisciplinary Inverurie Health Hub on the site of Inverurie's 1940s era Art Deco Hospital. The new health centre, possibly the largest in Scotland, opened in 2018 and boasts some forty consulting rooms for both GPs and other health professionals. Facilities include ultrasound and X-ray suites, speech therapy, birthing pools, a minor injury clinic, a dental suite and a community midwifery unit. Local schools such as Inverurie Academy and Market Place Primary are also being replaced. Delayed by the COVID-19 pandemic, a new £50 million 1,600-pupil capacity replacement Inverurie Academy opened in the town centre in autumn 2020, part-funded by the Scottish Government's £1.8 billion Schools for Future Programme. Market Place Primary closed its doors in 2017 being superseded by the purpose built Uryside Primary on Peregrine Drive just off the Meldrum Road. At heart though, Inverurie, despite the massive expansion of recent decades, remains a market town with a distinctively rural feel.

Traditional folk tales about the place range from the Hound and Hare mark on the bridge over the River Urie to the story of the Golden Cow. The Hound and Hare tale features a hare hunt in some forgotten year or other and involves a pack of the laird's foxhounds pursuing a solitary hare across the bridge over the Ury at the Bass. Depending on which version of the tale you adhere to, the hare either escapes by leaping from the parapet into the waters below or suffers blunt force trauma on the sharp rocks alongside the river, closely followed by the laird's pack of suicidal canines. The bridge parapet allegedly bears the faintly incised capital letter 'H' to mark the spot where the infamous leap took place. It's a hoary old tale indeed. However, the story of the golden cow has origins in real life events. Inverurie's golden cow tale involved a fibreglass ruminant which each day at dawn was wheeled onto the pavement outside the, now closed, Mitchells Dairy and each evening was dutifully wheeled back inside perhaps to avoid kidnap by rustlers. Originally a Friesian, the life-size animal was repainted in gold in honour of Inverurie athlete Hannah Miley's gold medal win at the 2014 Glasgow Commonwealth games in the four hundred metres individual swimming medley. Given the regularity of the Mitchells Dairy 'Changing of the Cow Ceremony' it seems surprising that the likes of VisitScotland failed to capitalise on the once-upon-a-time daily spectacle as a tourist attraction. Following the closure of the dairy the Golden Cow lived for a few months in the foyer of the newly completed Uryside Primary School before taking up residence at the local heritage museum. Market Place will never be the same again!

20
KEITH – THE FRIENDLY TOWN

On Saturday May the eighth 1650 a weary cavalcade of prisoners under heavy escort arrived at the Moray market town of Keith. Heading the sorry group of captives was John Graham Marquis of Montrose. Following his defeat at the battle of Philiphaugh near Selkirk in the September of 1645 Montrose had fled abroad, returning to Scotland in 1650 to head up the forces of Charles II. However, the battle of Carbisdale in Sutherland saw the Royalists soundly defeated by the Covenanting forces with Montrose's army of 1200 foot soldiers and perhaps forty mounted soldiers - many of whom were raw conscripts - being routed by a Covenanter cavalry charge almost without firing a shot. Montrose, although reportedly injured, escaped the field but was captured at Assynt a few days later and handed over to the Covenanters in exchange for a bounty. Then began the long trek to Edinburgh where Montrose and his fellow officers would face imprisonment and in some cases summary execution.

Captain General John Graham, Marquis of Montrose, to give him his full title, had been reserved for special treatment by his Covenanting captors and following several nights spent in the open he was dragged, bound and in filthy rags, to the parish church at Keith to be sat unceremoniously on the repentance stool. There he was subjected to a thunderous sermon delivered by William Kininmonth, a military chaplain, concerning the Old Testament slaughter of the Amalikites and hewing to pieces of Agag as described in the book of Samuel. When Montrose perceived the drift of the sermon he reportedly replied "Rail on Rabshekah" before turning his back on his tormentor. Montrose was well aware that he faced a sentence of death and indeed less than two weeks later the unfortunate Marquis was hung from a gibbet at the Mercat Cross in Edinburgh. There was no trial since the Scottish Parliament had already decided his fate and on his arrival at Leith in May 1650, he was taken straight to the Tollbooth. A few days later he took the short walk to the gallows. After reputedly paying the hangman four pieces of gold, Montrose delivered a brief but impassioned speech and was turned off. He was just thirty-eight years old when he died and his final words were "May Almighty God have mercy on this afflicted country."

The execution took place at three in the afternoon and three hours later Montrose's lifeless body was cut down. At the foot of the scaffold lay various instruments of butchery conveniently arranged alongside some small wooden coffins. These boxes were duly filled with the dead Marquis's limbs in preparation for their journey to various locations throughout Scotland. His head was placed on a spike at the Tolbooth and the mangled trunk was unceremoniously buried in a cesspit at the Burghmuir. In a strange postscript, a decade after what many termed a judicial murder, the Scottish Parliament ordered a state funeral for Montrose in order to make "reparation for that horrid and monstrous barbarity fixed on Royal authority on the person of the great Marquis of Montrose". Most of his scattered body parts were retrieved and in May 1661 the nobleman's remains were interred at Edinburgh's St Giles Cathedral.

Mid Street Keith - 2012

Fortunately, nowadays folk travelling through Keith will meet a much warmer welcome. Indeed, the signposts on the outskirts of town proclaim "Welcome to Keith, the Friendly Town." Situated in an upland valley overlooked by the likes of Ben Rinnes, Knock Hill and Cairds Hill - also known as the Hill of Friends - the town was for many years a focus for merchants from far and wide who converged on Keith for the Great Fair of Simmareve. The title is probably a corruption of St Maolrubha or St Rufus, the Seventh century Irish Saint after whom Keith Parish church is named. At one time Simmareve was probably the largest fair of its kind in Scotland and according to the Rev J.F.S. Gordon's 1880 tome *The Chronicles of Keith*, the event involved cattle, horse and general goods trade beginning on the first Tuesday of September and lasting for just over a week. The ancient fair was a good excuse for letting off steam since alongside the buying and selling of thousands of black cattle and horses plus acres of woollen cloth, Gordon informs the reader that "Male and female lay together in dozens and in scores upon straw, ... in all the pantries, barns and kilns of the town. Such was then the simplicity of manners."

Attracting visitors from near and far, the modern-day Keith Show at Seafield Park is much more sedate in nature and typically features the Scottish Beef Cattle Championships, vintage trucks, highland dancing, sheep shearing, show jumping, massed pipe bands plus a fair bit of traditional Haggis Hurling. The Haggis Hurling competition challenges all comers to beat the world hurling record of 66.142 metres. As with all public events, the show organisers had to take the difficult decision to cancel the 2020 event due to COVID-19 but with the 150th anniversary fast approaching plans are already underway for 2021 and beyond.

As to famous folk associated with Keith there have been quite a few including Brian Adam who served as the SNP Member of the Scottish Parliament for Aberdeen Donside and veteran broadcaster James Naughtie who was educated at Keith Grammar School. Then there is footballer Colin Hendry, perhaps Scotland's most famous defender aside from William Wallace. He played as striker for Keith FC and later Islavale FC before signing with Blackburn Rovers and famously captained Scotland in the 1998 World Cup in Paris. Then there is the martyred Saint John Ogilvie who was hanged at Glasgow in 1615 and who remains Scotland's only post Reformation Saint. Others include astronomer James Ferguson and John Ripley VC, a First War hero and survivor of the 1915 Battle of Aubers Ridge. Ripley made the headlines again when aged 65 he died after falling from a ladder. A second Keith-born Victoria Cross holder, George Sellar VC, won his medal in the Anglo Afghan war in 1879. His citation in the *London Gazette* reads:

"FOR CONSPICUOUS GALLANTRY displayed by him at the assault on the Asmai Heights, round Kabul, in December 1879, in having in a marked manner led the attack, under a heavy fire, and dashing on in front of the party up a slope, engaged in a desperate conflict with an Afghan who sprang out to meet him. In this encounter Lance Corporal Sellar was severely wounded."

Then there is James Gordon Bennett Senior (1795-1872) whose given names are often used as a convenient euphemism for expressions of surprise such as "cor blimey!" and "would you believe it!" Born at Enzie near Buckie, his family later moved to Newmill just outside Keith. He worked for a while in a local haberdashery on Mid Street before moving first to Aberdeen then to North

America where he drifted into the newspaper business. In 1835 he set up the *New York Herald* and began publishing amongst other things 'kiss and tell' stories. It seems that in 1836 for example, he offered a reward to any woman prepared to "set a trap for a Presbyterian parson and catch one of them *in flagrante delicto*." Described by a rival press baron as "an obscene foreign vagabond, a pestilential scoundrel, ass, rogue, habitual liar, loathsome and leprous slanderer and libeller" he was obviously a colourful character but he was also a shrewd newspaperman who sent out fast boats to meet the European ships before they made landfall in order to be first with the transatlantic news.

Bennett's son James Gordon Bennett Junior carried on the running of the family newspaper empire and despite his flamboyant and eccentric behaviour, which often scandalized the high society of the day, he continued to pursue sensational news stories. In 1869 for example he funded Henry Morton Stanley's successful expedition into deepest Africa in order to locate the Blantyre-born missionary David Livingstone. Stanley's mission was successful giving *The Herald* an exclusive account of Livingstone's various achievements. Perhaps Gordon Bennett Junior's most bizarre claim to fame however is his odd connection with Asteroid 305 Gordonia. Discovered in 1891 by French astronomer Auguste Honoré Charlois the heavenly body was named in honour of Gordon in recognition of his patronage of the Camille Flammarion Observatory near Paris. His headlines were sensational and perhaps suffered from glaring inaccuracies but at the end of the day he lent his name both to a figure of speech and to an interstellar piece of rock which was last seen hurtling around the universe at some thirty kilometres per second.

The Keith of today has a population of around 4491 and is an important staging post on the Speyside Malt Whisky Trail thanks in part to the Strathisla Distillery with its distinctive Doig Pagodas. Owned by Chivas, the visitor centre offers malt whisky tasting tours and is reputedly the oldest working distillery in the Highlands of Scotland. Keith also boasts a rapidly expanding craft brewery - Brewmeister - operating from the historic Isla Bank Mills. Brewmeister claims to brew the world's strongest beer at a reported 67.5 percent proof. The company's beers also include descriptive labels such as Snake Venom and Supersonic IPA. Alongside the whisky and beer making, the town has many fine examples of historic architecture ranging from the neo-Gothic design of St Rufus church to the breathtakingly beautiful St Thomas Roman Catholic Church with its distinctive copper dome and interior painting titled The Incredulity of Christ by Francois Dubois, commissioned the French King Charles X. The town centre boasts many fine buildings and a stroll down Mid Street reveals an outstanding range of Victorian architectural gems. The fifty-four narrow lanes which run through the town centre with names such as Pipers Lane, Ploo Lane, Fairmers Lane, and Sodgers Lane are worth exploring also.

Daniel Defoe once visited and records his passing through Keith in around 1719, the year his popular novel *The Life and Strange Surprizing Adventures of Robinson Crusoe, Mariner of York* made the bookshelves. A man of literature and widely published, he commented that the Auld Brig over the River Isla was "a very fine bridge." Had he been around to witness the crossing of the Auld Brig by Defoe, James Gordon Bennett Snr would have no doubt dug deep into Defoe's personal life and then written about the author's arrest and subsequent imprisonment for debt following the selling of dubious marine insurance during the naval war with France, his conviction for Seditious Libel and the alleged swindling of his mother-in-law in a failed Ponzi Scheme.

But the two writers inhabited Keith in two quite different eras. Almost three hundred years on from Defoe's crossing, the Auld Brig at Keith remains a very fine bridge indeed and is well worth a visit; not least to view Gaun's Pot just upstream where in olden days the townsfolk drowned the local witches. Fortunately, nowadays folk travelling through Keith will meet a much warmer welcome. Indeed, the signposts on the outskirts of town proclaim "Welcome to Keith, the Friendly Town." Situated in an upland valley overlooked by the likes of Ben Rinnes, Knock Hill and Cairds Hill - also known as the Hill of Friends - the town was for many years a focus for merchants from far and wide who converged on Keith for the Great Fair of Simmareve. The title is probably a corruption of St Maolrubha or St Rufus, the Seventh century Irish Saint after whom Keith Parish church is named. At one time Simmareve was probably the largest fair of its kind in Scotland and according to the Rev J.F.S. Gordon's 1880 tome The Chronicles of Keith, the event involved cattle, horse and general goods trade beginning on the first Tuesday of September and lasting for just over a week. The ancient fair was a good excuse for letting off of steam since alongside the buying and selling of literally thousands of black cattle and horses plus literally acres of woollen cloth, Gordon informs the reader that "Male and female lay together in dozens and in scores upon straw, ... in all the pantries, barns and kilns of the town. Such was then the simplicity of manners.". Attracting visitors from near and far the modern-day Keith Show at Seafield Park, is much more sedate in nature and typically features the Scottish Beef Cattle Championships, vintage trucks, highland dancing, sheep shearing, show jumping, massed pipe bands plus a fair bit of traditional Haggis Hurling. The Haggis Hurling competition challenges all comers to beat the world hurling record of 66.142m, or 217ft in real money. As with all public events, the show organisers had to take the difficult decision to cancel the 2020 event due to

COVID-19 but with the 150th anniversary fast approaching plans are already underway for 2021 and beyond.

21
KINTORE – A RIGHT ROYAL BURGH

A long gone road sign at Midmill, on the outskirts of Kintore, once revealed that the town, a Royal Burgh, lies some 686 miles from Land's End and 232 miles from John O' Groats. Seemingly Kintore lies further from Newcastle than from Thurso and is just twelve miles from Aberdeen. In fact, a total of around such fifty destinations were listed on the 1960s era signpost. A supermarket, several car showrooms and a new dental surgery now occupy the site and the only modern-day record of the signpost is a faded newspaper cutting held at the local public library. The advent of satnav has perhaps made such signposts redundant in any case. However, in a nod to the past, locals have expressed interest in recreating this historic signpost as a modern-day tourist attraction.

Kintore - Northern Road

In 1975 the town's official boundary signs were removed by the council and put into storage following local government boundary reforms. A style of local government dating from the Middle Ages was replaced with a new arrangement of regional and district councils. The burgh status became redundant in law and Kintore found itself within the governance of Gordon District which itself was within the greater governance of Grampian Region. Decades later, all this was to change yet again in a further local government shakeup.

Kintore claims to have gained a Royal Burgh Charter from Kenneth II in the Ninth century but there are seemingly no historical records which confirm this. The earliest extant Charter dates from 1506 and was granted by James IV. Although abolished in law, the title Royal Burgh is still used by many Scottish towns including Kintore and a long running dispute followed the removal of the iconic road signs. Following lengthy consultations between the Community Council, the Lord Lyon King of Arms, the Regional Council and the former Gordon District Council, the historical road signs bearing Kintore's historic coat of arms plus the town motto 'Truth is Strength' were finally taken out of storage. In 1981 they were re-erected at the town boundaries where to this day they welcome travellers to the non-existent Royal Burgh of Kintore.

Kintore at one time boasted two castles. Hallforest Castle stands a mile west of the town. Visited by Mary Queen of Scots in 1562, the tower house is visible from the A96 trunk road and is a rare example of a Scottish Fourteenth century keep. Traditionally described as a hunting lodge for King Robert Bruce, the tower is nowadays in ruin and trees grow amongst the tumbledown battlements. What remained of a second fortress on the Castle Hill in the centre of Kintore fell victim to the Victorian obsession with rail travel. Sited atop a conical mound over thirty feet high, the ruin has been compared to the historic Bass at Inverurie. Sadly, the Twelfth century monument at Kintore lay directly in the path of the Great North of Scotland Railway and was completely flattened in about 1854. Nowadays no obvious traces remain above ground.

The local Pictish stones have generally fared much better. As recently as September 1974 a symbol stone bearing a double square plus an elephant and mirror was unearthed in Henderson Crescent; and two carved stones preserved when the Castle Hill was removed by the railway engineers now form part of the permanent collection of the National Museum of Antiquities of Scotland in Edinburgh. A third carved stone stands alongside the war memorial arch within Kintore Parish Kirk yard. Known as the Ichthus Stone, it is sculpted on both faces with the front bearing fish and triple disc symbols and the back bearing a crescent and V-rod. Local author and poet Rev. Dawson Scott records in his 1953 publication *Story of Kintore* that the Ichthus Stone took up its present position in 1882 when the gravestones in the kirkyard were put into rows:

"Bit when gravestones were set in line
This stane wis pit aside the gate;
A welcome frai the deid an' gane,

This is God's Hoose, come pray, an' wait."

The Romans also left their mark on the local landscape in the form of a vast military camp at Deers Den. Surveyed by a Captain Courtney of the Royal Engineers in 1867, the site is reckoned to be unique in the Roman Empire in that it provides valuable insight into the activities of a Roman army in the field. Within this site there are also signs of at least seven roundhouses dating from the Iron-Age. Identifiable only as cropmarks in aerial photos these are, according to Ancient Monuments Scotland, "sited in pasture to the west of the A96 trunk road at Kintore, and lie around sixty metres above sea level and around 1.2 km west of the River Don". Both the modern day A96 Kintore Bypass and the Aberdeenshire Canal cut through the Roman camp at Deers Den and nowadays much of the land occupied by the Roman soldiers has been used for housing and occupied by the new primary school. Various excavations related to housing and highway development have revealed remains of forty Roman field ovens, several Roman rubbish pits and sections of a fortified perimeter ditch. Large enough to house ten thousand troops, the camp is classified as a marching camp and is just one of a vast network of similar military bases identified across Scotland. Frequently spaced a single day's march apart these were often temporary in nature being erected before dusk using prefabricated barricades then disassembled next day for reuse at the next overnight halt.

An important harbour and livery station for the Aberdeenshire Canal, Kintore at one time also boasted both a rail station and an aerodrome. The Canal connected the town to both Aberdeen and Inverurie for over half a century until 1854 when the Great North of Scotland Railway took over the route. Settlements such as Kintore became important staging posts both for the import and export of goods and as livery points for the horses which hauled the barges to and from Aberdeen. *The Annals of Aberdeen* record that in 1808 there were seventeen barges plus two Flyboats, or passenger boats, employed on the canal which indicates the scale of the enterprise. Exports included heavy goods such as granite and slate alongside wheat and oats. In 1833 alone over 2,180 tons of stone and 461 tons of slate, presumably extracted from the slate quarries at Colpy, left Port Elphinstone on the journey south to Aberdeen. In the same year 2829 tons of lime, 2184 tons of coal and 102 tons of dung - possibly the night-soil of the City of Aberdeen - made the journey north to Inverurie. Imports of bones for fertilizer amounted to 278 tons in 1835. By 1838 this figure had reached 1394 tons, hence the need for the bone mill at Port Elphinstone. Clearly the lime, dung and bonemeal were key inputs to the agricultural prosperity of

Aberdeenshire. There is a detailed history of the canal in my earlier book *The Little History of Aberdeenshire*. As for the night soil, despite the vagarious of the English language, it was probably the most sought after excrement in the whole of Scotland being just a fraction of the cost of imported South American Guano.

When the railway came, alongside the link south to Aberdeen and eventually north to Inverness, a sixteen-mile-long Alford Valley Railway extension linked Kintore, Kemnay, Monymusk and Alford. This spur line closed to passengers in 1949 although quarry traffic continued until 1967. A year later the track bed, minus rails and sleepers, featured as a stage on the Granite City Rally circuit. In more modern times Kintore's Tom's Forest Quarry, once ranked equal in importance to Aberdeen's Rubislaw and Northfield's Dancing Cairns, supplied much of the material for the Aberdeen Western Peripheral Route. Kintore's railway station ceased passenger operation in the 1960s. Fifty or so years on and as part of a major £170 million "Corridor of Prosperity" upgrade of Aberdeen to Inverness road and rail corridor, a new purpose-built station is under construction. Initially due for completion in March 2019, the project suffered delays in part due to the COVID-19 pandemic; but finally opened in 2020 without much fanfare. The long awaited station is generally welcomed by Kintore folk and also by Scotland's previous First Minister Alex Salmond who commented in 2014 that "The doubling of the line between Inverurie and Aberdeen, alongside the new station at Kintore will only serve to enhance these benefits of this essential transport link and help bring new people and opportunities to our local communities". In fact, as far back as 1900, a full year before Queen Victoria's demise, Inkson McConachie was recording in his guidebook about Donside that when the railway opened in Kintore great things were expected to happen. He writes that "Crowds of visitors will come out on holidays and pleasure excursions will be frequent … and Mr Gourley of the Kintore Arms will have enough to do to meet the demands of his larder and his good humour". There were even suggestions that "the merchant princes of Aberdeen" would be "erecting their villas by the side of the pretty Don" just as they had done over at Deeside. But it was not to be. Kintore had few attractions for the holiday crowd and those merchant princes seemingly had much better places to invest in.

Then there is Kintore's lost aerodrome. Situated alongside the A96 at Cairnhall, next to the graveyard, sits a fairly nondescript black corrugated iron building easily overlooked but with an interesting history. Constructed by local joiner Reggie Bisset the building is described by The Royal Commission on the Ancient and Historical Monuments of Scotland as Kintore Aircraft Hangar.

Kintore Aircraft Hangar - 2013

In fact, the building has experienced several incarnations. In recent decades the shed served as a Water Board store and is today occupied by an offshore equipment company. The category B listed building was in fact commissioned in 1934 by Scottish air pioneer, Captain Ernest Fresson, to house and service his airliners. Barnstormers such as Sir Alan Cobham's hugely popular Cobham's Flying Circus had performed at Kintore in the 1930s and although Captain Fresson was not averse to providing an occasional joy-ride, his mission at Cairnhall was to develop the aerodrome for passenger and airmail operations.

Fresson first became interested in aviation in 1908. As a youngster, he had witnessed early flights by aviation pioneers such as Brabazan and Short. With a military flying career including Royal Flying Corps service on U-boat patrol during the first war, he quickly grasped the potential of post war commercial flying and by 1934 was operating Britain's first airmail service to Orkney from Inverness. An Aberdeen to Orkney route quickly followed with daily flights operating from Seaton in Aberdeen. The coming of the Highland Show to Seaton in 1935 meant that his airline, Highland Airways, would have to find an alternative local aerodrome. Dyce was unavailable, being at the time in the hands of a rival airline headed by Eric Gandar Dower who operated Aberdeen (later Allied) Airways and the captain began a desperate search for a replacement landing ground.

In his memoir *The Air Road to the Isles* he records the history of Kintore Airfield. The Captain had recently purchased a DH60 Gipsy Moth biplane, a 1920s British manufactured touring aeroplane, from his close friend, the aviation pioneer Heloise Pauer and had been using this machine to scout out potential landing strips in the Aberdeenshire countryside. On arriving at Kintore he had approached a local farmer who, being unable to spare the grazing, recommended a neighbour who owned two fairly flat fields up by the cemetery. "It was a good omen" recalls Fresson "at least we would not have to look far in case of accident." Accidents were fairly common at the time and the captain was no stranger to them having crashed an aircraft into a stone wall while landing in mist at Wideford Aerodrome in 1933. Over a bottle of Malt, the Captain and Mr Barrack, the farmer at Cairnhall, struck a deal. A hangar and an airstrip could be built on the site and a long lease was available. To sweeten the deal, the two men agreed that between flights, which averaged perhaps two per day, the farmer's dairy herd could continue to graze the landing ground. Travel between Kintore and Orkney initially cost £5.50 return and the airline flew in and out of Kintore using mainly DH89A Dragon Rapide twin engine biplanes.

During WW2 Cairnhall and neighbouring East Fingask at Oldmeldrum became dispersal aerodromes for RAF Dyce, nowadays better known as Aberdeen International Airport. East Fingask was rarely used however although Alan Stewart's splendidly detailed book *North East Scotland at War* records that an entire flight of fifteen Avro Anson light bombers were evacuated there from Dyce airfield during a July 1940 'Red Alert'. Flight operations at Kintore were short lived and Highland Airways was soon swallowed up by nationalisation being eventually liquidated in 1940. One of Fresson's Kintore based airliners, a DH.84 Dragon1 biplane registered as G-ACIT and claimed to be Britain's oldest surviving airliner, is on display at the Science Museum at Wroughton. Renamed 'Orcadian' whilst in service with British Airways the machine has now been restored and repainted in the original Highland Airways Limited livery.

During the past few decades Kintore has been described variously as both the smallest Royal Burgh in Scotland and as the fastest growing town in Scotland. A century ago, in 1921, the population count was 2,281. Today the figure has more than doubled. The Inverurie and Kintore Capacity Study, an Aberdeenshire Council planning document, concluded that "By 2027 the level of growth considered in this study will result in Inverurie growing to a scale similar to the current size of Arbroath, and will result in Kintore growing to a scale similar to the current size of Portlethen." Portlethen recorded 7,130 inhabitants in the 2011 Census making it the seventh most populous settlement within Aberdeenshire. In the same Census, Kintore recorded 4,476 inhabitants.

Many locals, as well as wanting improved facilities are keen to retain the community feel of Kintore and are uneasy regarding the projected rate of growth. Recent projections indicate that the Aberdeenshire population is expected to rise by twenty-two percent by 2033, against a projected Scottish average increase of just seven percent for the same period. Kintore, as a dormitory town just twelve miles from the centre of the oil capital of Europe, seems poised to change out of all recognition. The 2015 Kintore Community Action Plan consultations took place as part of Kintore Summer Festival and a number of key areas were identified for further discussion. Respondents valued the community spirit, existing local facilities and ease of countryside access but recognised the needs of the rapidly expanding local population calling for more shops, a swimming pool and a new rail station. Kintore in 2015 had several cafés but lacked a public house and restaurant (now rectified following the reopening of the former Kintore Arms as The Square Bar and Lounge) and there were calls to block the proposed conversion of the former Torryburn Hotel into flats. As fate would have it, the hotel burned down in June 2015 making the arguments on either side largely redundant.

The Kintore of today is at a crossroads. The amenities available within the settlement clearly fail to meet the expectations of many of the residents living within this rapidly expanding community and yet most locals value the "small town" feel of the place and are reluctant to embrace major development. Traditional high street shops, such as family run butcher J. and G. Dossett, have long faced competition from the supermarkets at Inverurie and Aberdeen however now the big four are knocking at the front door. The recent opening of Sainsburys at Midmill represents a further challenge to the current high street line up which includes post office, newsagent, chipper, butcher, hairdresser and chemist. As the pace of development within the settlement gathers momentum it is difficult to imagine the Kintore of twenty-five years hence. A *Casablanca* style brief encounter between Bergman and Bogart at Cairnhall Aerodrome seems extremely unlikely but, in the big scheme of things, John O' Groats is still one third nearer to Kintore than to Land's End and Aberdeen remains a mere twelve miles away.

22
LENABO – THE BUCHAN BRIGADOON

The Scottish coastline is littered with the bones of ships and rumours of treasure laden Spanish galleons inhabit the folklore. The Armada ship Santa Catalina is said to lie amongst rocks just off Collieston. It foundered, according to various written accounts, off St Catherine's Dub in 1594 which is some six years after elements of the Spanish fleet were driven north from the Isle of Wight in that dreadful storm. The National Trust for Scotland stately home at Haddo House confidently claims to have a cannon salvaged from the wreck and commentators over the last several hundred years have repeated the unlikely tale one after the other in a chain of what can only be described as Chinese whispers.

Grampian historian Fenton Wyness investigated the mythology for his 1973 book *More Spots from the Leopard* and concluded that the local fishermen had maybe invented the tale to humour the government appointed surveyors of the Ordnance Survey who relied largely on local knowledge for the naming of such places. They marked the Ordnance Survey charts for Collieston with the helpful label 'Site of the Wreck of the St. Catherine'. But St Catherine's Dub, Wyness suggests, might well be a simple corruption of 'The Caterans Dub' which roughly translates as 'The Robbers Pool' and maybe has more to do with smuggling than with Spanish doubloons. Another Armada ship, the San Michael, seemingly lies amongst the Skerry Rocks at Boddam. Almost every castle in Scotland claims that Mary Queen of Scots slept there and almost every village along the Scottish coastline claims a connection to Spanish gold plus maybe a cannon or two salvaged from the shipwrecks of the Spanish Armada.

Mind you, there is the strange but maybe true tale of the wreck of the U-1206. A German U-boat dating from late in WW2, it lies off Cruden Bay and reputedly sank by virtue of a toilet malfunction. It's a hoary old tale. The U-1206 went into service in March 1944 and was assigned to active duty under the command of Kapitanleutnant Karl Adolf Schlitt. On April fourteenth 1945, just weeks prior to the end of hostilities, the submarine was cruising underwater just off the Buchan coast when a crew member, possibly the Captain, had a call of nature. Unfortunately, the U-1206 was fitted with a newly designed high pressure underwater flushing toilet. Previously crews often 'slopped out' using buckets which were taken topside at the earliest opportunity and emptied into the sea. The new system did away with this messy procedure and waste was passed through a series of valves before being fired at high pressure into the ocean in the form of a sort of poop-torpedo. The system however only worked safely at shallow depths and only crew members versed in the flushing procedure were authorised to operate the valves.

The Captain obviously hadn't read the manual and, as he attempted to flush the loo, something went badly wrong. A toilet specialist was summoned but misunderstood the situation and opened the wrong valve resulting in seawater entering the boat. The submarine's battery compartment was situated directly underneath the toilet floor and when the incoming saltwater combined with the battery acid, toxic chlorine gas was generated. Things soon got out of hand. Forced to surface in order to vent the fumes, the boat was quickly spotted and bombed by allied aircraft forcing the unfortunate Captain Schlitt to order the fifty crewmembers overboard before scuttling the vessel. One crew member died in the air attack and several more may have drowned in the North Sea as they abandoned ship. The surviving submariners made it to shore and spent the rest of the war in captivity.

But, alongside the hidden ships there are the hidden townships which lie below the shifting sands beside the sea. Culbin is well known. Buried, at least according to the folklore, in 1694 by a weather event called the 'Great Sand Drift' the sixteen local farms and the laird's big house at Culbin vanished under a tsunami of windblown sand in the course of a single day. Seemingly a ploughman abandoned his plough mid-furrow as the sand rolled in at speed to obliterate the farmland. Witchcraft was blamed but the true cause may have been more mundane. The local folk had been ripping up the marram grass for thatch and fuel unaware that they were uncovering the devil's dust. Without the grass to stabilise the dunes, the sands upped in the winter storm and smothered the township forever. Lesser known is Forvie at Newburgh which met the same fate but over nine days. A storm in 1688 overwhelmed the community and literally made the once fertile land into a desert. No witches were blamed although a trio of the laird's daughters were rumoured to have prayed for the land's destruction following a dispute over inheritance. Another archaic source cites papism and the ignorance of the villagers as the cause of the disaster, but the dates are wrong unless of course the place was resurrected then reburied by yet another tsunami of sand.

Another lost township lies seven miles inland at Longside in Buchan. Peat bogs were perhaps the problem here and not sand. In the making of the place a regiment of steam powered mechanical diggers and an army of navvies moved in to drain the land and strip the landscape of the stuff. Once the peat was out of the way hectares of concrete, kilometres of field drains and finally five miles of railway line were laid and paid for by the government of the day. It was late 1915 when Lenabo, literally 'the wet meadow of the cows', was finally completed. Brick by brick a township of hangars, engineering workshops and accommodation units had appeared in what had until ten months before been 1000 acres of subsistence farmland worked by the farms of Auchtydore, Torhendry and the aptly named Bogend. A cinema was built closely followed by a fire station and a waterworks. Finally came a gasworks and providentially a church. In short, a small town had been built on a peatbog and in less time than it would take to build a modern-day street of bungalows.

Lenabo Royal Naval Air Station in Buchan – the lair of the 'Silver Sausages'

The civil engineering company Tawse and Co had carried out the bulk of the work and in record time too, for this was wartime and the government contract stipulated that speed and only speed was of the essence. Even as the last bricks were being put in place, the new inhabitants moved in. Tawse had built the northernmost Royal Naval Air Station in Britain in record time and the military were eager to start work. By this point in the war, German U-boats were becoming a major threat to shipping and the newly formed Royal Naval Air Service had taken over the Army's small fleet of airships. A procurement programme quickly added to their numbers and soon they were being tasked with patrolling the sea lanes in search of enemy submarines. A succession of marques was produced, and by the time Lenabo was operational, the Coastal Class of airship was being produced in large numbers. Almost two-hundred feet long, these machines had an endurance of around twenty hours and the two engines - one pusher and one puller - propelled the craft at a heady fifty miles per hour on a good day. Armed with machine guns and bombs the crew of five were expected to attack submarines on the surface but given the sheer scale of these airships this could not have been very successful since manoeuvrability was poor and they were easily spotted. In practice they were mainly used as spotters although there was a naval theory that U-boat crews who didn't know this would be deterred from attacking merchant ships purely due to the imagined threat. A counter theory suggested that the mere presence of an airship hovering over a convoy would actually attract unwanted attention from enemy submarines and lead to even more losses.

As Tawse finished up construction at Lenabo, the first airships were brought in by road and rail in prefabricated sections. Following assembly in the vast hangers on the base, patrolling began over the North Sea. The sea lanes around Peterhead were seemingly infested with enemy submarines which passed by on their way into the Atlantic but the airbase's contribution the sea war seems to have been at best negligible and not a single U-boat was sunk by the Lenabo crews. A succession of RNAS airship types were housed at the base but all had the same fundamental set of problems. Known to locals as either Silver Sausages or Lenabo Soos (a reference to sows) and to the base personnel as Gasbags, they were cumbersome and difficult to handle in anything above a light breeze with engines that were at best unreliable. In 1917 one came down at Peterhead having collided with the weathercock on the roof of the Town House, another had to be 'ripped' to deflate the gas bags when it broke loose from a base landing party. A third, the Coastal Airship No. XXV (some accounts refer to it as HMA C-25), simply disappeared into some North Sea Bermuda Triangle while on patrol off the Buchan coast.

It was July 31st 1918 and the crew of the C 25 had been out along with other Coastal Class airships searching for German U-boats. The 196-foot machine was last sighted at 18:40 hours that evening some sixty miles out over the North Sea off Aberdeen. What happened next is subject to speculation. Some sources suggest that the crew sighted an enemy U-boat, attacked it and were shot down. Others suggest that the airship simply crashed into the sea following a mechanical failure. However, the truth will probably never be known although a twin bladed wooden propeller from the craft was picked up at sea by a passing ship the next day and is now on permanent display as a memorial to the crew at Longside Parish Church. The remains of the crew were never found and the men were presumed lost at sea. An obituary piece in the Essex County Chronicle records that: "Corpl-mech. Lewis G. Faiers R.A.F. only son of Mrs RE Faiers of 23 Moulsham Street is reported missing from August first. In a letter received from his station he is stated to have gone out on patrol duty in perfect weather and not returned."

Lewis had seemingly been a fishmonger in civilian life before training as an air mechanic in April 1917. A year later he was dead and the military township of Lenabo was about to follow in his footsteps.

Lenabo soldiered on for a couple of years beyond the Armistice. The base magazine - *The Battle Bag* - continued in print, but to a skeleton crew. Printed in Peterhead, the magazine cover featured the base motto "trans maria naves nos, in aethera" (Our ships crossed the ocean, into the heavens) - possibly a quote from Virgil's Aeneid - and consisted mainly of musings and reflective bits of poetry contributed by the base personnel. Finally, in 1920 the place was relegated to the Disposals Board of the War Office. Contracts were signed and contractors, in some cases the very same ones who five years before had built the base, arrived to take it all down. The airbase was stripped of everything of value and nowadays only the concrete slabs from the airship hangars remain alongside the foundations of the sixty or so buildings which once graced the site. Even the course of the old railway line is hard to find nowadays. It carried some 32,000 tons of supplies during its brief span of operation and the track was lifted a full century ago allowing nature to move in and cover the scar.

The line is mainly remembered nowadays as the site of Buchan's very first railway crossing fatality. There were seemingly two unmanned level crossings on the spur line, one at Kinmundy and one across the Banff to Peterhead main road. The theory was that trains had right of way over cars and in any case, there were few cars about to bother them. But in practice there was little warning and near misses were fairly common especially at Kinmundy where the engines were apt to emerge at speed from the trees beside the road. A local couple, a Peterhead businessman and his wife, were crossing the line at Flushing just where the line crosses the main road when a steam train appeared from the woods at Cairngall. The incident is graphically described by David Toulmin in his tale *The Last Journey*, part of his *Straw into Gold* miscellany:

"It happened in the last year of its [Lenabo's] existence in 1920 while Lenabo was still being demolished, that a Peterhead businessman and his wife, Mr. and Mrs Patterson (drapers) of 'London House', Chapel Street were killed in their veteran car on the level crossing …. The engine practically wiped the road with the car and the occupants were unrecognisable. A tragedy in our own day but

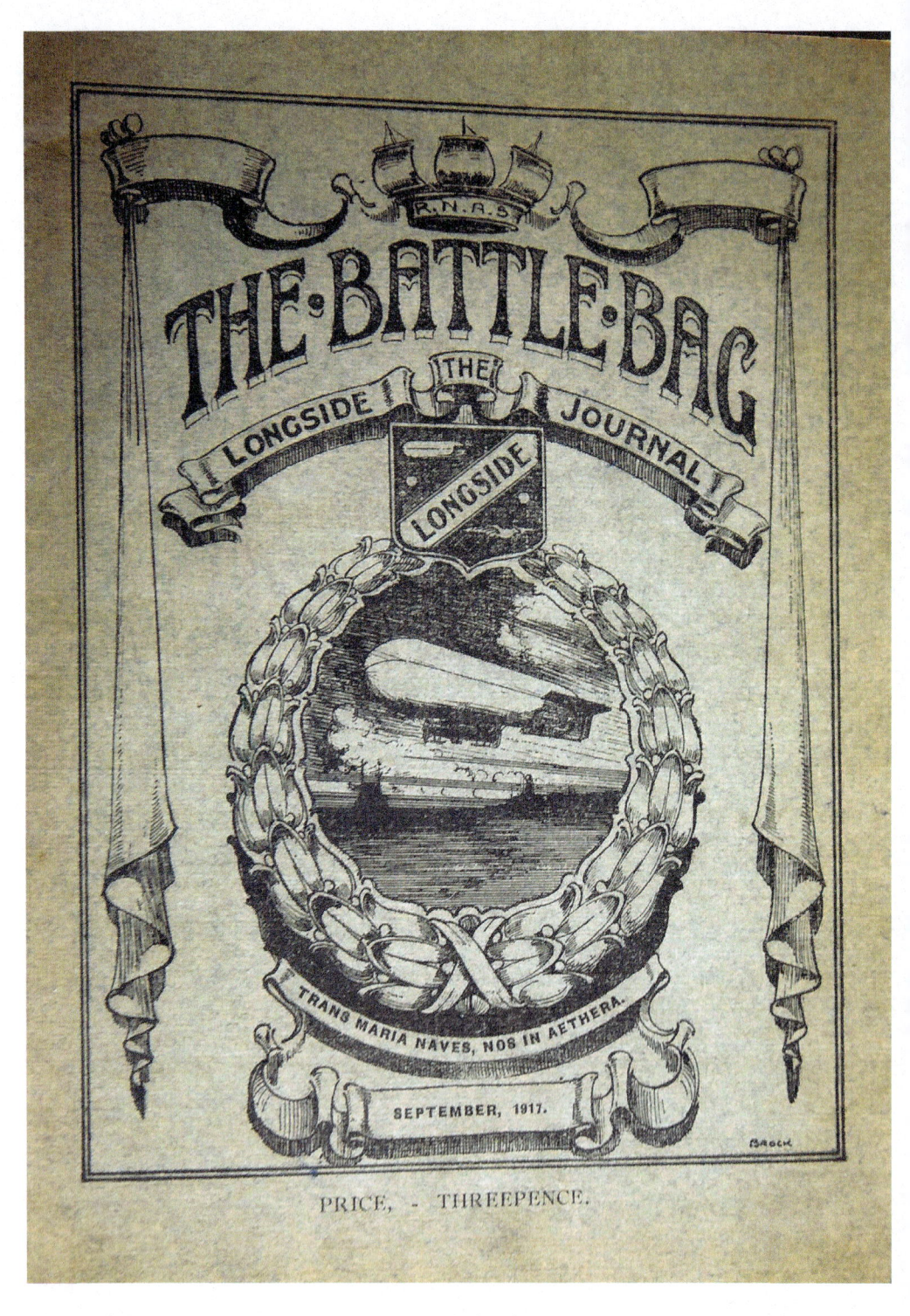

The Battle Bag – September 1917 (Courtesy of Aberdeenshire Library Service HQ)

you can imagine what it was like in a community practically free from road deaths."

When Lenabo was facing demolition, there were various suggestions as to what to do with the place. Local visionaries suggested that the military base would maybe make a fine site for a canning factory for processing canned vegetables, or beef or maybe even ox-tongues. Another notion, according to David Toulmin, was to convert the place into a hallelujah themed "pastoral precinct and call it New Kinmundy". Yet another idea was to use the site for large scale peat processing but obviously, someone along the timeline had completely forgotten that Tawse and Co had removed much of the peat and drained the land some five years previously. In the end the place was turned back to forestry and an eloquent Toulmin writes that Lenabo "had belonged to the old Keith domain of Ludquharn which, in turn, was part of the Aden estate, and it was said that Aden received £5,000 for the freehold of Lenabo. For a long time, the site lay derelict, until it was offered to the Forestry Commission, which has restored to a petrified forest a bountiful and fairyland garland of sylvan beauty."

David Toulmin, aka John Reid in his real life, almost got it right. He wrote that as the place was being torn down the original contractors were still engaged in maintaining and upgrading the base. The Tawse and Co trucks and diggers contracted to tear apart Lenabo were working side by side with the Tawse and Co trucks and diggers contracted by the government to keep the place from sinking back into the peat bog. The town of Lenabo had emerged from the peatlands for just a very few years before vanishing again under forestry. But every forty years or so when the time comes to harvest and replant the timber, the hidden remnants of the military township emerge briefly from the undergrowth like some ghostly Buchan Brigadoon, and to the sound of urgent chain saws and modern-day timber harvesters.

23
LOSSIEMOUTH – SCOTLAND'S BAY OF NAPLES

These are interesting times for Scotland. A Treaty of Union forged on the back of the Darien Scheme bankruptcy is again under scrutiny. The 1997 devolution referendum proved electric for many and the 2014 independence referendum led to a marginal 'no' victory with fifty-five percent (2,001,926) of the votes from an overall voter turnout of 84.5 percent voting to remain in the Union. First Minister Nicola Sturgeon forges ahead with matters of state and the internal politics of the four nations which currently comprise the United Kingdom, have changed forever.

From an ordinary family in Irvine, the First Minister's father was an electrician and her mother a dental nurse. The family weren't particularly political and she recalls that her upbringing was unremarkable saying that "there was nothing in my childhood that said I'm going to be First Minister of the country one day."

Despite the political divides, in some ways her background and rise to influence echoes the story of Lossiemouth man James Ramsay MacDonald (1866-1937). From humble beginnings he too rose to a pinnacle and became not only the first ever Labour Prime Minister but coincidently one of the first members of parliament to embrace aviation as a routine means of transport to and from his Lossiemouth home to the powerhouse of Westminster. In pre-RAF Lossiemouth days, he regularly flew south to Croydon Aerodrome from a grass airstrip on the outskirts of the seaside town.

Born in 1866 he entered Parliament in 1906 as MP for Leicester following an early career as a journalist. A fierce critic of the Boer Wars (1880-1881 and 1889-1902), he was also outspoken in his opposition to WW1. His pacifist convictions and unshakeable socialist stance quickly made him a hate figure both locally and nationally. Widely attacked in the establishment press he was blackballed by Moray Golf Club in 1916 and vilified in the likes of *John Bull* magazine as "A traitor and a coward, a libeller and a slanderer of his country … he is nothing more than the illegitimate son of a Scotch servant girl!" Strong words indeed from a magazine founded and edited by Horatio William Bottomley, himself from humble origins having been brought up in an orphanage. Bottomley's career path embraced bankruptcy and eventual disgrace following his conviction as a war bonds fraudster. MacDonald's career, although blighted by an unforgiving Labour Party who regarded him as a turncoat due his role in forming a National Government in 1931, embraced two prime ministerships and eventual recognition - well after his death in 1937 - for his pivotal role (alongside Keir Hardie and Arthur Henderson) in the formation of the Labour Party. As the First War dragged on and the painful losses mounted, Ramsay MacDonald's public reputation slowly recovered. To their credit, Moray Golf Club later revised their decision to expel him and in 1929 - some fourteen years after the event - offered to reinstate him as a member. Still stung by the impact of his expulsion, MacDonald declined and continued happily playing golf at neighbouring Spey Bay.

Birthplace of Ramsay MacDonald – Gregory Place, Lossiemouth

Lossiemouth remains quite proud of the MacDonald connection and there are interpretation boards around the town proclaiming the fact. He was born in a modest end terrace cottage in Gregory Place and later lived at The Hillocks in Moray Street, a house he built for his mother. The Hillocks remains in family ownership and is occasionally open to the public during Scottish Civic Trust Doors Open Days. The Gregory Place cottage, a listed Grade B building, is little changed on the outside and is in private ownership. Lossiemouth Fisheries and Community Museum on the harbour front contains a replica of the great man's study complete with personal effects, books and his parliamentary dispatch case. Ramsay Macdonald died aged seventy-one in November 1937 on board the ocean liner *MV Reina del Pacifico* during a sea cruise which friends had hoped might restore his failing health. Following a Westminster Abbey state funeral, his ashes were brought north to be buried alongside his wife Margaret in Spynie Cemetery.

MacDonald labelled the golden stretch of sand from Covesea lighthouse to Lossiemouth as "Our Bay of Naples" and the town has long proved popular with business folk from the likes of Elgin and Nairn who in many cases built grand holiday mansions overlooking the bay. The coming of the railways opened up the Moray coast to both day trippers and folk from much further afield. When the Elgin to Lossiemouth line, which opened in 1852, was finally linked to the national rail grid this led to an influx of holidaymakers from as far away as London and the south of England. The line closed to passengers in 1964 and freight services ceased in 1966. Much of the old line is now incorporated within the Moray Coastal Trail. Some original track is visible at the harbour and local rumours suggest that a number of early railway carriages dating from around 1900 lie buried amongst the dunes of the East Beach.

Half way between Inverness and Peterhead by sea, Lossiemouth was once the seaport for Elgin. In common with most coastal settlements on the Moray Firth, fishing was once the main industry with the herring fisheries starting in about 1819 alongside a long tradition of harvesting cod, skate, halibut and haddock. Nowadays there are just a few commercial boats and local seafaring consists in the main of pleasure craft, the bulk of which are moored in the town's state of the art marina. Billed as a top destination for sea fishing, the waters off the harbour mouth are frequented by bottlenose dolphins which range up and down the Moray Firth along with the occasional minke whale. With two large caravan parks, a good range of hotel accommodation plus a microclimate which offers above average temperatures throughout the year it's no great surprise that Lossiemouth's main industry today is tourism. Add to the mix Moray Golf Club's two eighteen-hole courses - appropriately named the Old Course and the New Course - and it is easy to see why the resort has remained popular with holidaymakers for over 150 years.

It's surprisingly difficult to obtain an exact population figure for Lossiemouth. The 2011 Census records a resident town population of 7,705 but it is unclear if this figure includes the residents of the RAF base. In December 2007 the Highlands and Islands Development Board estimated a more likely population figure of 8,921 with a growth rate almost four times the Scottish average. Whatever the truth of the matter it is clear that RAF Lossiemouth is key to the town's economy. In 2014 the base generated over 3,300 civilian jobs both on site and in the wider community. Contributing an estimated £90 million to the local economy annually, new businesses ranging from the Windswept

Lossiemouth Marina

micro-brewery to a local PR company have been set up by retired RAF personnel using resettlement packages. The base also hosts a privately owned state of the art flight simulator staffed by ex RAF aircrew. On the first of September 2014 Royal Air Force Lossiemouth began a new era when it took on the role of Quick Reaction Alert (Interceptor) North. With a ten-minute launch window, the first Quick Reaction Alert (QRA) took place in September 2014 when newly arrived state of the art Typhoon jets scrambled to challenge Russian bears massing just off the Scottish coastline. It's a sobering thought really, but the RAF remains Britain's prime defence against bears. The mammals in question are Russian Tupolev Tu-95 reconnaissance aircraft. Often said to be the noisiest and most obvious spy planes in history, the giant Soviet turboprop aircraft make regular passes just off the twelve nautical mile limit leading to the launch of interceptor aircraft to both identify and if necessary, escort them firmly but politely into international airspace. A base spokesperson commented "You have to admire Soviet technology. These ancient Russian aircraft actually have a means to communicate with submerged Soviet submarines. A two-mile length of aerial cable is wound out of the back of the aeroplane and the subs are able to send and receive messages … quite agricultural really but it appears to work!"

The QRA role is just the latest in the history of the Lossiemouth base.

Currently the busiest fast jet base in Europe, the 1100-acre site rivals the adjacent town of Lossiemouth in size. Although grass topped agricultural fields at Couldarbank and Newlands of Dronie - where Ramsay MacDonald flew from on his parliamentary journeys - had been used as commercial airstrips during the 1920s it was not until December 1938 that the Air Ministry requisitioned an initial 550 acres of farmland to allow for the construction of the airbase. The political situation on the continent was fast deteriorating and the very obvious threat of a second continental war led to the establishment of a flying training school. The first flying course began in June 1939 just weeks before the declaration of war and amidst the chaos of a partially constructed airfield. Bomber aircraft quickly followed including the iconic Vickers Wellingtons of 99 Squadron tasked with attacking enemy shipping off the Danish coast.

One of the last major operations carried out by aircraft from a wartime RAF Lossiemouth was Operation Paravane, an attack on the German battleship Tirpitz in September 1944. A frequent target of both the RAF and elements of the Royal Navy, the giant battleship had lain at anchor in a Norwegian Fjord for two years posing a threat to allied shipping including the Arctic convoys taking munitions to Murmansk. Using twenty-seven Avro Lancaster bombers from both 617 and 9 Squadrons armed with a combination of 12,000lb Tallboy deep-penetration bombs and anti-shipping mines, the threat from the Tirpitz was only partially eliminated. Badly damaged in the raid, she was towed to Tromso to be patched up and recommissioned as a long-range naval artillery battery.

Finally, in November 1944, in a further attack named Operation Catechism, a combined force of thirty-six aircraft of 617 (Dambusters) Squadron and 9 Squadron plus a solitary film unit Lancaster manned by an Australian crew from 463 Squadron, took off from RAF Lossiemouth, RAF Kinloss and RAF Milltown heading for Tromso in Arctic Norway. Three bombs hit the giant ship which capsized killing over a thousand of its crew. Handed over to the Royal Navy in 1946 and renamed HMS Fulmar, the air station once again became RAF Lossiemouth in 1972 and remains to this day a frontline RAF Station. Although ruled out of the government shortlist of UK aerodromes under consideration to host a proposed UK Spaceport, the Lossiemouth base along with its strong historical, social and economic links to the neighbouring town looks to have a secure long-term future.

In February 2015, Royal Mail published a commemorative stamp set entitled Working Sail and featuring the work of so the called 'Pier-head Painters'. Working at speed in order to finish and deliver ship portraits before the subject left port, pier-head painters such as Aberdeen fish porter Alexander Harwood (1873-1943) produced hundreds of paintings of North East fishing vessels including the herring drifter Briar (BCK.42) which features in the Royal Mail commemorative set. The tradition continues to this day with the work of Hebridean artist Margaret MacLean who was recently commissioned to paint a portrait of Northern Light (INS.56), a Zulu class herring drifter owned and operated in the late Nineteenth century by Hopeman man Daniel Sutherland, better known locally as 'Junties Dan'. Described in some quarters as "the most noble looking sailing craft ever designed", the Zulu class became popular with many examples being converted to motor power. Carrying large and heavy sails on masts up to sixty feet in height these were fast boats capable of around twelve knots and were quite able to outrun the more modern coal fired steam drifters which progressively took over from them.

The origins of the Zulu are legendary. A Lossiemouth fisherman by the name of William Campbell is credited with the original design. In the 1870s, and driven by the need to fish in more distant waters, a demand for fast powerful boats emerged and Campbell's groundbreaking design fitted the bill. Built by Alexander Wood of Lossiemouth in 1879 the new boat combined the best features from two existing successful fishing boat designs, the steeply raking stern of the Scaffie and the near vertical stem of the Fifie. The result was a fast and highly manoeuvrable carvel planked hybrid. The Zulu wars were in full swing at the time with reports of both military disasters and victories regularly featured in the press and for reasons best known to himself Campbell had obviously decided to name his new design after the Zulu warriors of King Cetshwayo.

A much more romantic version of the origins of the Zulu features a marriage between a Lossiemouth fisherman and a fisher woman from Buckie. On deciding to commission a new boat, they failed to agree on the final design. The husband had always sailed in a boat of the Fifie class and quite naturally wanted to build one after this model. But the wife's family were used to the Scaffie and she obstinately insisted on that design; rightly pointing out that she was after all providing half of the funding for the new craft. After much discussion a compromise was reached. The newlyweds agreed to combine the two designs, the husband got his way as regards the bow and the wife got her way as regards the stern. The boat was duly built and christened Nonesuch due to being neither one nor the other. Eventually thousands of Zulus would be built and they remained popular well into the age of steam drifters with some folk referring to them as 'The King of the Sea-boats'.

The original Lossiemouth Zulu, the Nonesuch, had her registration closed in 1901 after being broken up; however the Scottish Fisheries Museum at Anstruther has a full size dry berthed example of a Zulu drifter on display. And of course, Lossiemouth Fisheries and Community Museum on the harbour front of Ramsay MacDonald's Bay of Naples, holds a wealth of exhibits relating to both the Zulu and to Lossiemouth in general.

24
MACDUFF – PARAFFIN SANDWICHES AND PONDMASTERS

The planned township of Macduff has a relatively short history. As recently as 1759 rent-rolls for the settlement, known then variously as Down or Doune, recorded just thirty-four tenancies along with around four hundred inhabitants who subsisted largely through crofting and fishing from what was probably a very basic harbour. The population in 2017 was around 3,850. Burgh status came in 1783 and in that year the first town council assembled to deliberate on the improvement of the town. Markets were organised, vagrants were ostracised and residents forbidden to throw dung and general rubbish onto the streets.

The various Earls of Fife invested heavily in the town and encouraged improvements in agricultural practices. They appear to have understood the potential of exploiting the natural resources of the sea and began harbour improvements in the 1760s. The harbour has been upgraded at regular intervals up to the present day with ownership passing from James Duff the second Earl of Fife to the town council in the March of 1897 for what was then described as a nominal fee of £10,000. The second Earl inherited the Lands of Doune in 1773 on the death of his father and within a few years the thorny question of what to call his new town arose. In a letter to his factor, a man by the name of William Rose, dated twenty-sixth of August 1781 the Earl writes "If I change the name of Down, I would change it altogether and call it Macduff, as if we were to say Down Duff, wits would explain it as knocking Down my family." The canny laird must have had a sixth sense as well as a wry sense of humour since some 230 years later in 2006, a mysterious Hollywood style sign spelling out, in giant letters, the word MACDUFF unexpectedly appeared above the town on top of the Doune Hill. Over the succeeding two weeks the giant sign seemingly morphed into the words DUFFCAM, MADCUFF and finally MACFFUD at which point the council felt obliged to enforce removal of the offending anagram. The 2006 Hollywood sign was the work of pranksters but more recently a campaign group, convinced of the sign's marketing potential, gathered 2,059 signatures in a petition demanding its reinstatement.

Neighbouring Banff has its Brodies but Macduff has its Bodies. Author Peter Anson records in his 1969 book *Life on Low Shore*, an autobiographical account of his twenty years residence in Macduff, that when his close friend Campbell Cowie died in the September of 1941 the celebrated Scottish sculptor Hew Lorimer (1907-1993) marked out the new lettering on the young man's family gravestone. "Thus it was, that Macduff acquired an example of the work of this now famous sculptor" writes Anson. Campbell lies buried in Doune Kirkyard not far from the family plot of one of Macduff's more celebrated residents, Aberdeen born Dr Walford Bodie (1869 -1939).

The Bodie Mansion - Macduff

Sometimes known as the Laird of Macduff, he was variously billed as The Electric Wizard of the North and The Most Remarkable Man on Earth during his long and successful career. A talented magician and illusionist, Bodie was never a man to shy away from publicity. An early career with The National Telephone Company provided him with a basic understanding of electricity which he used to great advantage on stage. A popular stunt saw Bodie discharging of thousands of volts of low amperage electricity from his fingertips in the form of bolts of lightning before inviting members of the audience to step right up and take a seat in his electric chair; whereupon the unsuspecting volunteer would reputedly be publicly electrocuted to the point of unconsciousness. Bodie would then revive the blue lipped subjects using several slaps about the face. Health and safety was conspicuously absent from early Twentieth century stages and at the time it was common practice for showmen to adopt the spurious title of Doctor. Walford Bodie later added the letters MD to his name but never publicly revealed what the capital letters actually meant.

In 1919, Bodie, according to one unsubstantiated account, is said to have electrocuted his glamorous assistant, La Belle Electra, during a performance in Glasgow. He had lost all five tons of his stage-props when, after touring South Africa, his ship was torpedoed off Malta by a German U-boat in 1916. Replacement props, including a new electric chair, were hurriedly manufactured and the Bodie Show resumed touring when hostilities ceased. During the Glasgow performance however, something went badly wrong with the electric chair illusion and the unfortunate La Belle Electra received a massive electric shock. She supposedly died the next day and is buried in the family plot at Doune. Surprisingly perhaps Bodie was never charged in respect of her demise. A descendant however casts doubt on the authenticity of this tale and has evidence that La Belle Electra - in reality Bodie's sister-in-law Isabella Henry - in fact died of natural causes. Perhaps the death by electrocution theory came about due to Bodie's potent and often extravagant promotional material.

Even today the mention of his name elicits memories. Maud resident Avril Wilson recalls a family tale about the man. "Auntie Fanny often spoke about how Uncle Jim went away on his bike to Bodie's concert at Mintlaw Hall. It was the 1920s I suppose and Bodie was touring the local halls. While he was off watching the performance, she gave birth to twins and Jim missed the birth. Bodie was quite a draw you see."

Walford Bodie was a high earner throughout the majority of his stage career. Alongside the Manor House on Macduff's Skene Street, he owned London properties including a night club, several hotels and a houseboat on which he entertained celebrities including Edward VIII and Wallis Simpson. He enhanced his income by endorsing a range of Electric Ointments including Electric Life Pills, Electric Dentifrice and Electric Liniment. Today's Trading Standards would have had a field day. Generous to his adopted town he sponsored Macduff Walford FC, financed the public baths and bankrolled the Royal Tarlair Golf Club. He was seemingly first to tee off on the club's opening day in 1926. The club history records that:

> "The opening tee shot at Royal Tarlair was taken by the incomparable Dr Walford Bodie; probably the town's most famous son, whose real name was Samuel Murphy Bodie (1869–1939). He was a Scottish showman, hypnotist, ventriloquist and stage magician, famous for his 'mock' electrocutions involving a replica of 'The Electric Chair'. He also performed an act of 'Bloodless Surgery' claiming he could use electricity, hypnosis and manipulation to cure 'all kinds of ailments and disabilities' although with the grip he demonstrates in the picture above he might have trouble curing slices! His performances though were enormously popular in the early Twentieth century, and inspired both Harry Houdini and Charlie Chaplin."

A fountain, in memory of Bodie's daughter Jeannie, stands in Macduff's Maritime Memorial Garden alongside the Peter Anson memorial sculpture. Known as the Bodie Fountain, it was gifted to the town by the Bodie family in 1910, a year after Jeannie's death aged just nineteen and bears the poignant inscription "Drink thirsty soul and thank God."

Perhaps not quite on a par with the Italian Chapel on Orkney or Macduff's magnificent Parish Church on Doune Hill, the cramped attic space of Peter Anson's house at Number 2 Low Shore attracted national interest when the *Sunday Express* gave it nationwide publicity in 1946 when first Mass was celebrated. The oratory, dedicated to Our Lady of the Ships and St Peter the Fisherman, was for some years the only chapel on the Scottish mainland dedicated to the spiritual needs of mariners. The Harbour Head Loft Chapel sported an altar made by local joiner Geordie Watt with a canvas altar cover sewn by Jim Blair the local sailmaker. The building later served as a net store before being demolished to make way for harbour improvements leaving both Macduff and Scotland much the poorer. On leaving Macduff in 1952, Peter dismantled the oratory and shipped the contents to France for re-use by the Mission de la Mer. There are no traces nowadays of either Peter's house or of the oratory.

Macduff was for many years a popular holiday destination attracting visitors from all parts of the North East and beyond. The medicinal mineral well at Tarlair was popular with health tourists although the flow was apparently disrupted during WW2 when a sea mine drifted and exploded nearby. Some accounts attribute the explosion to a stray bomb from a German raider; however, local soft drink producer 'Macb Flavoured Water' the successor to the Sangs brand, until recently referred to their use of water from "The lost Well of Tarlair" in their manufacturing process.

A major Macduff holiday attraction was the Art Deco style Tarlair outdoor saltwater swimming pool. In the inter-war period 169 such pool complexes, often known as Lidos, operated at coastal resorts all around the UK and the Tarlair Lido is one of only a very few remaining Scottish examples. Other Scottish towns, such as Wick and Gourock, still boast outdoor pools and at Wick the 'Trinkie Pool' is still in regular use although it cannot claim Art Deco status. Commissioned by Macduff Burgh Council, Tarlair Open Air Pool opened to the public in summer 1930 in partially completed form. Funding had come via public subscription and also from the government's Unemployment Grants Committee, a 1930s style Job Creation Scheme. In 1935 the town council secured a seven thousand pound loan enabling final completion of the ambitious project. Unlike the Stonehaven heated outdoor pool, Tarlair relied on

Tarlair Art Deco Pool

the vagaries of the sun to warm the salt water which given the Scottish climate could be a hit or miss affair. The main pool boasted a diving board and a chute and there were paddling pools, a restaurant, sandpits and even a boating pond. Swimming lessons could be arranged via a mysterious man known as the Pondmaster and on summer Sundays a brass band played to the crowds.

Eyewitness to Tarlair's glory days, Inverurie-born Anne Strachan has mixed memories of the pool. As a child in the 1940s she, along with her family, made the annual pilgrimage from Inverurie to Macduff by train before walking the mile or so to Tarlair. "We went every summer holiday and took the train from Inverurie" she recalls "My Uncle Dan would be in charge. He carried the pillowcase full of sandwiches plus a small paraffin stove to heat the kettle. One year the stove must have leaked so there was nothing else to do but eat the paraffin and cheese sandwiches. Another year, I nearly drowned when I came down the chute but surfaced underneath an inflatable dingy. Your family were supposed to look out for you but mine took not a blind bit of notice! I don't think there were any lifeguards in those days."

Tarlair's popularity waned in the later part of the Twentieth century and the pool was closed to swimmers in 1996. A few years after the closure there were attempts to re-invent the complex as a concert venue. In the 1980s and with Woodstock firmly in mind, the pool witnessed pop group Wet Wet Wet land by helicopter on the local golf course to perform before a crowd of several thousand, and more recently there were plans to open a lobster hatchery on the site. On the National Buildings at Risk register since 2008 and Grade A listed the lido owners, Aberdeenshire Council, recently completed a three hundred thousand pound refurbishment designed to stabilise the structure. Full re-instatement is likely to cost a further £2.2 million according to consultancy firm Addison Conservation and Design, and campaign group Friends of Tarlair are actively fundraising with the intention of restoring the historic lido to full working order.

Although situated on a fairly exposed section of the Moray Firth, Macduff remains an important general cargo port for the North East. Operated by Aberdeenshire Harbour Authority the port, like many on the Moray coast, is gearing up to provide a comprehensive range of services for the offshore energy sector. Facilities include four modern hydraulic vertical boat cradles, each capable of hauling vessels of up to 350 tonnes onto the council owned slipway. Additionally, there are substantial local chandlery and fabrication facilities. The major employer in the town is Macduff Shipyards which, with a workforce of around 180 skilled workers and apprentices, builds and refits a wide range of vessels including pilot boats, research vessels, ferries and motor yachts. The group also offers big-lift crane hire via a subsidiary company and provides ship-painting, engineering and general fabrication services.

With Duff House - a satellite of the National Galleries of Scotland and itself a Category A listed building - on the outskirts and the Macduff Distillery just down the road, the town is well placed to attract tourists. Macduff also hosts one of Aberdeenshire's top visitor attractions in the form of Macduff Aquarium where visitors can get up close to a wide range of marine life including wolf-fish, seahorses and sharks. Alongside the marine exhibits, in the summer months a video-link offers visitors easy access to the cliffs at nearby Troup Head, the only mainland gannet colony in Scotland. It might be a few years before the pool at Tarlair re-opens and the re-instatement of the Hollywood sign on Doune Hill remains a fairly distant prospect. But all good things are worth the wait.

25
MAGGIEKNOCKATER – THE BEES KNEES

The road to Maggieknockater - 2021

Cartographers are seemingly in the habit of inserting fake towns into maps in order to expose plagiarism. By including a trivial piece of false information in a larger work, it is easier to demonstrate subsequent plagiarism if the fictitious insert is copied without the approval of the copyright owner. Known as copyright traps in legal parlance such entries have included Dickinson Street in central Manchester falsely named Philpott Street and the phantom town of Argletown in Lancashire which allegedly appeared for a time on Google Maps. Then of course there is Maggieknockater which despite the appearance of being a copyright trap for the unwary, actually exists.

For those not in the know, Maggieknockater or in the Scots Gaelic 'Mathg an Fhucadair', is a tiny village on the A95 between Craigallachie and Keith. Well known in Scottish Dance Music circles, it lies just down the road from Dufftown's distilleries and in cattle droving days there would have been a shebeen in the place. It's quite a mouthful though. When asked whereabouts they come from, locals jokingly sometimes tell the enquirer Craigallachie or even Dufftown rather than the truth. Seemingly if they admit to living in

Maggieknockater, the enquirer is liable to collapse laughing.

Folk in the Scottish villages of Glass, Lost, Jericho and Knock apparently have the same problem. Then there's Maggie Glutton on the outskirts of Inverurie. Named allegedly after 'Meg the Glutton' who once owned a local croft, the name at least reflects what it says on the tin. There's also a World's End in Buchan, but let's not go there! And spare a thought for the folk who live in the Angus village of Waterybutts. Indeed, returning to Lost, the road signs in the village have a habit of disappearing overnight, no doubt to grace some student flat or other on the Aberdeen University campus. For those living in the village of Premnay just north of Inverurie, the situation is even more problematic since both the Ordnance Survey Maps and the roadside signposts spell Premnay as Auchleven meaning that no one can even find the place never mind laugh at the residents!

If you check the web for the meaning of the name Maggieknockater you are likely to find explanations ranging from "arable land on the forest's lower slopes" to "the fuller's field". However, there is much more to the place than that. For a start, Mary Queen of Scots may well have stayed at the nearby Gauldwell Castle during her gad about Scotland in 1561. Mind you she stayed at some seventy Scottish castles during her travels so perhaps Maggieknockater requires a somewhat greater claim to fame to justify the long name. The Maggieknockater school was closed in the 1960s and the old mission hall was deconsecrated and turned into a dwelling house in 1946. What was once a smithy is now a garage but still in the hands of the MacLean family who have lived there for quite a few generations. Maggieknockater formerly had a post office which seemingly opened in June 1876 and closed as long ago as 1940. So, at first glance it might appear that there is not much going for the place; that is unless you count the bees.

Up until the late 1960s there was large apiary in the village. It was started by an Aberdonian by the name of George McLean who made heather honey on a grand scale and sold it far and wide. Crate loads of the stuff went to Ireland and to outlets all over the UK. But the best was sold at the roadside to passing motorists who saw the Maggieknockater Apiary as a welcome pit stop on the road to either Craigellachie or Keith. George was in fact one of the most prominent beekeepers in Scotland. A farmer, grocer and blacksmith, he was also the secretary of the North of Scotland Beekeepers' Association for a time. The bee skeps are long gone from the roadside and George McLean died some years ago at a very ripe old age but his legacy lives on in the Scottish Country Dance *The Bees of Maggieknockater*. Internationally famous and a favourite of those in the know, it goes something like this:

"1- 8 1s cross RH and cast 1 place, dance RH across with 3s and end 1M+3L also 1L+3M in prom hold facing out to pass corner person RSh. 9-24 All dance 4x½ Reels of 3 on sides (to right to start, then left, right and left) with 1s+3s changing partners in centre at end of each ½ Reel to progress Men clockwise and Ladies anticlockwise. End in centre 1s facing down and 3s facing up. 25-32 1s dance between 3s turning 3s with nearer hand 1½ times, crossing over to own sides and turn 4th person 1½ times (Men RH and Ladies LH). 2341."

Devised by an Englishman by the name of John Drewry (1923-2014), the dance comprises a 32-step jig, requiring four couples to dance facing each other. Forres Country Dance is the usual tune used. Seemingly John, a biochemist working at Aberdeen University, was inspired by the banks of beehives at Maggieknockater although in fact he seemingly never took the time to stop and buy any of George's honey! A prolific composer, John composed some 800 country dances including his 1998 Thomas Glover's Reel in memory of the legendary 'Scottish Samurai'. But *The Bees of Maggieknockater* is perhaps one of his best known compositions. While visiting Banff, Alberta in the 1980s he witnessed a comedy sketch of the dance written to Rimsky Korsakov's *Flight of the Bumble Bee*. Sadly, honey farmer George McLean missed it by a few years but he would probably have been entranced by the spectacle. Next time you are on the A95 between Craigallachie and Keith, take a wee minute to remember both George and John as you pass through the village. After all they combined to make Maggieknockater internationally famous, and not just because of the long name.

26
MONTROSE – CAMELS, BEARS AND GABLE ENDIES

With a High Street as broad as any in Scotland overlooked by a liberal sprinkling of centuries old gable ended mansions, the casual visitor to Montrose might be forgiven for imagining that they had stumbled upon a Flemish townscape on the northern Angus borders. The Montrose High Street would still be instantly recognisable to the likes of James Boswell and his travelling companion Samuel Johnston. The literary pair stopped overnight at the town's Ship Inn in the August of 1773 *en route* to the Western Isles to eventually meet up with Flora Macdonald. Flora is best known as the legendary Jacobite heroine who in June 1746 aided the fugitive 'Young Pretender' Charles Edward Stuart in his escape following the military disaster at Culloden.

The Angus town of Montrose had long been sympathetic to the Jacobite cause. Indeed, it was here that James Edward Stuart, the Old Pretender 'The King Over the Water' had spent his final night in Scotland before sailing into exile in France. Not that Johnson necessarily either liked or disliked Montrose. In fact, a typically grumpy Johnson, in uncharacteristically mellow tones, recorded in his journal of the trip 'A Journey to the Western Isles of Scotland', that "many of the houses are built with their ends to the street, which looks awkward." Boswell on the other hand wrote more positively that they had found the town "well built, airy and clean."

Today's High Street sports many post-Boswell additions including the superb flying buttressed Auld Kirk spire which was completed in 1834 and designed by Dunblane-born architect James Gillespie Graham. At almost sixty-seven metres high it is the defining 'town mark' of modern Montrose and appears in the work of many of the town's artists including Scottish Surrealist Edward Baird and William Lamb, a gifted sculptor and fortunate survivor of the 1914-18 lost generation.

A good place to start an exploration of the Angus town is at Montrose Museum on Panmure Place. Alongside displays to do with the town's seafaring history - mainly whaling and tobacco - and the various exhibits to do with William Lamb and the doomed Marquis of Montrose, there is a solitary death mask purporting to be one of only a very few made of the dead Napoleon Bonaparte. Authentic Bonaparte masks have a provenance dating from May the sixth 1821 when a military surgeon by the name of Dr Francis Burton conspired with François Carlo Antommarchi - who was Napoleon's physician - to cash in on the French emperor's death. A second cast was made later on the same day by a visiting English artist and both moulds went on to be reproduced on an

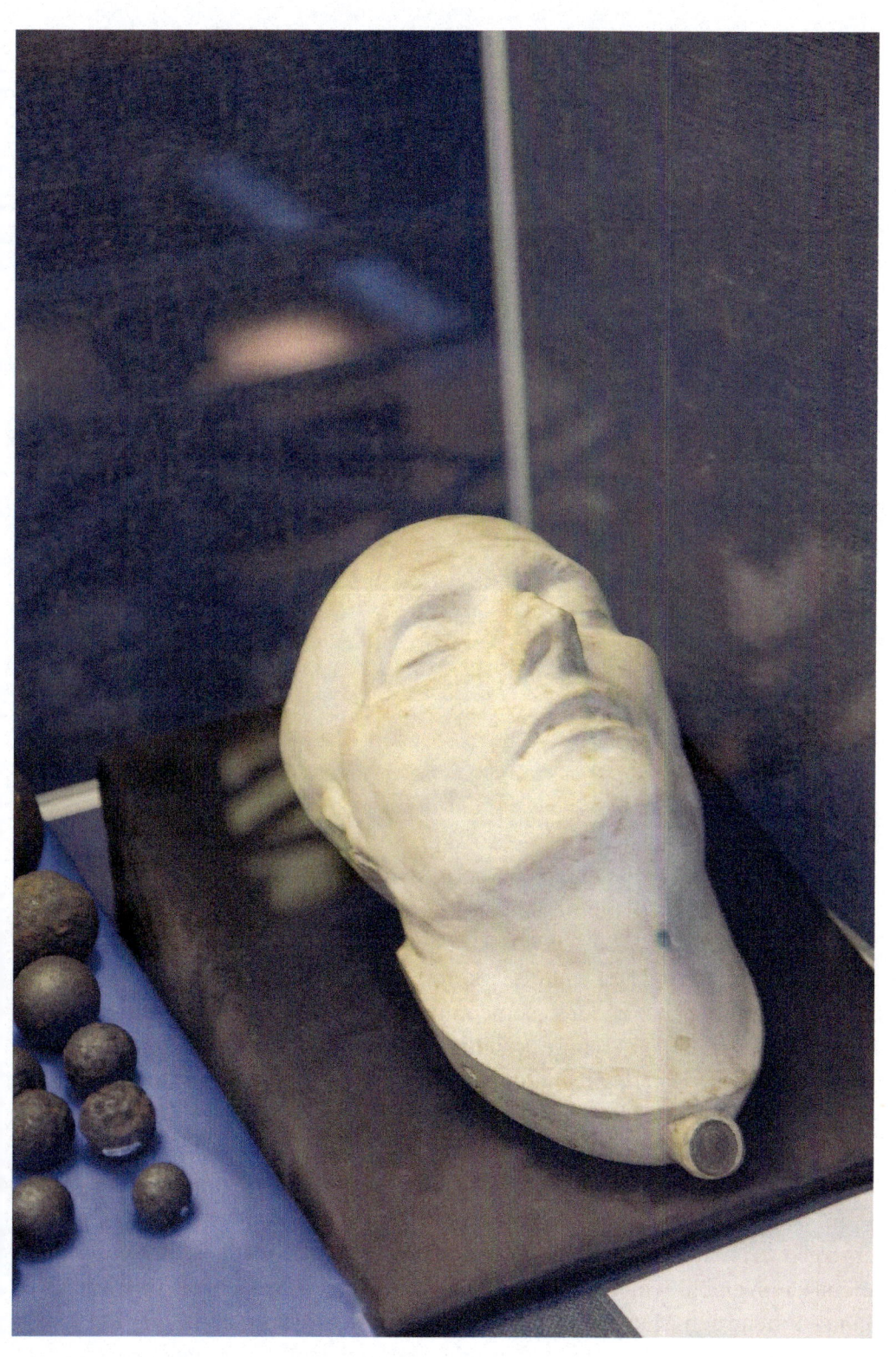

Napoleon's death mask on display at Montrose Museum

industrial scale. The Montrose copy was presented to Montrose Natural History and Antiquarian Society eighteen years after the French emperor's death in 1821, and given its historical significance, it does take the breath away.

Lamb's 1932 bronze busts of Princess Margaret, Princess Elizabeth and the Queen Mother

Montrose Museum also holds keys to William Lamb's studio. Much is known about Lamb (1893-1951) and an authoritative account of his life exists in the form of John Stanfield's thoroughly researched book *The People's Sculptor – The Life and Art of William Lamb*. A first war veteran, Lamb was greatly troubled by physical and mental scars from the trenches where he suffered several injuries. Lamb endured some nineteen post-war operations to repair a badly injured right hand before resigning himself to his disability and adapting his sculpting and drawing technique to compensate. Lamb was well acquainted with Christopher Murray Grieve, best known by his pen name Hugh MacDiarmid, who alongside reporting for and editing the *Montrose Review* during the 1920s, was instrumental in promoting the new Scottish Renaissance. From being a hotbed of rebellious Jacobite sentiment Montrose had by 1924 emerged as an unlikely cultural hub of a new Scottish artistic, political and literary movement which resonates even to this day. The likes of Neil Gunn, James Pittendrigh MacGillivray, Violet Jacob, Neil Munro and Compton McKenzie - to name but a very few - flocked to the town to create new work and debate a new direction for Scottish arts and letters.

A prolific water colourist, engraver and sculptor, Lamb often used locals as his subjects. A good example is 'The Minesweeper'. Modelled using local man James Dolan as a sitter and exhibited at the Royal Society of Arts in 1944, this life size sculpture is just one of his legacies. Tasked with spotting anti-shipping mines drifting ashore onto the Montrose foreshore, a modern day reproduction of the green tinged bronze sculpture stands on the beachfront links gazing intently out to sea. The original white plaster maquette, complete with Lamb's signature drawn in characteristic block capitals on its base, can be seen in Lamb's studio as can his simply stunning 1932 bronze busts of the young Princess Margaret Rose, her sister Princess Elizabeth and their mother, the Queen Mother, who was then Duchess of York.

Lamb died at Stracathro Hospital in January 1951 but when you enter his studio on the town's Market Street today there is a strong sense that the artist has just stepped outside for a bite to eat or perhaps a midday stroll around the town. The sense of Lamb's presence pervades the space and it is at first hard to comprehend that nearly seventy years have passed since the artist, in a death bed gesture reminiscent of Rodin's gift of the Musee Rodin to the French Nation, gifted his work place to the people of Montrose.

Once Scotland's principal tobacco port, the Montrose of today still sports a busy commercial harbour. In days past, the harbour was a hub for shipmasters trading in both tobacco and slaves. Not that slaves actually made landfall in the town. They had been shipped as cargo on the West Africa to America leg of the journey and then traded for tobacco. It's not a pretty story and Montrose Museum holds documents revealing the town's complicity in this unsavoury trade in human misery. One such record reveals that a Montrose owned vessel, the Virginia built 'Potomac Merchant', made landfall at South Potomac in Virginia in July 1752 with "197 passengers from Africa" on board. Montrose's part in the triangular trade was seemingly short-lived and by the later part of the Eighteenth century, the town council were discussing petitioning Parliament to bring about an end to the slave trade. By this point in time, local ships were engaging in direct trade with the tobacco colonies which probably oiled the wheels of change; and the likes of Thomas Douglass and Company of Montrose had by 1751 begun the switch from transporting slaves to shipping tobacco from Virginia in a two-way trade, missing out the long Africa leg of the journey completely.

The slavers and the whalers may be long gone but, in common with several Scottish seaports up and down the North Sea coast, Montrose's deep-water berths are shared by oil and gas industry service vessels alongside cargo ships

Montrose from Kirkton of Craig

full of timber, grain and fertiliser. The recently completed four million pound quay upgrade by Montrose Port Authority underlines the importance of the harbour's role as one of the busiest in Scotland. Handling most of the wood pulp imported into Scotland and with a proven track record in the landing of bulky components for onshore windfarms, the port's future looks favourable. The harbour was an enemy target during both Twentieth century wars and Westhill composer Gordon Duthie recently recalled a war time event in which his great grandfather's fishing vessel, the Fraserburgh registered Steam Drifter SS Duthies was sunk in Montrose Harbour by the young men of the Luftwaffe. Alongside titles such as *Whisky Disco* and *Feel Loon did a Wildpoepen*, Gordon's tribute to the Sandhaven built FR106 Duthies is just one of ten provocative numbers on his album *Thran*. The boat had been on anti-submarine duty towing steel nets across the harbour mouth when it was sunk. In his 2001 book *Steam Drifters Recalled - Whitehills to St. Combs* local author J. Reid records the following details:

"Built 1914 of wood by Forbes of Sandhaven for Lewis Duthie, Cairnbulg; William Duthie, Alex. Duthie, Inverallochy and Geo. Walker, Fraserburgh. Named DUTHIES and registered in Fraserburgh (FR 106). Dimensions: 89 G.R.T. Length 88.70ft, Breadth 19.40ft., Depth 9.60ft. 16-inch expansion engine by Lewis, Torry, Kincardine. Boiler by John Lewis, and Sons, Torry, Kincardine. Requisitioned for war service 1915-1919 as an anti-submarine net vessel fitted with a three-pounder gun; and again 1939-1940. Lost on Admiralty service 25th October 1940, wrecked by parachute mine, Registry cancelled 26th November 1940."

The vessel had in fact served in both wars having been requisitioned by the Admiralty (as AD 2378) between 1915 and 1919. Having survived the Kaiser's lengthy war, the steam ketch never saw VE day in the next war although her eight-strong crew survived the sinking.

Nowadays the coastal salmon fisheries around the Scottish coast remain an important local industry, with records dating back to at least 1506 detailing Crown Charters granting the town monopolies over the packing and exporting of salmon caught off neighbouring settlements such as Gourdon and Stonehaven. The old jute mill factories of Montrose may have closed for good but new industries such as that at the local GlaxoSmithKline (GSK) factory provide employment for around 130 people out of a current town population of around 12,000. A company spokesman for GSK recently commented that "Currently, Montrose produces active ingredients for a number of medicines in important disease areas such as respiratory and HIV/AIDS and is a major employer in the town." It's a far cry from the more traditional local industry but, in a way, reflects the ability of the town to move with the times.

No take on the Angus town would be complete without mention of James Graham, the First Marquis of Montrose. Allegedly born in 1604 on the High Street site currently occupied by the local Job Centre Plus, he is popularly thought to have burned his hometown of Montrose to the ground in an act of military barbarism. As one of the first to sign the National Covenant at Greyfriars in Edinburgh in the February of 1638, the Marquis rose to prominence in a Scotland torn asunder by religious and civil strife. Outlining radical demands for change in Scotland's governance, the Covenant quickly led to a civil war in Scotland and would ultimately lead James Graham to the gallows in Edinburgh. Following his sacking of Aberdeen in 1644, a portion of his army, led by Alexander Irvine of Drum, entered Montrose with the intention of seizing the town's two brass cannon. Meeting local opposition, the Marquis's troops seemingly destroyed the artillery pieces and plundered the town before withdrawing north for fear of counter attack. The 1882 *Ordnance Gazetteer of Scotland* disputes the birthplace theory however and reports that "The great Marquis of Montrose was born at Old Montrose in Maryton parish; but some of his dealings with the neighbouring town of Montrose were of doubtful advantage thereto." Whatever the truth of the matter it is clear that the Marquis was, at the very least, a local man with some attitude.

Nowadays the Usan based Scottish Wild Salmon Company exports locally caught Scottish wild salmon across Europe with netting stations operating along the Angus Coast from Montrose to Arbroath. Usan also has a strong association with accordions and was once headlined as 'The Accordion Capital of the Mearns'. Four miles south of Montrose, Fishtown of Usan - to use the Sunday name - was home to retired salmon fisher Dave Pullar (1929-2020) a man known in musical circles as "The man with a thousand accordions". Dave's clifftop cottage, overlooked the rugged Mearns coastline from which he made his living from salmon netting for a large part of his working life. His view out to sea was interrupted only by a Victorian era turf roofed icehouse which, although originally used to store ice brought in from abroad, is nowadays used as a packing house for the family salmon business. In retirement, Dave began collecting in what some might term an obsessive way. Initially, he gathered a large collection of vintage cars, Austin Sevens and the like, but these were disposed of in favour of accordions; literally hundreds of them. In 2001, he fell in love with the instrument while attending a memorial concert to celebrate the life of virtuoso accordionist John Huband whose collaboration with Jim Reid, via albums such as Freewheeling Now, had won widespread popularity with classic lines such as:

> "I'm getting ower the hill it seems,
> Tho ma hert it still feels young,
> But to say when half a hunders here,
> Your flings should aa be flung."

At the end of the concert, Dave announced his intention to purchase an accordion and from then on, began collecting the instruments big time. The first in the collection was a Hohner Vox 4, and this was followed within a few days by the purchase of a second instrument. Word quickly spread that Dave was in the mood for more. Soon, accordions began to appear at his door. Some were brought to him as gifts from friends. Some were bought up at roups. And just a few were found in skips and dusty attics. Very soon, he had, by his own estimate, more than a thousand of the instruments filling his house and outbuildings and by his own admission, taking over his life: "It's like an infection and given a choice between buying groceries or an accordion, the instrument would usually win hands down," he joked.

Being a left hander, Dave had to overcome the right hand bias of the keyboard and he would dismiss any suggestion that by simply turning the

Dave Pullar playing Jimmy Shand's 'Gold Shand Morino' at Fishtown of Usan

accordion upside down he could rectify the issue. Seemingly you'll never see a left-handed power saw and the same is true of accordions. He played well, though, and enjoyed toe-tapping sessions with fellow musicians, including those from the Montrose Fiddle and Accordion Club and even the Buttons and Bows Club, the home club of the late Jimmy Shand. Indeed, Dave's favourite instrument, and one which he kept in a glass display case in the restored net store beneath his home, was a Gold Shand Morino made by Hohner especially for Sir Jimmy Shand. The instrument sat beside Sir Jimmy's piano in Dave's accordion room alongside other Shand memorabilia including the great man's hall mirror. "It's maybe a strange thing to bring home but I like to think on the fact that Jimmy gazed into this mirror each and every day of his life" recalled Dave. The autographed Shand Gold Morino has an extra row of buttons, designed to allow the maestro to play ever more complex pieces. Not at all put off by this, Dave would, if asked nicely, happily fetch the accordion from the glass case and play it for visitors before placing the iconic instrument reverently back inside his display cabinet.

Repair and overhaul of the instruments was a big part of the hobby. "If they are not played, the reeds, at the very least, need attention. These are instruments that are meant to be used regularly, after all," he explained. Originally a joiner to trade, Dave enjoyed repairing accordions almost as much as playing them.

However, given the size of his collection, he would he said in 2014 "need to take on a few extra hands to cope with the job!" With this in mind, he advised that he had recently disposed of a few and estimated that the total was now down to "about 800". Dave liked to think that his collection might be eventually be preserved intact, especially given the additional musical memorabilia he had collected along the way. Posters, photographs and myriad related ornaments and artefacts covered every spare shelf and wall throughout his home and piano accordions, chromatic boxes and melodeons sat stacked, often three high, in sheds throughout the property. "It's time to move them on soon. I have had my pleasure out of them and it's time other folk were able to enjoy them now," he once said. The late Sir Jimmy Shand would no doubt have approved of Dave's collection. In fact, had he been alive today, he would probably have encouraged the creation of a 'Scottish National Accordion Museum' to house the whole kit and caboodle!

But, back to the salmon fishing. The Pullar family have in recent years, expanded the business of the Scottish Wild Salmon Company Ltd as far as Murkle/Castlehill, on the northern coast, and Gardenstown on the Moray Firth. Dave's son George commented "To have the rights on the north coast is a particular pleasure, as these were the fisheries our father leased from the Crown Estate when we were children. Owning them now really represents a return to our roots." When Dave first leased the fishing rights at Usan the fishing station was in a dilapidated state. The Crown leasing agent agreed to a peppercorn rent for the first few seasons with a view to reviewing the station's viability and rental value at a later date. Inevitably, the rent was re-valued upwards, after Dave and his family worked hard to make the fishing viable again. Nowadays, the Fishtown of Usan salmon station sports modern buildings and state-of-the-art fishing gear, a testament to Dave's determination and positive outlook. But, as Dave pointed out, it wasn't always so: "Before the big shed was built, we had to stand for hours in often freezing conditions, sorting out the nets; now it's much more pleasant working indoors out of the wind." The old ice house at Usan remains an imposing structure, topped by a turf roof, which Dave advised was more than just decorative: "The turf is not there to look nice or provide insulation. If you think about it, you can probably understand that the grass roof is permanently wet from the rain and the sea. The evaporation of moisture has a cooling effect on the interior of the building, helping to keep the place cold enough to preserve the ice."

Designated a Grade C listed building, the stone structure sits on land once occupied by three salt pans at Usan dating from around 1790. Sea water was trapped in a rock basin and, particularly in summer, evaporation increased the salt concentration of the brine. A channel was cut through the rock to supply the pans with salt water at high tide. Archaeological notes, published by RCAHMS (The Royal Commission on the Ancient and Historical Monuments for Scotland), describe the salt making process:

"A massive coursed-rubble building, with the usual vaulted roof, on the foreshore where sloops of 40 to 50 tons used the channel to land coal. It took approximately six tons of coal to boil enough water to produce one ton of salt. Salt had been an expensive commodity but when the duty on it entering Scotland was repealed in January 1823, cheaply mined rock salt flooded the market and all of the Scottish sea-salt works became unprofitable and were shut down soon afterwards. This surviving salt pan, or boiling house, was converted into an ice house to store local salmon catches."

Although many ice houses were built near country estate ponds during the seventeenth and eighteenth centuries, to take advantage of the winter ice harvest, Dave Pullar reckoned that the Usan ice house would have been stocked with imported ice from either Norway or Greenland. The international ice trade was in full swing when the structure was built and it would probably have been filled by transporting imported block ice from the port of Montrose by horse drawn 'coup cart', before being tipped into the vaulted chamber via a roof hatch. With the advent of industrial ice manufacturing, the trade in imported ice, or 'Frozen Water' as it was often known as, gradually died out. However, the ice houses of Scotland largely survive as a testament to the craftsmen who built them. You just need to know where to look and Usan is certainly a good starting point.

Scotland's seaport histories often tell tales of foreign wild animals such as polar bears, parrots and even pet monkeys roaming the streets having been brought back by seafarers as trophies and objects of wonder. Montrose is no exception. One such tale involves a bear cub, no doubt brought from the Americas as a result of the Triangular Trade in which goods were exported to Africa whereupon slaves were purchased for export to America where tobacco was purchased for import to Europe. Seemingly the poor bear was kept imprisoned within the walled garden of Sunnyside Psychiatric Hospital just outside Montrose until it reached adulthood, whereupon it was shot and stuffed before being exhibited locally. Borrowed from the local museum for a celebration a few years ago it was never returned. Angus Museum staff are keen to hear of the animal's current whereabouts.

Aside from bears, Montrose has an association with camels; Sopwith Camels to be precise. In 1913, Montrose Air Station, at Upper Dysart Farm, some three miles south of Montrose, became the first permanent military aerodrome in Britain. Ideally positioned to send patrols over the North Sea, the aerodrome was a key element in the defence of the Rosyth and Cromarty Naval Bases against the looming menace of the German High Seas Fleet. By the outbreak of war in August 1914 the air base had re-located to Broomfield Farm on the edge of the town links and the airfield's No 2 Squadron, led by a Major Burke, became one of the early units to fly over the battlegrounds of France and Belgium. The very first aeroplanes to arrive at Montrose in 1913 had been fragile Maurice Farman biplanes. Resembling powered kites, they were ultra-light and could be easily lifted off the ground by two or three adults. By 1917 though, the Air Station was flying the very latest in aircraft design, the Sopwith Camel.

The Camel, once mastered, was a highly manoeuvrable fighter plane but when it stalled in flight, it spun badly and crashes were common. The French designed Clerget-Blin rotary engine was particularly sensitive to fuel mixture control and incorrect settings could cause the engine to cut out on take-off, killing many trainees. Health and safety was conspicuously absent in 1917 and even parachutes were frowned upon lest they encourage cowardice. So, a quick learning curve and a modicum of luck were essential flying requirements. James Bigglesworth, the W.E. Johns fictional hero of the air war in France, flew Camels with the equally fictional 266 Squadron. In the very first Biggles book *Biggles and the Flying Camel* he achieved thirty-two kills and survived being shot down eight times. The author was however being somewhat economical with the truth since the chances of surviving even a few weeks of aerial combat in the skies over the Western Front were slim. Indeed, the chances of surviving flight training were equally bleak.

Approximately 5,490 Camels were built. A replica Sopwith F.1 Camel is on display at Montrose Air Station Heritage Centre and there are persistent local rumours to the effect that several of these biplanes lie buried in the sands following crashes into Montrose Basin. Captain Ernest Fresson (1891-1963) the founder of Kintore based Highland Airways, liked nothing better than to entertain dinner guests with daring tales of the early days of Scottish aviation. One such story involved the search for a missing RAF Avro Anson aeroplane during the spring of 1941. While flying over the Cairngorms, Captain Fresson had not only located the 1941 crash site but claimed to have spotted the remains of a much older crash dating from the winter of 1917. Seemingly the wreck was that of a Royal Flying Corps Camel which had gone missing without trace on a training flight out of Montrose. The Captain's tale concludes with a vivid description of the tattered wreckage wedged in a corrie with the goggled and helmeted pilot's skeleton still aboard! Daniel Paton of Montrose Air Station Heritage Centre doubts the authenticity of this story commenting that "We know about this incident which was reported in the Journal of the Observer Corps in 1941 … the version I heard a long time ago is that the skeleton of the pilot was still in the wreckage but that is not, I think correct. It was difficult to locate missing aircraft in the mountains and there were certainly cases of aircraft and the remains of their occupants being found months after they were reported missing."

Whatever the truth of the matter, it does make for an interesting tale. There are some 132 Commonwealth War Graves at Montrose's aptly named Sleepyhillock Cemetery including the graves of many airmen who served at Montrose Air Station. Thirty-nine of these date from the First World War, with ninety-three from the Second World War. The majority of the dead flyers buried at Sleepyhillock died in training accidents although one grave contains the remains of Lt. Desmond Arthur who was killed in 1913 when his aircraft reportedly broke up over Lunan Bay. Unfairly blamed for the accident, his ghost is said to haunt the hangars at Montrose Air Museum to this very day!

No history of Montrose would be complete without reference to the story of George James Ramsay, the man who died before he was born. The tiny cliff top cemetery at Boddin Point is well worth a visit just to see George's headstone. Sited just above the coastal path between Boddin Limekiln and Ferryden the graveyard is a little bit out of the way nowadays, but is clearly marked on the Ordnance Survey maps. It's a graveyard with a difference though, since George's weathered granite headstone reads: 'IN MEMORY OF GEORGE JAMES RAMSAY. BORN NOVEMBER 24 1859. DIED DECEMBER 17 1840'. Nothing more is known about the man aside from the assertion that he died some nineteen years before he was born! Now there's a mystery worthy of some attention!

27
OLDMELDRUM – PETROSPHERES AND CORNKISTERS

Birthplace of Mary Mitchell (1821-1866) the mother of missionary Mary Slessor and Patrick Manson (1844-1922) - the founder of the London School of Tropical Medicine - late Eighteenth century Oldmeldrum outclassed the neighbouring burgh of Inverurie in terms both of economic importance and population. A distillery town and onetime centre for the hosiery trade, Oldmeldrum's population in 1790 approached eight-hundred at a time when Inverurie's population was just 360. Today's inhabitants number around 3,230. The completion of the Aberdeen to Banff Turnpike in 1804 and the town's road link to the port of Newburgh provided further impetus for growth but by 1850 Oldmeldrum's economy was in freefall. The hosiery trade had collapsed and the construction of the Aberdeenshire Canal linking Inverurie to Aberdeen, later followed by the late arrival of the railways to Oldmeldrum, favoured Inverurie as the main market town in the Garioch. So it was that Meldrum missed out on both canal and railway at a pivotal point in the economic development of the North East of Scotland.

Nowadays new industries have moved into the town's rapidly expanding industrial estates and various leisure businesses have been established to meet the leisure needs of the wider Aberdeenshire population. Just off the A920 Colpy Road, Lochter Activity Centre and Fishery offers activities as diverse as corporate team building, fly fishing and body zorbing while on the Inverurie Road Hoodles offers grass sledging, carting plus an activity packed playbarn for younger folks. Two miles south on the Inverurie Road, Barra Berries hosts seasonal pop-up shops selling soft fruit and Christmas turkeys. The town's Glen Garioch Distillery, alongside producing fine single malt whisky, offers distillery tours and corporate entertainment as well as the opportunity to bottle your own unique blend. Oil related businesses abound and one fabrication company even made the front pages when in 2018 the letter 'H' from the original 1923 Hollywood Sign arrived in the North Meadows yard of James Fisher. The giant letter - the height of four double decker buses - had been in storage for four decades and was in for repairs before heading off on a world tour celebrating the centenary of the erection of the original signage in the Santa Monica Mountains above Los Angeles.

Oldmeldrum is no stranger to public art. North East Scotland is littered with structures as old as the pyramids of both Egypt and Peru. Most settlements in the region boast a standing stone or two. A lucky few are home to stone circles rivalling Stonehenge and a select few are home to ancient artefacts in the shape of 4000-year-old carved stone balls. Known as Petrospheres and dating from Neolithic times these are typically seven centimetres in diameter with as many as 160 protruding knobs on their surface. They could be weapons, coinage, loom weights or religious objects. No one really knows for sure and the finely detailed stone carvings have been found in their hundreds all over the North East.

Scotland currently boasts two public art installations themed on these mysterious objects. Festival Square in Edinburgh features First Conundrum by artist Remco de Fouw. Created for the Millennium, it consists of a series of Neolithic carved balls made from various materials and set within the heart of Edinburgh's financial district. The second installation dominates Market Square at Oldmeldrum. Sculpted by Deeside artist Janet McEwan, a graduate of Gray's School of Art, the piece was financed in 2011 by the Scottish Government's Town Centre Regeneration Fund supported by Aberdeenshire Arts Development Team. The Oldmeldrum artwork consists of three large granite spheres jointly titled 'The Eternal Present: GNEISS GRANITE GABBRO'. Constructed using three varieties of local stone (gneiss, granite and gabbro) the design was inspired by a group of Petrospheres found at Barra Hill, traditionally held to be the encampment of the Comyn at the Battle of Old Meldrum, and at nearby Bourtie. Alongside the commissioning of the sculpture, extensive work was undertaken to revitalise the town square and a new "Courtesy traffic calming system" was put in place at the road junctions throughout the historic town centre. Based on the psychological principle that uncertainty is likely to reduce traffic speed, the junction markings and all traffic signage on the main square were removed, forcing drivers to negotiate priorities at junctions rather than take them as of right. Residents continue to have mixed feelings regarding the experimental scheme and drivers continue to be confused by the lack of guidance.

At the last count there were twenty-eight listed buildings within the Oldmeldrum Conservation Area including the Sailor Mannie statue beside the Meldrum Arms, Morris's Hotel and the Town Hall in the Market Square. Morris's Hotel is probably the oldest building in town and the gable end of Jock's Bar, a 1673 former coffee house, sports several plaques commemorating past residents including Willie Kemp (1889-1965) The King o' the Cornkisters and George Morris, writer of many popular Doric comic songs. Willie was signed to the Beltona record label and made frequent radio broadcasts from the BBC's Aberdeen studios in the 1920s. A popular entertainer, his output

Morris's Hotel – home o' the Cornkisters

included gems such as *Willie Gillander's Goat* and *The Weddin' o' McGinnis to his Cross-Eyed Pet*. Known as The Buchan Chiel, George Morris (1876-1958) married Willie's sister Agnes in 1912 and moved to Oldmeldrum where he too signed with Beltona. His output included many bothy ballads including *The Buchan Bobby, Aikey Brae* and *A New Lum Hat*. Perhaps his best-known composition, widely sung today, is *A Pair o Nicky-tams* which includes the immortal lines:

> "Though unco sweir, I took them aff, the lassie for the please,
> But aye my breeks they lirkit up, a roon aboot my knees.
> A wasp gaed crawlin up my leg, in the middle o the Psalms,
> So niver again will I rig the kirk withoot my Nicky Tams."

Nicky Tams were bindings tied tightly below the knee to stop dubs and wee beasties getting to where they shouldn't be. Often termed 'taums', they made the wearer's breeks resemble knickerbockers. For the uninitiated, dubs are wee bits of sticky mud and other sorts of unpleasant farmyard stuff.

The railway arrived late to Oldmeldrum and then only in the form of a single track branch line from Inverurie with halts at Lethanty Mill and at Fingask. The six miles of track terminated at Strathmeldrum at the foot of the town in a small marshalling yard complete with wooden ticket office. The line opened with great fanfare in June 1856 and operated for 109 years until closure in 1965. The opening ceremony made local headlines and was celebrated with a banquet held in the new engine shed where three hundred invited guests drank some thirty toasts to the success of the new venture. The eventual closure of the line also made headlines and featured on BBC television news perhaps due to the romanticism associated with the line's locomotives. The closure was just one of many throughout both Scotland and the UK as a whole and as the railways contracted, the Meldrum spur found a final use as a storage facility for hundreds of now redundant pieces of rolling stock. Auctioned off to local farmers the long lines of wagons and carriages were said by some to have taken up the entire six mile length of the track between Inverurie and Meldrum. Even today the farms of the North East sport railway relics from those days. Put to use for storage or in some cases hen sheds and even as temporary accommodation, the cattle trucks and passenger coaches have long outlived the steam engines which once hauled them around the countryside.

Meldrum's few steam trains ranked high in the affection of locals, who nicknamed successive engines 'Meldrum Meg'. Seemingly Aberdeenshire poet and humourist Dufton Scott (1880-1944) had referred to an early steam locomotive in one of his local poetry readings as 'Meldrum Meg'. The label stuck and from then on, every engine used on the line adopted the name. Another local poem, in this case not a Dufton Scott piece, records that:

"Meldrum Meg has gone at last
An' her racing days are past
Nae mair ye'll hear me sing the auld refrain
So I think that me an' you
Should drink her health in mountain dew
For we'll never see anither like the Meldrum Train."

In the Twenty-first century, portions of the track bed remain although the bridges in many cases have long gone for scrap and the station buildings have been variously demolished or have found new use. For many years the wooden station building at Meldrum functioned as an office. In 2012 the Crathes based Royal Deeside Railway - a railway preservation group - obtained and relocated the fragile 1890 building to form part of the refurbished Milton of Crathes Station. More recently Meldrum Paths Group completed a feasibility study regarding Meldrum Meg Way, a proposed pathway linking Meldrum to Inverurie along the old railway route, and Aberdeenshire Council contracted engineering consultants Grontmij Ltd to conduct a feasibility study. Wayleave issues, missing bridges and ploughed over track were identified as problematic and to date (2021) the jury is still out on the project.

Meldrum Sports were first held in 1930 on the site of what is now Provost Drive. Events included a tug of war between single and married men - there is no record as to which team won - plus various athletic competitions and sideshows. Proceeds were donated to a School Cocoa Fund for the children of the town. In 2015 Oldmeldrum Pleasure Park saw the eighty-fifth Oldmeldrum Sports and Highland Games take place and to mark the occasion the new sports pavilion was officially opened for use by community groups. Part of the Glenfiddich Grampian Games Series, the 2015 event was opened by local resident and Commonwealth Games men's freestyle wrestling Bronze Medallist Viorel Etko. Previous openings have been carried out by celebrities such as journalist Jack Webster, Sooty and Sweep, The Two Crankies, Rod Hull's Emu and Alex Salmond. In 1980 the Scotland the What comedy team brought tears of laughter to the proceedings when comedian Steve Robertson used the public address system to play the part of Meldrum Sports Convener Sandy Thomson and made an impassioned spoof phone call to the Queen at Balmoral inviting her to open the 1981 event. The committee are still awaiting Her Majesty's response. Nowadays the Meldrum Sports features an array of traditional Highland Games alongside Highland dancing, field events, heavyweights plus a 'Massed Pipe Bands Salute to the Chieftain'.

1955 saw the very first celebrity opening of the games when broadcaster Sir Richard Dimbleby kicked off proceedings in front of a record crowd of fifteen thousand people. Dimbleby was a close friend and broadcasting colleague of Robert Beauchamp Duff (1915-1990), the thirty-second and last hereditary Laird of Oldmeldrum. Aberdeenshire born Duff inherited both his lairdship and Meldrum House, the family ancestral home, from his uncle in 1954. A Cambridge graduate, war reporter and news anchor man, he worked as a presenter then as a radio journalist for the BBC and during World War Two famously stood on various London rooftops during the Blitz describing in graphic detail, and in the required BBC clipped tones of the period, the night bombing of the city by the Luftwaffe.

In an interview just two years before his death in 1990 aged seventy-five, Robert recalled his long and quite distinguished career. He had covered the liberation of Europe, reported from the Normandy beaches during the allied landings and been shot at by a sniper during the liberation of Paris. Post-war he returned to France to record the Radio Scotland series *Duff's War* in which he recounted his journey through the battlefields of Europe. Less well known is the fact that he was perhaps the very first newsman to broadcast an expletive on the normally sedate BBC Radio News. While reporting on the London Blitz, his recording van was strafed by a German plane which he recalled "would have machine-gunned all of the reporting crew given the chance". He quite naturally let loose with a few strong words which, after careful consideration, the news editors at the BBC and the wartime censors passed for broadcast.

On inheriting Meldrum House from his uncle, he converted a large part of the building into a luxury hotel. Alongside clientele including entertainers, politicians and even rock stars, a frequent visitor was ballet mega-star Dame Margot Fontaine, a lifelong friend whose autobiography he co-wrote. Chairman of Scottish Ballet from 1973 until 1982 Robert is buried at St Matthew and St George's Episcopal Church on Oldmeldrum's Banff Road. Meldrum House Hotel continues to pick up awards. In 2015 the hotel, for the third year in a row, won the 'Aberdeen City and Shire Tourism Award for Most Hospitable Hotel'.

Known locally as 'The Mannie', Meldrum's 'Sailor Boy Statue' is a life size stone sculpture of a mariner in period costume standing proudly outside the Meldrum Arms Hotel on South Road. Rumours abound regarding his provenance. Few know his true origins but some claim that Spanish gold lies buried beneath his feet. Originally, he held a claypipe in one hand and an anchor in the other however the bowl of his pipe has disappeared over the years. Clad in the style of a Nineteenth century French sailor he is apparently sculpted from Portland Stone, the same material which from which Whitehall's Cenotaph is made, and was purchased by Alford's Postie Lawson - inventor of the steam powered Craigievar Express - at a local farm sale for just five shillings many years ago. Alford Transport Museum confirms that the statue stood outside Lawson's house at Craigievar until 1938 after which he was relocated to Oldmeldrum. If the Portland Stone connection is accurate, before taking up residence at Oldmeldrum, the old salt may have made his way to Aberdeenshire via Dorset where he is rumoured to have been commissioned by the widow of a drowned seafarer. A listed Grade C statue, Oldmeldrum's Mannie mariner would no doubt appreciate being reunited with the missing portion of his clay pipe.

28
PETERHEAD – HERRING, HARBOURS AND JACOBITES

When farm servant John Reid wrote about his native North East in his guise as David Toulmin, he penned some memorable stories. Amongst the crowded pages his short story *Snowfire* springs to mind. Hitler's armies are at the very gates of Moscow and the Russians are fighting for their lives in the siege of Leningrad. It is 1942 and he writes that the folk of Buchan were getting the tail end of the Russian winter "so you dug the snow from the turnip drills ... and all you'd get for an afternoons wark was enough to fill a horse cart." A dramatic sequence of events ensues. During a blizzard, the steading water trough freezes over leaving the livestock with nothing much to drink. When the beasts are let out onto the frozen river to sup from a break in the ice, a German bomber appears overhead and the aircraft gunner sprays the ice with bullets sending the thirst crazed animals to a watery doom. But not all of his Buchan tales were quite as dramatic. In his social history piece *Clarkie's and Aubrey's* he recounts the cinematic history of Peterhead. For a while at least, he lived just three miles outside the town and when money wasn't tight, he would cycle in to see the latest Hollywood offering.

Now, a man called Clarkie was the local ironmonger who, alongside studying the stock market, found time to run the Palace Theatre in Hanover Street. Previously known as the Electric Theatre, in earlier days it had been a skating rink. Unkind folk knew the place as The Bug Palace. Seemingly "you sometimes got flechs at Clarkie's." Up the road in the main square, James Aubrey ran The Picture House in the old Music Hall building. Described as "a real posh place" it was the first variety house in town to convert exclusively to film and showed mainly love stories. During WW1 Peterhead had become used to the sight of airships, from the nearby Royal Naval Air Station at Lenabo, overflying the town. Nicknamed 'Silver Sausages' by the townsfolk these early airships often suffered mechanical breakdown. For example, in 1917 a North Sea Class Airship got into difficulties over Peterhead. Experiencing engine failure and forced to lose height the machine collided with the Townhouse weathercock on Broad Street. Fortunately, the aircraft was only lightly damaged and managed to land on the Smith Embankment where a crowd of spectators hung grimly onto the mooring ropes until a lorry load of naval ratings arrived to take over. But it could have been disastrous! Toulmin also recounts how, during the winter of 1926, the Town House steeple toppled over during a storm and fell through the roof of Aubrey's Picture House to the consternation of those who had just left the building following the evening performance. Apart from his description of the event no record appears in the public domain. It is a matter of record however that in 1936, Aubrey's picture house burned down following a showing of the Gracie Fields' Ealing musical comedy *Queen of Hearts*. Toulmin's description of the hurricane includes the poignant lines "monstrous waves spiralled over the lighthouse and cascaded along the outer piers. Shipping dragged their anchors in the bay and their mast lights reeled like a drunk in the dark." Fine words by the North East's master story teller!

Peterhead Prison - 2017

Things however might have been much worse had the Admiralty not set in motion an ambitious scheme to build a gigantic breakwater across Peterhead Bay. Completed in 1956, following an astounding seventy years of construction, the Harbour of Refuge is one of Peterhead's iconic landmarks providing safe haven for North Sea shipping in all weathers. To cut costs, it had been decided to employ convict labour and the 1886 Harbour of Refuge Act provided for the building of a convict prison on the outskirts of the town at Invernettie. The use of forced labour was not at all a new idea. In fact, the Admiralty was involved in a similar project for Dover using convicts housed at Langdon Prison. At

Peterhead, Aberdeen firm MacAndrew & Co began constructing the first cell blocks in 1886 and on completion these housed the captive labour force needed to build both the rest of the prison and the sea defences. A two mile long narrow gauge railway, at the time probably the only state owned railway in the whole of Scotland, was laid between the Admiralty Yard at Salthousehead and the granite quarry up on Stirlinghill. The mammoth task of constructing the huge granite breakwaters then began.

Other projects including the Stevenson lighthouse at Rattray Head just to the west of the town were also constructed using convict labour. Rattray Head is a wild place and the sands around are full of the bones of ships. The lighthouse tower dates from the 1890s and at low tide can almost be reached from the shore. In the early years the keepers used semaphore and even megaphones to communicate with the shore, but in the 1950s - or so the story goes - an overhead phone line was installed at the personal expense of the lighthouse keepers, between the beach and the lighthouse. You can still see what appears to be a line of wooden telegraph poles running along the dunes. Seemingly an RAF Shackleton air sea rescue aircraft from Lossiemouth was on a low flying mission in 1960 when it flew past the lighthouse just above sea level and cut the cable.

Conditions were harsh at both the quarry and the prison. The Civil Guards on the outside work details were armed with rifles and prison warders wielded cutlasses. Seemingly these were not just for show. There were escape attempts. In July 1932 for example, a Strichen man serving seven years for armed robbery was shot dead attempting escape from the quarry. Infamous inmates included Gentle Johnny Ramensky, Glasgow hardman Jimmy Boyle and Godfather Arthur Thompson. Less infamous were those innocents imprisoned within the Peterhead Prison walls such as Paddy Meehan and Oscar Slater. Both men suffered serious miscarriages of justice. In 1918 Peterhead Prison played host to the Scottish Socialist leader John McLean. A fierce opponent of WW1 he was convicted of sedition. He spent five months on hunger strike at Peterhead before being released in ruined health in December 1918 as part of a raft of concessions following government fears of a post war Marxist Scottish Revolution. In 2013 'Scotland's Gulag' as the old Peterhead Prison had come to be known was replaced with a modern purpose built £150 million super-jail capable of housing 552 men, women and young offenders supervised by 360 staff. The old jail, or at least remnants of it, is now a tourist attraction visited by folk curious to reflect on a punitive regime which contained the worst of the worst from the Scottish prison population. The days of forced manual labour have probably gone forever though, and in a programme designed to aid integration back into the community prisoners at the new Peterhead facility are nowadays encouraged, amongst other things, to learn call centre skills. Perhaps next time you order a pizza or make a ScotRail enquiry the helpful voice at the end of the line will be speaking from a prison workshop in the Blue Toon.

Besides the Admiralty's investment in the harbour of refuge, Peterhead was built on the profits from seafaring and fishing. Peterhead whalers in particular sometimes made fortunes from the harvesting of whales and Greenland seals. Whaling was big business despite the dangers; and voyages, which could last up to six months, started in late spring in the hope that the ships could return home before the onset of the Arctic winter.

An adult whale carcass could yield maybe ten tons of oil plus a rich harvest of blubber and baleen. The oil lit the nations lamps and was used in the manufacture of jute. Baleen, the bony filter plates which hang from the whale's jaw bones, was used to make a wide variety of products including carriage springs, umbrella spokes and stays for corsets. Even the 'whalebones' which once were a feature of most harbours along the Scottish coastline, yielded a small bounty. Full of oil and difficult to drain, they were often hung from the masts of the whaling ships on the long journey south from Greenland in order to allow the last few gallons of whale oil drip into the ship's barrels.

Mind you, the Scottish whaling fleets of the eighteenth and Nineteenth century, aside from bringing back seal and whale oil to feed the nation's lamps were not averse to a bit of a bit of human trafficking. Alongside the odd polar bear an occasional Eskimo ended up in warmer climes on the return trip from the Arctic. Encouraged perhaps by the Admiralty, who were keen to map new trade routes through the ice, a number of lads from Greenland and Baffin Island ended up heading south to Scottish ports as guests of the ship-masters. These northerners were not just Arctic curiosities however. They often had valuable insight into the migration habits of whales and could sometimes provide assistance to cartographers in the making of navigational charts. One such visitor was a man by the name of Eenoolooapik who ended up in Aberdeen in the winter of 1839. Nicknamed Bobbie since few in the Granite City could pronounce his name, he hailed from Tenudiakbeek Gulf in Arctic Keimooksook and was seemingly a big hit at dinner parties. A local paper recorded that he went out on the River Dee to hunt ducks in his kayak although it does sound a bit contrived if you ask me. There is a story that he was later put on stage at the Theatre Royal in Aberdeen's Marischal Street but I'm not sure if that actually happened either. Eventually, in late 1840, Bobbie left Aberdeen to sail home to the Arctic where he seemingly died of tuberculosis.

Peterhead in its turn played host to a Baffin Islander named Nouyabik. There were no cameras around in the days of Eenoolooapik but Nouyabik was a much later visitor and there are images of him dressed in western clothes in various local history archives. He stayed in Peterhead for maybe a few months in around 1925 before returning home. Interestingly, during his Scottish sojourn, he was on at least one occasion invited to appear at a meeting of Aberdeen University Anatomical Society. The Arbuthnot Museum, one of Aberdeenshire's oldest museums, holds a wealth of information from those profitable but highly dangerous days. In common with many seaports, souvenirs in the form of live animals were sometimes brought back as trophies. A fully grown Greenland polar bear, donated by a local whaling skipper, stands among the nautical exhibits. The Arbuthnot Museum is also home to an important Inuit collection, whaling memorabilia and vintage photographs of both Peterhead and the surrounding area.

Aberdeenshire's Peterhead Profile indicated a 2012 population figure for Peterhead of 18,450 with a projected three percent ten year growth rate. For 2014, house prices were recorded as being just forty-five percent of the county average and unemployment three percent compared to the Aberdeenshire average of just one percent. Despite these dismal figures, a 2015 survey commissioned by Peterhead Port Authority indicated that trade through the port contributed £0.8 billion annually to the Scottish economy and supported ten thousand jobs throughout the entire North East.

Although in recent years Peterhead has seen several high profile business closures, the growth of the oil and gas sector combined with the town's status as the UK's largest white and pelagic fish port have combined to provide fresh employment opportunities. Enterprises as diverse as National Grid Transco, British Gas and the Scottish Prison Service are major employers. The fishing remains important though and in 2012 for example, 150,000 tons of fish valued at over £150m was handled through Peterhead. By 2019, the local fish market was selling ten-thousand fish boxes a day and recording an annual turnover of £126m with total fish landings at the port being put at £200 million per annum. The Port Authority's policy of continual investment and upgrading of port facilities combined with diversification of local processors from the traditional species of herring and mackerel into a range of other types including Blue Whiting, which was previously processed into fishmeal, has encouraged skippers of large foreign vessels to consign their fish for sale at Peterhead. A £33 million deep water expansion at Smith Quay was completed in 2010 and plans have been recently unveiled for a £47 million state of the art fishing hub to include the deepening of the inner harbours to 6.5 metres and provision of an even larger fish market. John Wallace, Chief Executive of Peterhead Port

Authority recently said "the development will have a tremendous impact on the port, town and subsequently the local business community. This investment will ensure the port meets the current and future needs of the sector and should bring confidence to others about future opportunities in this industry".

But back to the older history of Peterhead in the form of a Jacobite link. Amongst the 17 million exhibits held by the Museums Victoria in Melbourne, Australia is a curious silver guinea dated 1716 but struck in 1828 by Mathew Young of London probably from dies manufactured in France in preparation for what was intended to be a new Scottish coinage for James VIII in anticipation of his ascent to the throne. The British Museum houses a set of the original dies. The coin's face depicts the draped bust of James with the reverse showing four crowned shields set to form a cross around a thistle with the inscription SCO AN FRA ET HIB REX 1716. Known widely as Pretender Coinage the dies for the coins were made by Norbert Roettiers, a Paris based engraver appointed by the exiled Stuarts. When George I was chosen to rule over Britain in preference to James, many Scots were sympathetic to the Jacobite cause. Although recognised by his cousin Louis XIV of France as the rightful king of England, Scotland and Ireland, James's refusal to renounce Catholicism made accession to the Protestant throne impossible and the only course of action left to him was a military one. A previous planned invasion in 1708, again aided by France, had been thwarted before James could even set foot in Scotland. Seven years later, in 1715, things would he imagined be different. Accordingly, some three hundred years ago on December the twenty second 1715, the man who would be king landed by sea at Peterhead. Crucially, he brought with him no guns or troops and reputedly no treasure chest. As if to emphasise his isolation, the French ship which delivered him to Scotland immediately made off back to Europe fearful that ships of the English navy might intervene.

Whether Peterhead was chosen by accident or design is not clear. However, in September 1715, the town had made known its Jacobite sympathies via a proclamation for King James at the Mercat Cross on the Broadgate. A meeting of the Magistrates and Town Council on October the fifth 1715 decided that due to the "hazard and danger the Town may sustain by the inconvenience of the present tymes ... the said Town for their own safety and defence keep Guaird by calling out the rexive Inhabitants." A gathering was called for at 10 am the following day at which all the "ffenceable men" were encouraged to enlist and carry arms in defence of the town. In all 138 men, and indeed ten women, were issued with "ane sufficient gun, charged with powder and bullets, and ffour shots besides, and ane sufficient suord." Additionally, several cannon, reputedly salvaged from the wreck of the Spanish ship St Michael, were set up around the

Peterhead Harbour

harbour mouths to defend the seaward approaches. But, when the prospective king finally arrived at Peterhead three days before Christmas in 1715, the rebellion was already melting away. The Royal Standard had been raised at Braemar on September the sixth 1715 and the Scottish pro-Jacobite army, headed up by the Earl of Mar, had marched on Perth. Results were mixed and indecisively, the key Jacobite battle at Sheriffmuir was fought and seemingly won by both sides in November 1715. Dundee bard William Topaz McGonagall records that:

> "The success on either side is doubtful to this day,
> And all that can be said is, both armies ran away."

In some ways McGonagall's take on the battle reflected the black comedy of a later conflict in which a deluded Marshall Petain told Churchill that the battle for France was not yet lost and advised the Prime Minister to phone back tomorrow since his "victory against the Germans could of course go either way". Both Petain's troops and the British Expeditionary Force also ran away and the butcher's bill was eventually to be in the millions. The Jacobite butcher's bill was much more localised but took Scotland by surprise. Entente was on hold and a vengeful England demanded blood for forgiveness. And it was not long in coming.

Robert Burns took perhaps a more balanced view of the Jacobite action in his 1789 account *The Battle o' Sherramuir*:

"But had you seen the philibegs,
And skyrin tartan trews, man;
When in the teeth they dar'd our Whigs
And covenant true blues, man;
In lines extended lang and large,
When bayonets opposed the targe,
And thousands hasten'd to the charge,
Wi' Highland wrath they frae the sheath,
Drew blades o' death, 'till, out o' breath,
They fled like frighted doos, man."

Following further strategic withdrawals, James finally found himself at the Angus town of Montrose in early February 1716 where he and his commander, the Earl of Mar, boarded a small vessel and sailed for France. He never set foot in Scotland again. A plaque in Peterhead's Park Lane commemorates the site of the house, owned by a local merchant named as James Park, where the king in waiting lodged overnight prior to his journey south. Seemingly James penned a grateful letter to the folk of Peterhead thanking them for their valued assistance in promoting the failed rebellion. The Old Chevalier as he was popularly called obviously had no qualms about incriminating his now abandoned supporters. To commemorate the tricentenary of the king in waiting's landing, local community group Peterhead 1715 performed a play at Drummer's Corner on the three hundredth anniversary of the landing.

For a town which lays claim to seeing all four seasons in just the one day, Peterhead can appear a bit dreich and dreary if you catch it on the wrong time of day. But if you delve into the history of what must surely be the easterly most point in the whole landmass of Scotland, the place is surely worth a trip. And if the weather catches you out, there's always the local prison museum to explore. Who knows, you might even be lucky enough to spend time in the very cell once inhabited by Gentle Johnny Ramensky. And if Peterhead grabs you by the gills, there is a splendid documentary film about the place titled *Peterhead Harbours 1993* on YouTube shot by Grampian film maker James Taylor reflecting on the long strike action by Aberdeen Harbour's stevedores which led to the Granite City's fish merchants upping sticks to head north to cement Peterhead's rightful place as the premier EU port for the UK fishing industry during the 1980s and maybe even to the present day.

29
PORTSOY – THE VILLAGE OF THE DRAMMED

Known nowadays as a setting for Peaky Blinders and Whisky Galore, Portsoy at one time boasted a herring fleet of around fifty-seven boats. As steam drifters gradually took over from the more traditional sail driven Zulus and Skaffies during the late Nineteenth century, harbour traffic declined and the majority of local boats gravitated to the larger harbours such as Buckie, Fraserburgh and Macduff. By the end of that century the town's role as a seaport had all but disappeared, killed off in part at least by the railways. A branch line from Tillynaught connected the harbour to the Great North of Scotland Railway (GNSR) main line at Grange but the completion of the Moray Coast Line in the May of 1886 effectively made the Portsoy Harbour spur line with its steep 1:30 gradient redundant.

Few records of this short spur remain although local lore suggests that it was in use for less than thirty years and was so steep that the shunting engines could only haul a single wagon at a time on the return journey up the hill (some sources quote four) between the harbour yard and the goods yard on the main line. It closed in 1888 and the track bed is now a footpath. Coastal trade in general merchandise, grain and timber moved to the larger North East ports where movement of goods by rail was much easier and by 1910 the Portsoy harbour line had closed. A final death blow was dealt to the Portsoy harbour trade when the outbreak of the First War severed the town's links with former European trading partners. The Russian Civil War further disrupted trade from the Baltic states although by that time the harbour trade had by most accounts migrated to the bigger ports in any case.

Writer and priest Peter Anson devoted just two pages to Portsoy in his classic study *Fishing Boats and Fishing Boats on the North East of Scotland*, about as much as he devoted to the likes of Sandend and Cairnbulg. In sharp contrast - in that book at least - he spends ten pages recording the maritime history of Buckie. Aside from recording that in 1929 there were just nine steam drifters and four motor boats operating from the Portsoy harbour, he writes that "Of all the ports on the south side of the Moray Firth, Portsoy strikes the visitor as being perhaps the most derelict. The whole place looks abandoned and ruinous, owing largely to the number of great warehouses, now deserted and falling into ruin which stand around the harbour".

In sharp contrast, when newspaper columnist Cuthbert Graham wrote about Portsoy in 1963, things had obviously changed for the better. He commented that the town was one of the most progressive communities on the Moray Firth. In his travel column *This is My Country* he wrote about the "triumphant success" of the town's efforts to encourage tourism and the discussions then taking place regarding the rehabilitation of Loch Soy. Now, in the days before the advent of ice making on a commercial basis, ice for the preserving of Scottish fish was either shipped in from places such as Greenland via the international ice trade or more likely harvested locally from ponds and rivers during the winter months. Portsoy's Loch Soy was at one time the main source of ice for the local salmon fishing industry and also provided water power for local mills such as MacDonald Brothers engineering works. By the middle of the Twentieth century however, the loch had become a weed strewn eyesore and the local Town Improvement Association stepped in to address the issue. Following extensive landscaping, Loch Soy was officially reopened as a leisure park and boating loch in June 1973. The MacDonald Brothers mill had closed in 1968. In operation for around 112 years, the company operated as an engineering business complete with foundry and fabrication sheds and at its peak employed over twenty engineers, craftsmen and draftsmen.

Catering largely for the needs of fisher folk, MacDonalds patented a number of innovative maritime engineering designs including one for a "patent twin screw auxiliary propeller" driven by the same coal fuelled engine employed for the boat's steam capstan. This innovative design was intended to solve the problem of sail driven boats becoming becalmed. The *Banffshire Reporter* in May 1902, recorded how "this invention … makes it possible for a boat to move at a speed of 3 to 4 knots   an hour when a favourable breeze fails to fill the sails … we venture to state that many a fisherman, when wind fails him, may be enabled to realise from a night's shot considerably more than the little expense his propelling gear has cost him."

Perhaps though, the factory's most famous product was the MacDonald Steam Capstan. As the need for herring drifters to venture further offshore led to the building of larger boats, so the difficulties of both hauling in nets and raising ever larger sails increased. The larger drifters had masts over sixty feet in height and the effort of manually raising the heavy canvas sails, especially in a damp breeze, was an exhausting and difficult job for the crews. The patented MacDonald Steam Capstan took the heavy work in its stride and very soon became an international success. Although competing companies manufactured similar products, the innovative reverse gear and ease of operation of the MacDonald model made it a market leader. The Scottish Fisheries Museum's extensively restored 1902 seventy foot herring drifter Reaper (FR 958) sports perhaps the very last of the - made in Portsoy - MacDonald Steam Capstans.

The MacDonald Steam Capstan aboard Reaper (FR 958)

Now converted to operate using compressed air, this machine is in regular use on the Sandhaven built boat which is now part of the Core Collection of the National Historic Ships Fleet.

Chosen as a film location for the remake of the Ealing comedy *Whisky Galore*, Portsoy has recently been rebranded as "The Village of the Drammed" by film publicists. Quite what *Whisky Galore* author Sir Compton Mackenzie would have made of it all is unclear, however by a fortunate coincidence, just as casting began, London Auctioneer Bonham's listed a rare bottle of Glen Boyne Old Scotch Whisky, bottled and labelled by Portsoy grocer G.G. McRobbie in the late Nineteenth century, for sale. There is some doubt regarding the exact provenance of the spirit since although Portsoy had a distillery in Burnside Street in pre-railway days, this probably pre-dates the Bonhams item leading to the suspicion that the Glen Boyne might have been distilled at nearby Glenglassaugh Distillery before being bottled by Mr McRobbie. Founded in 1875, the Glenglassaugh Distillery Company is now part of the Edinburgh based Ben Riach Distillery Company. Sited beside the iconic 'Cup and Saucer' of Abercrombie's Windmill on the A98 just outside Portsoy, the facility is currently being upgraded. As part of a £25 million investment strategy, Ben Riach plans to lay down stocks of premium brand malt in order to meet rapidly expanding demand in the Far East, particularly Taiwan. It's a far cry from the back shop of McRobbie's grocery store, but on the other hand maybe a few bottles of his Glen Boyne malt reached foreign shores courtesy of Portsoy's trade with the continent.

The town is particularly famed for Portsoy Marble, quarried from a vein of serpentine which runs across the braes to the west of the Old Harbour. Although widely used for decorative architectural purposes, there is little evidence, aside from one building on Shorehead and another beside Loch Soy, of the use of Portsoy Marble in the external facings of the town's buildings. Strictly speaking Portsoy Marble is in fact serpentine, a colourful but very soft stone suited mainly for decorative purposes including funeral monuments, sundials and souvenir ware. Admired for its lustre it was shipped abroad in past times for use in the interiors of grand buildings such as the Palace of Versailles and The Hermitage at St. Petersburg. Closer to home, Cullen House at one time boasted gravel paths and even fireplaces made from the local serpentine. Although large scale quarrying using dynamite has long ceased, the Portsoy Marble Shop at the old harbour stocks locally made Portsoy Marble souvenirs alongside locally fired pottery and knitwear.

There are a good few famous folk associated with Portsoy. Premier League midfielder Eoin Jess played for the Dons, Coventry City and Northampton Town. Born in Portsoy in 1970, he was capped for Scotland eighteen times before becoming coach for Nottingham Forest Youth Team. Traditional singer Jimmy MacBeath was born in Portsoy in 1894 and is buried in the town. A Gordon Highlander during the First War, he hailed from travelling folk and was prone to tramp the highways and the byways of Scotland earning money along the way through singing at fairs and markets as he went. In 1951 he had his big break when Hamish Henderson heard about him. Jimmy signed with Columbia Records and carved a professional career performing the likes of *The Barnyards of Delgaty* and *Fae Would Be a Fisherman's Wife?* both on the folk circuit and in early BBC television folk programmes. Then there is James Abercrombie of Glassaugh, builder of the Glassaugh Windmill which sits a few miles east of the town next to the distillery. At first glance, the ivy-covered structure can easily be mistaken for a Pictish Broch or even a Martello Tower. A scheduled monument the building is described by Historic Scotland as:

"Mid-18th century, possibly 1761. 4-storey tapering circular windmill encompassed by circular platform base. Rubble, tooled ashlar dressings. 2 doorways at 1st floor level give on to roof of circular base (which forms wall-walk) around 1st floor of windmill; 3 1st, 2nd and 3rd floor windows of diminishing size set one above the other at regular intervals around tower; 4

segmental-headed wide openings in ground floor. Wallhead crowned with dressed ashlar cope; 2 small holes visible in S side of cope, these formerly retained pinion rings for staying sails."

Known locally as the Cup and Saucer because of its distinctive shape and set back over five hundred metres from the A98 between Portsoy and Banff the structure has a covering of ivy which masks the outline of the building and suggests a ruined tower house with a walled garden encircling the base. Nothing could be further from the truth however! In common with much of the Banff and Buchan coastline, the area around Portsoy is full of Pictish remains. These are often built over or indeed incorporated in later structures such as farm houses, churches and dykes. The Glassaugh Windmill is just such a building.

General James Abercrombie of Glassaugh was as his title suggests a military man. He was born in 1706 to a wealthy Banffshire family and as was the custom of the time, he purchased a major's commission to enter the army in 1742. He was promoted to colonel in 1746 and major general in 1756. The General is credited with having particularly good organisational skills but very little understanding of the art of warfare. Unfortunately, in the July of 1758 he met his 'Charge of the Light Brigade' moment when he directed troops to make a frontal assault on a fortified French position without the benefit of artillery support. More than 2,000 of his force of 15,000 were killed or wounded resulting in the general being recalled to Britain where he duly became a Member of Parliament in a government committed to supporting the cause of British dominion over the Northern Territories of America and Canada.

When Major General Abercrombie MP returned to his native Scotland, he took over the running of the family estate at Glassaugh and, possibly lacking much to do in the parliament of the day, he began organising the improvement of the agricultural economy of the estate. This was a time of land improvement and land enclosure. Labour was plentiful and cheap as a large number of Irish Catholics had been dispossessed by the influx of English and Scottish aristocracy and had sought work on the land in Scotland. He had been a poor general but, as has already been said, he had good organisational skills. In the true spirit of Jaroslav Hašek's Good Soldier Švejk which is essentially a series of absurdly comic episodes, Abercrombie decided to build a giant windmill. Now, in those far off days, the majority of mills were powered by water. There are tens of thousands of watermills in the UK and at a guess there must be at least one in every inhabited town and village in Aberdeenshire. Transport was improving during the 1750s but local grain mills were still the order of the day. Windmills were not unknown in the North East, but were not common due to the ease and availability of waterpower. The good General however decided that wind was the way to go.

As any engineer will know, the biggest challenge in building large structures is the sourcing of building materials. If you need to build a wall then you will require large quantities of heavy and difficult to transport stone. The shorter the journey from quarry to building site the better. Fortunately, Abercrombie had a ready-made supply of building materials in the form of a Bronze Age burial cist. The folk who had built the cairn would have no objections to its recycling after all and at that time there was no legislation in force to protect the ancient structure. The 'Cup and Saucer' was born. Using the materials from the ancient monument, Abercrombie bade his workers to build an enormous windmill four stories high complete with a tapering tower topped with white sails. It must have been the sight of the century for folk who had never travelled further than Sandend or Portsoy. How long Abercrombie's windmill was at full tilt is not recorded, however in a letter dated twenty third of August 1761, the general advised his eldest daughter that high winds had almost blown off "the pompon of the wind mill which was only set up yesterday." The ivy clad granite stump of the structure is however all that remains today to remind us of the man who had the vision to build it all those years ago. In a 1979 article, local Portsoy historian Mary Mackie describes an old painting of nearby Glassaugh House which clearly shows an image of the Glassaugh Windmill in full sail. She also suggests that the path connecting the nearby Glenglassaugh Distillery passed through the windmill by the north and south arches linking the windmill to a nearby public house known as the Black Jug. So, there we have it. The Glassaugh windmill, known locally as the Cup and Saucer, also sports a black jug.

Perhaps the best known of Portsoy's modern day sons is trombonist Big Jim Paterson of Dexys Midnight Runners fame. Formed in 1978 and named in honour of the recreational drug Dexedrine, the group's debut album *Searching for the Young Soul Rebels* made the top ten in 1980. Famed for big line ups, the group's hit singles include *Geno* and *Come on Eileen*. They disbanded in 1986 reforming as Dexys in 2003 with Big Jim Patterson on trombone. Jim is now back living in his native town and regularly performs at the annual Portsoy Harbour Festival.

Although not born in the town, Peter Anson, writer, artist and some-time priest, lived in the harbour area in 1936 prior to his moves to Banff, Macduff and Montrose. A co-founder of the Apostleship of the Sea and known as "a skeely drawer o' boats an' haibers an' fisher fowk" Anson's extensive body of work includes quite a few mentions of Portsoy harbour life. For example, in 1936 Portsoy gained international fame as the home port of the drifter Boy

Portsoy Harbour at Boat Festival time

Andrew which that year won the Prunier Trophy with a catch of 231 crans, or around a quarter of a million fish. The prize, instituted by Parisian restaurant owner Madame Simone Prunier, was awarded annually to the drifter netting the highest crannage of herring in one shot and, alongside the trophy, involved the crew being invited to dine at her fashionable London restaurant all expenses paid. Uncharacteristically, Anson writes acidly of the win "It seems strange that it should need the enterprising proprietress of a fashionable London restaurant to bring Portsoy onto the national headlines."

Alongside the rehabilitation of Loch Soy, Portsoy has in recent years capitalised on its connection with the sea. In 1994 the town hosted the very first Scottish Traditional Boat Festival, an event which in 2019 celebrated twenty-five years of development work by the town. The 1994 event firmly placed Portsoy on the tourist map and visitor numbers regularly swell the resident population of 1,800 to a giddy 18,000 on festival weekend. 1994 saw a world record first, the landing of a radio-controlled model helicopter on the deck of the world's largest model aircraft carrier - Duncan Cameron's thirty-one foot HMS Invincible - within the shelter of the Seventeenth century Old Harbour. Nowadays an annual fixture and undoubted leader of the harbour festival pack, the Portsoy Harbour Festival lays special emphasis on heritage, boat building and sailing ships backed up with music, story-telling and traditional crafts. In tandem with the Harbour Festival, in 2008, after decades of neglect, Portsoy's historic Salmon Bothy opened its doors for events following a major restoration. Originally operated by the Seafield Estate, the bothy dates from 1834 and features an ice house, fish processing room and net loft. Nowadays owned and operated by the Scottish Traditional Boat Festival, the building hosts regular folk and theatre events plus a museum dedicated to local history. Recent events have included showings of the 2016 remake of *Whisky Galore* starring Gregor Fisher, Eddie Izzard, Sean Biggerstaff and Naomi Battrick.

Portsoy through the years has seen a multitude of changes. The fishing, the railway and the shipping trade have all gone. The focus on tourism and heritage has clearly paid dividends. A recent exhibition mounted by the Scottish Traditional Boat Festival at the Scottish Parliament showcased the Portsoy Organisation for Restoration and Training's (PORT) construction of a unique Moray Firth fishing coble. Banffshire and Buchan MSP Stewart Stevenson commented "The work that the Scottish Traditional Boat Festival is doing on the construction of a traditional coble will be invaluable for generations to come as they are documenting a process previously passed on by word of mouth."

In one respect though, time has not moved on in Portsoy. If church clocks are a measure of progress, then the former parish church in Seafield Street has a bit of catching up to do. Three faces of the Portsoy Parish Church clock conform to the accepted practice of counting the hours in a one through to twelve sequence. The northerly facing dial unaccountably has no nine but a choice of elevens. Church clock errors are not uncommon. Perhaps the craftsmen were semi-literate and simply copied by rote. Such anomalies occur occasionally on gravestones also and there is even one infamous example in the Mearns where a local man is recorded as having died several years before he was born (see chapter 26).

The clock at the St Mary Magdalene Church at Whitgift, East Yorkshire is also a good example and bears Roman numerals to the value of thirteen instead of the more usual twelve and Crimond Kirk near Fraserburgh sports a timepiece with an extra minute between the numerals eleven and twelve resulting in a sixty-one minute hour. Local investigation regarding the Portsoy clock's duplicity of elevens and lack of a nine led one resident to comment "it's about time someone did something about this horological joke."

30
STONEHAVEN – A GOOD DEAL ROMANTIC

Stonehaven Harbour

With a fast-growing population, approaching 11,000 in 2020, and a broad coastal outlook its quite easy to see why people are attracted to Stonehaven today. The former fishing port boasts several Art Deco buildings including the quite stunning Carron Restaurant and the Stonehaven Open Air Swimming Pool the town is geared up to welcome tourists and visitors throughout the year. Events such as the annual Harbour Festival, the New Year Fireball Ceremony and the summer Feein' Market bring folk from far and wide to the town. Although no longer a substantial fishing port, Stonehaven retains its historic connections with the sea with over 140 regular moorings available to pleasure craft within the harbour's three sheltered basins. Fresh seafood including langoustine, lobster and mackerel from the local day boats is a staple of the local restaurants and takeaways. Indeed, Peter Anson records in his 1930 book *Fisher Folk and Fisher Folk in the North East of Scotland* that fishing at Stonehaven has had a chequered history. Boat numbers have fluctuated widely over the years he writes and, in common with many other ports, the post 1918 period was particularly hard on the towns fisherfolk. By 1929 he writes that just thirty-three boats were left manned by "seventy-eight mainly old men or middle aged none of whom were below fifty in years". He candidly records that when asked why the young men refused to go to sea, a typical response would be "It's because they will na' work and prefer to live on the dole!" He continues "Whatever the true cause of the decline, the fisherman's quarter of Stonehaven gives one the impression of tragic decay."

As you munch on your neeps and haggis on Burns Night, its maybe worth remembering that Scotland has two bards named Robert Burns. The one we know and celebrate each January had a creative counterpart in the Mearns just a few miles inland from Dunnottar Castle in Aberdeenshire. And, some 230 years ago, they both met up to exchange pleasantries and down a few drams in a farmhouse just outside Stonehaven.

In the September of 1787 Robert Burns the younger was nearing the end of his third 'Vacation Tour' of his native Scotland. Along with travelling companion Willie Nicol, he had left Edinburgh in the May of that year with the intention of collecting the national songs of Scotland as part of a collaboration with the Edinburgh music publisher James Johnson. Armed with letters of introduction they had dined and been wined by both lairds and cottars the length and breadth of the land and by the end of the trip had collected around 160 ballads for inclusion in Johnson's six volume collection: *The Scots Musical Museum*.

Burns however needed no letter of introduction on arrival in Stonehaven however since his family had long roots at the farm of Clochnahill in Dunnottar Parish, birthplace of the bard's father. In the course of the short visit, he met up with his Mearns relatives before proceeding south to Laurencekirk and then on to Montrose. A civic garden alongside the Cowie River commemorates the Burns connection and features a sandstone bust of the bard in classic pose sculpted by local monumental mason 'Ghosty Bob'. "Near Stonehive" Burns writes in his diary of the trip, "the coast a good deal romantic. Met my relations. Robert Burns, writer in Stonehive, one of those who love fun, a gill, and a good punning joke, and have not a bad heart … his wife a sweet, hospitable body, without any affectation of what is now called town-breeding." Referring to the Mearns, he comments "It is a rich and cultivated, but still unenclosed country."

At first glance however he might well have taken Stonehaven for a town under siege. A First century Roman camp sits high on the hillside above the coastal town. Arguably the finest example of a marching camp in Scotland, the fortification at Raedykes occupies a thirty-hectare site large enough to house several thousand troops. Kempstone Hill, to the east of Raedykes was once a favoured location for the battle of Mons Graupius however the debate continues as to the actual battleground and very little in the way of Roman artefacts appears to have been unearthed at Raedykes although a Roman coin hoard, including denarii dating from the rule of Septimius Severus (circa 211 AD), was found on nearby Cowie Common in 1843.

The cliff top ruins of Dunnottar Castle

To the south of Stonehaven, the stunning cliff top ruins of Dunnottar castle tell of a different era. Alongside featuring as a screensaver on Microsoft Windows the castle is also well remembered as the defender and saviour of the Scottish Crown Jewels. The Regalia had been kept within the fortress prior to Cromwell's siege of 1651 before being smuggled out by a local clergyman to be hidden at Kinneff Church. One of the most impregnable fortresses in Scotland due to its clifftop location, Dunnottar has been besieged many times by both foreign invaders - such as the Vikings - and by the home grown armies of Cromwell, James Graham the First Marquis of Montrose, and William Wallace. Cromwell and Montrose seem to have contented themselves with the pillaging of Stonehaven town while Wallace infamously burned down the castle's church in 1297 with the English garrison imprisoned inside. Blind Harry, the Scots Makar, recounts the event in the epic poem *Wallace*:

"Therefore a fire was brought speedily,
Which burnt the church, and all those South'ron boys,

Out o'er the rock the rest rush'd great noise;
Some hung on craigs, and loath were to die,
Some lap, some fell, some flutter'd in the sea,
And perish'd all, not one remain'd alive."

Then there are the more recent wartime coastal defences. In 1940, fear of invasion via German occupied Norway led to the construction of beach defences on a truly epic scale along the entire east coast of Scotland and while the cliffs around Stonehaven made seaborne landings unlikely, the bay itself was seen as vulnerable with an easy exit inland which could be exploited by invading mechanised troops. Accordingly, a defensive line running from the mouth of the mouth of the Cowie Water all the way inland as far as Braemar was constructed. One of three defensive lines, or 'Stop Lines', constructed in the Aberdeen area the Cowie Defence Line was by far the most extensive when compared to those on the Rivers Dee and Don. Exploiting the natural features of the landscape, pillboxes and anti-tank blocks were placed at strategic points such as road and rail bridges and the river banks were cut away in many places to divert and slow down enemy mechanised transport long enough to allow counter attacks to be organised. Although much of Stonehaven town's WW2 concrete defence work appears to have been incorporated into the town's flood defences, the area around Ury House retains many classic structures from those troubled times.

Identified by military planners as a vulnerable crossing point over the river, the two old bridges on Ury estate were obstructed by anti-tank blocks with covering fire from a rare granite faced Type 22 pillbox. The river banks were steepened also and a moveable railway block was placed on Glenury Viaduct. There was also a Fougasse emplacement built into an embankment on the Slug Road just down from the railway bridge and it may well still be there. A particularly nasty weapon, these devices consisted of a concealed flame thrower fed by a forty-gallon tank of napalm, designed to incinerate passing troops or armoured vehicles. Remotely controlled and operated usually by Home Guard soldiers the Fougasse in some ways was a forerunner to the modern day IED. Fortunately, these defences were never tested although the town did experience the direct effects of Twentieth century warfare on more than one occasion. In the January of 1940 the SS Gowrie was bombed and sunk just four miles offshore and in the August of that year, in a highly unusual action during which a force of German seaplanes attacked a convoy south of the town, a cargo ship, the SS Highlander, made port in Aberdeen with the remains of a crashed enemy bomber on the foredeck. Also, anti-shipping mines often floated ashore all along the east coast and although many were spotted by coastal defence observers before being detonated by rifle fire or defused and made safe this was not always the case and Stonehaven's oldest harbour building, the Tolbooth, fell victim to one such device in 1944 when a massive explosion severely damaged the building. Another, more tragic, explosion occurred in late January 1941 when the Stonehaven Coastguard hut blew up while the occupants were examining an explosive device. Three people were killed in the tragedy. It was not until 1963 that the Tollbooth building was fully restored prompting a visit by the late Queen Elizabeth The Queen Mother to perform the official re-opening. Originally built in the Sixteenth century as a harbour storehouse the Tolbooth currently functions as the town museum and houses a fine seafood restaurant on the upper floor.

In a strange quirk of fate, Stonehaven Golf Club actually benefited from those difficult days of 1940. Founded in 1888 and with dramatic short holes played over deep gullies along the top of a set of steep cliffs, the Stonehaven course is described by the club as "a challenging cliff top course lying on the Braes of Cowie, overlooking the North Sea." The first fairway features 'Hitler's Bunker', which to the uninitiated consists of a bomb crater created by the young men of the Luftwaffe during an air raid on the town in August 1940. Originally thirty feet wide and ten feet deep the bunker is nowadays much reduced in size but is still a talking point amongst members who will also point to the fact that the golf course spans the Highland Boundary Fault which not only divides Scotland from east to west but divides the thirteenth and fifteenth holes with golfers requiring to carry their clubs over a gap known locally as 'The Gully'.

The railway delivered prosperity when it arrived in 1849 and by 1863 *Bradshaw's Railway Guide* was describing the settlement as "The county town of Kincardineshire with a population of about 3,240 who are principally engaged in the herring trade fisheries, distilleries and breweries." Bradshaw goes on to state that the railway station is one and a half miles from the sea and that there was one telegraph station in the town.

On that fateful day of the event known locally as the 'Stonehaven Railway Riot of January 1848' the telegraph station was yet to be built. The local constabulary, consisting of six constables headed by Superintendent of Police Alexander Weir, were completely outnumbered when faced with a drunken mob of over two hundred railway navvies, and they had no easy way to summon help.

The previous weekend, the navvies had fought with locals and on this holiday weekend they had seemingly decided to gain the upper hand by taking over the town. Windows were smashed at various points in the town and the

Mill Inn was vandalised, townsfolk were jostled and, in some cases, bludgeoned by the mob. After almost six hours of rampage the mob dispersed and calm prevailed. A local man by the name of William Murray lay dead however, having been violently assaulted in the town's Allardyce Street. Someone would have to pay. The transcript for the Circuit Court of Justiciary for the County of Aberdeen for Monday April the tenth 1848 records the punishment handed out to the usual suspects:

"George Keith, age 13 from Banff, guilty of burglary - 18 months in Perth Prison. Elizabeth Milne, theft of 15 sovereigns from Lazarus Myres, a Jewish travelling hawker in Aberdeen: 15 months imprisonment. Two men convicted of highway robbery outside Huntly: 14 years transportation."

There followed the trial of several men charged with organising and leading the Stonehaven riot. Witnesses were called but, as with all good trials involving mobbing and rioting, the evidence became blurred if not completely contradictory. The alleged ring leader, Daniel Donald Davidson a railway navvy from Inverness was variously described as striking the fatal blow and of being simply a participant. At one point a witness even portrayed him as the man who had defended local men James Walker and John Carnegie from the actions of the mob. But whatever the evidence, there was only one possible outcome, an example had to be made.

There were six accused of mobbing and rioting. Five received custodial sentences. The sixth, Daniel Davidson was sentenced in April 1848 to seven years Penal Servitude in Van Diemens Land (nowadays Tasmania). Transported on the sailing ship Nile II alongside 299 fellow convicts he reached his destination in the October of 1850 after a voyage lasting 109 days. His great great-grand daughter Vicki Pearce of Shearwater in modern day Tasmania has researched his story. She writes:

"Daniel Donald married Margaret Griffin 19 July 1853 at Bellerive, Tasmania. They lived at Kangaroo Point on the eastern shore, so called because of the large numbers of kangaroo to be seen on the beach. They had 7 children and lived at Triabunna on the east coast of Tasmania. Daniel worked at the sandstone quarries. He was admitted to the General Hospital on 19/8/1874 suffering from pneumonia and died on 31/8/1874."

The official penal record states that on the day of his demise, he was "free by servitude" having spent a total of twenty-four years in the colony and that he was buried by friends. Daniel was but one of some 75,000 convicts transported to Tasmania from the UK.

No tale about Stonehaven would be complete without the story of the Flying Farmer. Sex parties are nothing new and in the shadowy world of swinging, the jingling of car keys in a tartan bonnet, although perhaps a bit dodgy has a long history. London entrepreneur and convicted fraudster 'Fast Eddie' Davenport reputedly hosted a number of 'Gate Crasher Balls' in the 1980s and in more recent years, London swingers could seemingly associate freely with fellow clubbers for a mere £100 entrance fee at Emma Sayle's Killing Kittens Club. Not to be outdone, Aberdeenshire - alongside boasting several alleged dogging sites - has a story or two to tell about sex-clubbing. And the tale of Kinky Cottage and the Flying Farmer stands supreme not least because of the resultant and very public trial.

To all intents and purposes, it was the trial of the century. A media sensation, the so called Garvie Trial captured the public imagination. Folk all across the Mearns choked over their porridge as the lurid headlines spread across the globe. The decomposed body of Maxwell Garvie, a wealthy Mearns farmer, had been discovered in an underground tunnel at Lauriston Castle near St Cyrus and his wife Sheila along with two co-accused, Brian Tevendale and Alan Peters, had been remanded in custody charged with his murder. On November eighth 1968 all three accused appeared at Stonehaven Sheriff Court for a pleading diet. The charges alleged that: "on May fourteen or fifteen 1968, in the farmhouse at West Cairnbeg near Fordoun, the accused had assaulted Maxwell Robert Garvie by striking him on the head with a solid object before shooting him in the head and murdering him."

All three pleaded not guilty and the case was sent for trial at the High Court in Aberdeen. In the meantime, bail was refused and the trio were held on remand at Aberdeen's Victorian era Craiginches Prison, the final resting place of Henry Burnett. Burnett had been hanged in the August of 1963 and was the very last convicted murderer to be executed in Britain before capital punishment was abolished. As things turned out, the two of the three accused who were eventually convicted in the Garvie murder case were very lucky indeed not to have joined Henry in the prison graveyard. In fact, they missed the hangman by a mere five years.

The trial proper began on Tuesday November nineteenth and it soon became apparent that both press and public interest was high. By 7 am on day one, a full three hours before the doors of the courthouse were due to open, an excited queue had formed. By 10 am some three-hundred people were jostling for the sixty or so seats on the public benches. Local police were out in force and, strangely perhaps, a contingent of infantrymen from Gordon Barracks were on hand in case of trouble.

It was December second 1968 when the trial finally concluded. Both Sheila Garvie and Brian Tevendale were convicted of the murder and each was sentenced to ten years imprisonment while Peters was to walk free following a Not Proven verdict. However, alongside the lurid details of the actual murder, an equally lurid tale of drink, drugs and swingers was gradually revealed to a hungry court audience in the course of the trial. Seemingly the murdered Maxwell was not averse to a bit of wife swapping and it soon emerged that the initially reluctant Sheila eventually gave in to his sexual demands. Tales of orgies at a private nudist club, known locally as 'Kinky Cottage', over at Alford emerged and allegations that Maxwell enjoyed the company of both sexes emerged when a missing person report previously published in the *Police Gazette* was produced in evidence:

"Spends freely, is a heavy spirit drinker and often consumes tranquilisers and Pro-Plus tablets when drinking. Is fond of female company but has strong homosexual tendencies and is often in the company of young men."

In point of fact, Maxwell Garvie had been listed as missing some four months prior to his body being discovered. An enthusiastic flyer and owner of a light plane, Maxwell had seemingly been in the habit of 'shooting up' cars on the roads around Stonehaven in an apparent attempt to show off and intimidate drivers. When he repeated the exercise at the harbour at Stonehaven, flying at mast height over the breakwater, he was reported to the police and charged. Having failed to appear in court to answer the charge of dangerous flying and having also failed to turn up at a local SNP meeting - he was an ardent supporter of Scottish Independence - the alarm was raised and first his sister Hilda and then his wife Sheila reported him as a missing person.

The full truth of what happened on the night of the murder will never be known and all three accused are now deceased. Forensics had indicated that Maxwell had been shot in the head and in a theatrical move which shocked those present at the trial, the murdered man's yellowing skull was produced in court as part of the evidence. It was day three of the proceedings and a box containing the Garvie skull had in fact been briefly shown to a Crown witness the day before. On this later occasion however, the gruesome exhibit was produced for all to see. Labelled 'Exhibit 14', the skull was removed from its packaging and amidst gasps from the public benches was subjected to a detailed examination by an enthusiastic forensic expert, a Dr McBain. A bullet exit wound behind the right ear was pointed out and a graphic account of the projectile's path through the dead man's head was given before the yellowing artifact was returned to its place of temporary rest within the carboard box. A brief recess was then called to allow the accused - and indeed the jury - to regain composure following the presentation of this dramatic piece of evidence. The outcome was perhaps predictable. Although Alan Peters was to walk free due to that uniquely Scottish 'Not Proven' verdict, both Sheila Garvie and Brian Tevendale were to spend a long time in prison.

Compared by some to both Lady Macbeth and Lady Chatterley, Sheila perhaps gained most notoriety. Not only did she profess her love for Tevendale in the courtroom, but many commentators have forcefully pointed out that she spent several months following Maxwell's murder in the company of the man who quite possibly had pulled the trigger and who almost certainly disposed of the body. In reality though, the Garvie trial was not simply a murder trial. Public morality was on trial also. Indeed, there are strong parallels with the writings of Lewis Grassic Gibbon in the Garvie tale since behind the 'shock and disgust', many of those who followed the court case had what can only be described as 'intimate knowledge' of Garvie's adventurous behaviour.

Brought up at Arbuthnot, not that far from the Garvies West Cairnbeg farmhouse, Lewis Grassic Gibbon (1901-1935) produced some seventeen novels during his short literary career. Perhaps his best known published work is a trilogy set in the Mearns and collectively known as *A Scots Quair* in which he tells a story of family tragedy, sexual depravity and heartbreak in the land around during the early part of the Twentieth century. When he published *A Scots Quair*, some readers were utterly shocked at the content, not so much because of the *expose* of a moral depravity which inhabited the pages but because many of the characters were easily identifiable and were still alive and kicking and oft-times living just down the road! Gibbon's name changes were in reality a poor disguise for the guilty parties.

The Garvie trial in its turn exposed a portion of the local populace to the reality that living amongst them were neighbours who had been part of Maxwell Garvie's inner circle. The parties and the orgies at Kinky Cottage and elsewhere had made national headlines and inevitably left folk wondering who amongst their neighbours might have been willing participants in the lurid events laid out in court and which culminated in the murder of the Flying Farmer. Decades on, the gossip rumbles on just as it did with the Grassic Gibbon book revelations.

Following his release from Perth Prison in 1978, Brian Tevendale ran a public house in Scone. He died in 2003. Sheila was also released in 1978 following her ten year incarceration, first at Gateside Prison Greenock and then at Cornton Vale Prison near Stirling. Marrying twice more, she ran a bed and breakfast establishment in her native Stonehaven for many years. In 1980 she published an account of her harrowing life under the title *Marriage to Murder* which she described as a "poignant account of a harrowing marriage, trial and subsequent imprisonment". She died in 2014.

On a more orthodox note, Stonehaven can boast a decent number of less infamous folk amongst the sons of the town, Lord Reith for one. Reith became the first Director General of the BBC, and was born in Stonehaven during a brief but memorable family holiday. Another well-known inhabitant was George Donald Petrie of the Glen Ury Cycle Works who in 1901 patented what he termed "An improved design for a Better Rifle Carrier for Bicycles".

A lesser known Stonehaven resident forged links with Moscow. Tom McEwan was born in the seaside town in 1891. Orphaned young he was taken in at age nine by an aunt in Catterline until as a teenager he moved to Aberdeen to work on the railways. Marriage and children followed and in 1912 he emigrated to Manitoba where he worked for a while as a blacksmith before joining the Socialist Party of Canada. By 1929 Tom had become the party's industrial director and a few years later he was lobbying the Canadian government for employment insurance for unemployed workers. His demands were rejected by the prime minister of the day who vowed "Never will I or any government of which I am a part, put a premium on idleness or put our people on the dole!" Needless to say, Tom's links with the Soviets led to led to distrust and on the outbreak of WW2 he and many like him were arrested and imprisoned. He served maybe two years hard labour before an Orwellian change of alliance meant that the Soviets were no longer the enemy. Hitler had invaded Russia and the previously banned Communist Party of Canada was now permitted to rebadge as The Canadian Progressive Party. Tom McEwan went on to secure Canadian workers' rights, enhanced employee pensions and campaigned for equality for Canadian indigenous people before dying at the ripe old age of 97 in 1988. In 1974 he published an autobiography *The Forge Glows Red*. And yet, few in his native Stonehaven have ever heard of him.

Then there is the unresolved tale of the origin of the pneumatic tyre. Stonehaven inventor Robert Thomson seemingly first patented his 'Aerial Wheels' in 1845 with the ambitious claim that the new invention might run for 1200 miles without needing attention. A rival in Ayrshire was to make similar claims and the row still rumbles on to this day. But of course, another Robert had already taken to the roads to make Stonehaven famous. Widely known as Captain Pedestrian, Captain Robert Barclay-Allardyce was born in 1779. An avid walker, he tramped his way into history as the father of the sport of Pedestrianism. Aged just seventeen, in 1796, he wagered that he could cover the six miles from Croydon to the outskirts of London in under an hour. He won and collected 100 guineas. More walks and more wagers followed.

In 1805 he famously walked 72 miles "between breakfast and dinner". 1807 saw him cover 78 miles on hilly roads in just fourteen hours. In the summer of 1808, he reached his zenith when he completed 1,000 miles in 1,000 successive hours to win 1,000 guineas. It took him forty-two days and he seemingly lost two stone in weight along the way. *The Times* newspaper followed the story and reported that:

"The gentleman on Wednesday completed his arduous pedestrian undertaking, to walk a thousand miles in a thousand successive hours, at the rate of a mile in each and every hour. He had until four o'clock P.M. to finish his task; but he performed his last mile in the quarter of an hour after three, with perfect ease and great spirit, amidst an immense concourse of spectators."

Both Lord Reith and the inventor of the Aerial Wheel have blue plaques in the seaside town. As for Captain Pedestrian's wee blue plaque? He's still biding his time.

31
TOMINTOUL – WHERE NOT MUCH HAPPENS?

Main Street, Tomintoul

The sign over the door of the Highland Market on Tomintoul's Main Street reads "On this spot in 1832 nothing much happened"; but in reality, nothing could be further from the truth. A planned village founded in around 1775 by the Fourth Duke of Gordon, Tomintoul sits firmly astride the old military road linking Deeside to Inverness. Nestling within the very heart of the Cairngorms National Park the place is a popular stopping off point for travellers exploring the Malt Whisky Trail. At an altitude of around 1164ft above sea level the settlement can probably lay claim to be the highest village in the Highlands but not perhaps the highest village in Scotland. That accolade probably belongs to Wanlockhead which sits at an ear popping 1,531ft amidst the lowland Lowther Hills.

Tomintoul has on occasion been ridiculed by those who should perhaps have known better. Described by monarch and diarist Queen Victoria as "the most tumble-down, poor looking place I ever saw ... a long street with three inns and miserable, dirty looking houses and people, and a sad look of wretchedness about it." To cap it all, the parish was dismissed in the Old Statistical Account of Scotland as being a place where "All of them sell whisky and all of them drink it". Whisky is still sold in the village, as any visitor to the Whisky Castle on Main Street will tell you, however nowadays excise duty is paid on each and every dram and the old whisky trails which head off in all directions are the preserve of hill walkers rather than bootleggers intent on dodging the exciseman. Getting to Tomintoul is fairly straightforward nowadays although in the very depths of winter and with the snow gates poised to close, it may be quite a different story. From Deeside the A939 snakes its way northwards via Corgarff Castle - a government barracks used after Culloden to suppress the Highlands - before heading up the Lecht past the Ski Centre and the Wells of Lecht. Travellers arriving from the Grantown-on-Spey side have perhaps an easier time of it and the final approach is marked by the Fodderletter Lums. A set of roadside freestanding stone chimneys, the Lums are easily mistaken for the gable ends of old cotter houses however the structures were actually built by early road builders who would place portable shelters against the chimney stacks before settling in for the night.

Tomintoul is no stranger to tales of the unexpected. The local museum records tales of a derelict manganese mine on the Lecht and has on display a relic from the First War in the shape of a rusting 1917 German artillery piece no doubt gifted by a grateful government in recognition of the sacrifice of local sons during that awful conflict. Located in the village square and operated by Tomintoul and Glenlivet Development Trust, the museum displays also feature a reconstructed crofter's kitchen, a village blacksmith's smiddy alongside various artefacts and photographs recalling the history of Tomintoul and Glenlivet. There's no obvious mention amongst the exhibits though of a set of events which elevated this tiny settlement to national prominence in the more recent past; the tale of the Laird of Tomintoul.

In the 1990s Anthony Williams, a serving Metropolitan Police deputy finance director invested several million pounds into the village economy. Over the course of a decade his holding company - Tomintoul Enterprises - renovated the Clockhouse Restaurant, redeveloped several local properties and spent around £1.5m of public money renovating the Gordon Arms Hotel, now renamed The Balfour Manor, in the square. Seemingly Anthony had unbridled access to secret public funds intended to pay for informers, create safe houses and conduct surveillance operations against both the IRA and organised crime. Eventually the bobbies caught up with the man. Sentenced in 1995 to a lengthy jail sentence following the £5.3m fraud Williams, locally titled The Laird of Tomintoul, is nowadays regarded by some as a sort of local hero. While many locals refuse to discuss the matter, one man, firmly ensconced in the bar of the Richmond Arms, commented that "if it were not for that money, Tomintoul would be in a right state today. We nicknamed the man the Laird and he literally revived the place. It's maybe a case of the oil money coming back from London. I would shake his hand if I met him today."

Most locals steadfastly declined to say more about the affair however a damning report by the House of Commons Select Committee on Public Accounts concluded that it was completely unacceptable that the Metropolitan Police had failed to pick up on the lavish lifestyle that Williams financed with plundered public money. London police supremo of the time, Paul Condon, was called to account for the embarrassing fiasco which included the misuse of public funds to pay for a police pipe band to play at the Tomintoul Highland Games. Released from jail in 1999, the current whereabouts of Anthony Williams are unknown although a Google search reveals that he worked for a time after release as a bus driver. In recognition of his contribution to the local economy, a local micro-brewery brought out an ale labelled The Laird of Tomintoul.

On a lighter note, the village also made the national headlines in 1999 when breakfast radio presenter Terry Wogan criticised the Moray Council snow clearance record along the A939 road from Cockbridge over to Tomintoul. The Radio Two DJ told listeners "Every year since God was a boy, the road at this time of the year gets closed due to bad weather and it always seems to come as a surprise to the authorities". A heated debate between a grumpy Wogan and his loyal but annoyed listeners ensued and infamously he went on to state that "Well, you know, it's fairly easy to get up the nose of a Scotsman, even by criticising his snowdrifts." Then a few weeks later, a local from Tomintoul phoned the show to point out that it was not in fact the council who had responsibility for snow clearance in the village, but rather Mrs MacKay the local postmistress. She was doing the best she could under difficult circumstances he said; but given that she only had the one shovel she had an almost impossible task, what with the constant blizzards and her having to keep the post office open as well. The banter rumbled on for years with listeners regularly phoning the show in snowy weather - which in Tomintoul can start as early as August - to update Terry on the mythical Mrs MacKay's snow shovelling progress. In point of fact though, there are typically at least three snowploughs and a snow blower stationed in the Highland village during the worst of the winter months.

In his tale of kidnap, intrigue and adventure *Biggles and the Poor Rich Boy*, Captain W.E. Johns writes: "Biggles continued … how in the world did you hear of a place like Tomintoul?" The answer is that the popular author spent the latter part of the 1940s living in and around the Highland village. Although he was later to take up residence at Pitchroy Lodge near Ballindalloch, it seems likely that he penned some dozen of the hundred or so Biggles books while staying at the Richmond Hotel in the square at Tomintoul. Hotel owner Martin Hutchinson has investigated the Biggles connection and keeps copies of books which mention the village behind the hotel bar. When asked what attracted the writer to Tomintoul he replies "the fishing of course, the area offers the finest salmon fishing in the whole of the Highlands." There is much more than a grain of truth in this since a previous owner of the Richmond Arms, Duncan McNiven, not only knew Captain Johns personally but was described in fly-fisher Richard Waddington's biography as "the greatest all round salmon fisherman I ever knew." Seemingly, prior to dispatching his catch, he would always look at it for a moment in silent contemplation before saying in his soft Highland voice "Cheerio old lad, goodbye."

Having survived First War combat with the Royal Flying Corps and spent time as a POW after being shot down during a bombing raid over Mannheim, Captain Johns was quick to take up Duncan McNiven's offer of a fishing holiday in Tomintoul. London in 1944 was under enemy attack. The bombers of the Luftwaffe had given way to the unmanned flying bombs which struck daily terror into the populace and, commenting that "Enemy action has at last forced me to leave my home" the author travelled north to confront the salmon of the River Avon.

The fictional manhunt described in *Biggles and the Poor Rich Boy* mirrors in some ways a real manhunt which took place just south of the village in far off 1920. It was mid-May and Percy Toplis, an out of work ex-soldier, appeared in Tomintoul. The villagers took pity on him and found him work on the deer forest at Inchrory. Unknown to them Toplis, a confidence trickster and black marketeer, was on the run following the murder of a taxi driver in Thruxton. Toplis took up residence in a lonely cottage on the Lecht where he began, without the owner's permission, to burn the furniture and tear down a neighbouring farmer's sheep pens for firewood. This was too much for the farmer and on the first day of June 1920 he enlisted the help of the keeper of the cottage, a Mr McKenzie, and the local bobby. At around 11 pm all three men set off to confront Toplis who was at this time tucked up in front of the fire. Events soon spiralled out of control. The intention of the village policeman had been simply to issue a stern warning but when challenged, Toplis lured the men into a narrow corridor at the back of the cottage before pulling out a service revolver and firing point blank into the huddled group. Both the policeman and the farmer were badly injured but, by some miracle, McKenzie was unhurt. Following the shooting, Toplis made off by bicycle to Aberdeen where he is said to have boarded a southbound train.

Toplis Cottage alongside the A939

Percy Toplis was eventually cornered near Penrith and shot dead following a running fight with armed police. He was just twenty-three years old when he died. In 1986, and under the title *The Monocled Mutineer*, the BBC aired a four part adaptation of the Toplis story, penned by playwright Alan Bleasdale and starring Paul McGann, of *Withnail and I fame*, as Percy. Criticised at the time as being "riddled with error", the television dramatization of the Topliss story not only glorified the so-called English Dillinger, but also failed to use the actual location in which the Lecht shootings took place; instead substituting an ornate, red roofed bungalow of uncertain origin. The genuine location, locally known as Toplis Cottage, lies in full view of passing traffic on the A939 not far from the Lecht Ski Centre.

A further strange but probably quite accurate account of the monocled mutineer's connection with Aberdeenshire appears in an article published in *Leopard Magazine* some years ago and penned by local author Alastair Stupart. Seemingly prior to his sojourn on the Lecht, Toplis resided for a short while at number fifteen Holburn Street in Aberdeen city centre. Shortly before her death, Alastair's aunt, Margaret Mitchel recounted meeting Toplis at the lodging house. The fugitive had rented a room at the back of the Holburn Street property for just a few days and he most probably had his service revolver handy just in case of awkward callers. Margaret had mentioned her meeting with Toplis to many acquaintances over the years but, until the screening of Bleasdale's take on the story on the BBC in the autumn of 1986, few took much notice of her recollections. Alastair writes that she had paid a call to her aunt Lizzie McDermott, the proprietor of the lodging house. Expecting to be met by her aunt, Margaret was surprised to be greeted at the door by a smart looking gentleman who promised to tell Mrs McDermott that she had called past. Alastair writes that "at this time Margaret was a student and was some three years younger than the Holburn Street lodger". Seemingly Toplis "on leaving Aberdeen made his way up Donside and stopped at Alford for a shave". Now there's a part of the story that playwright Bleasdale failed to pick up on.

In a final twist of the Toplis tale, Alastair records that when the doomed and by now penniless fugitive stowed away on the south-bound train at Aberdeen's Joint Station at the start of his final journey south, he was soon discovered hiding behind some fish boxes by the guard. "The train guard clearly did not recognise the country's number one fugitive" he writes "and not only did he not report Percy but he shared sandwiches with him on the long journey south." "Perhaps" writes Alastair, "this was the final bit of compassion shown to Toplis" before his "well documented death at the hands of three armed police officers and their vigilante inspired chief constable's son at Penrith."

Many decades after these tragic events, Police Scotland presented medals and official commendations to the surviving relatives of the victims of Percy's violent rampage on the Lecht.

The March 1992 edition of *Leopard Magazine* carried an article by Alasdair Roberts describing the most northerly portion of Peter Anson and Anthony Rowe's epic journey around Scotland. In the long hot summer of 1934, they drove a horse drawn caravan into Tomintoul and then went on, probably on foot, to visit nearby Scalan College at Glenlivet. Compton Mackenzie, in his foreword to Peter's 1938 travelogue about the journey *The Caravan Pilgrim* commented that "The particular object of the pilgrimage was to visit and record ... the various Catholic churches on that long road to the north." Anson of course was an authority on religious themes and was at the time contracted to contribute sketches and descriptions of churches for publication in The Catholic Universe.

So, what is Scalan and why is it an important part of the story of Tomintoul and indeed the North East? Scalan at the time of Anson's visit was little more than a tumbledown croft inhabited by a subsistence farming family and there was little to suggest that, in the day - between 1717 and 1799 - the place had been a clandestine school for Catholic boys tutored by fugitive 'heather priests'.

"It must have been a thrilling experience" he writes, "to have been present that morning in 1725 when Bishop Gordon ordained two students to the priesthood". He recorded that "It was sad to find this venerable sanctuary in such a neglected state. For over a century it has been used as a farm and its present condition is a reproach to its owners". Better days were to come and although burned by government forces at least the once after Culloden, Scalan has been rebuilt several times over the years and remains a potent symbol of the fragility of both civil rights and religious freedom in Scotland.

Often described in the historical literature as a college for the training of several hundred Catholic priests, it was perhaps nothing of the sort. Figures vary, but a recent academic study by John Watts titled *The Forbidden College*, caps the number of recorded graduate students at sixty-three during the entire period of the school's operation. The current building was constructed in the 1860s and although by the time of Anson's visit in 1934 (he was to return in 1948 while researching his final book *Underground Catholicism in Scotland*) the place was by then in a state of ruin and had in some ways become an ecclesiastical embarrassment. But as a result of pressure by Anson and others, the Scalan as we see it today has been rebuilt and re-energised as a potent symbol of the resistance to the suppression of the Catholic faith in the North East.

In fact, the College of Scalan, alongside Blairs College near Aberdeen and the old College at Aquhorthies near Inverurie all in their turn played a vital role in the post-Reformation recovery of the Roman Catholic Church in Scotland following the repression which followed the passing of the Penal Laws forbidding the celebration of Mass. The Scalan Association nowadays both manages the site and holds an annual Pilgrimage Mass each June. Today the once secret seminary attracts a steady stream of visitors who stop off along the old whisky trail linking Glenlivet to the Lecht to take time to revisit the history of those long years of religious intolerance.

The Church of Scotland in Tomintoul was to fare much better. Especially after the Napoleonic Wars. Originally built as one of Thomas Telford's Parliamentary Churches, Tomintoul Church on Main Street opened for worship in 1827. Probably the least known of Telford's creations, the Parliamentary Churches resulted from a government commission set up to erect churches and manses throughout the Highlands in what appears to have been an afterthought following the erection of 214 English 'Commissioners Churches' built or refurbished as an expression of gratitude to God following victory in the Napoleonic Wars. The English Parliament sanctioned £1,000,000 in 1819 for the project, with a further £500,000 in 1824, for the building of churches and

The Telford 'Cheap John' Parliamentary Kirk at Tomintoul

chapels for the Church of England.

A similar proposal to provide a mere £200,000 for the Church of Scotland was delayed for years by political difficulties, English parliamentary indifference and outright obstruction from Anglican objectors. When an amended Bill was eventually passed in 1824, it provided just £50,000 for the entirety of the Highlands. No more than thirty-two kirks with manses were to be built, and no more than £1500 was to be spent on any one site.

Telford got the contract although his company cannot have made much in the way of profit from the Westminster inspired scheme. The Telford Kirk at Tomintoul was completed in under a year to the Telford standardised design for such buildings (typically single storey with two windows flanked by two doors of the same plain unornamented shape, and a thin belfry to the left as you view the main elevation) and came in fourteen pounds under budget with kirk and manse costing just £1486 and five shillings in total. Much altered nowadays the original Tomintoul Telford Kirk has pretty much vanished behind subsequent extensions and much needed improvements. Stone buttresses were added in 1900 and the building now sports an elegant gothic interior. A pipe organ by E. F. Walcker & Co was installed in 1903 and a Communion Table was added in 1911. Telford and his team of engineers would nowadays be hard put to recognise the original piece of 'Cheap John' parliamentary work.

Tomintoul has many such rich stories to tell. So, in the big scheme of things and despite Queen Victoria's comments about it being "the most tumbledown place I ever saw", what is there not to like about the place?

32
TORPHINS – A PLEASANT VILLAGE IN ROYAL DEESIDE

The picturesque settlement of Torphins lies roughly twenty-two miles from Aberdeen, eighteen miles from Ballater and just a couple of miles from the site of Macbeth's last stand at the Battle of Lumphanan in the August of 1057. A later battlefield is recorded in the tumble-down stones of the local war memorial which lists some 160 lads from the village who embraced the romantic myth of the 1914 European great adventure but never made it back home to Torphins. There are just three local names from 1939-1946 recorded on the monument which is perhaps testimony to the scarcity of men who returned from the trenches of that earlier conflict to sustain the local population.

St Combs author James Buchan recalls in an interview recorded by Doric film maker James Taylor how he once met a man who had actually worked on the making of the Torphins war memorial. A mason to trade, the man admitted in his drink that he'd killed some eighteen of the enemy in that earlier war, gained a medal for his efforts and here he was earning a living commemorating the bloodletting. James later penned a play for the BBC about the meeting and highlighted the paradox. Mind you, such seemingly absurd events are mirrored also in the work of Montrose sculptor William Lamb who, having spent three years in the killing fields of the European trenches, returned home to sculpt not one but two Angus war memorials.

While neighbouring settlements such as Kincardine O' Neil, Tarland and Tornaveen struggled economically during the Nineteenth century, the completion of the Royal Deeside Railway's Aboyne Extension in 1859 gave Torphins a golden key to economic growth. Not that there had been much in the way of housing in the settlement prior to the coming of the railway. But by 1901, according to Sydney Wood, in his book *The Shaping of Nineteenth Century Aberdeenshire*, some four hundred people were living in a brand-new village centred around the railway station. He records that "Torphins developed from being but a house or two into a village." Alongside providing access to new markets for timber and agricultural products, the rail expansion fuelled a surge in tourist traffic which previously had relied on a less than adequate road network. A journey previously taking perhaps twenty hours by coach could now be done in a tenth of that time by rail and at half the cost. So, in common with Aboyne, Banchory and Ballater, Torphins had become a holiday destination for city folk from Aberdeen and beyond.

The Deeside Railway initially opened as a single-track line linking Aberdeen to Banchory in the September of 1853. The Upper Deeside Extension to Aboyne followed in December 1859 and a further extension to Ballater became operational in 1866. Although the original plan involved running the Deeside line through Kincardine O'Neil, the final route diverted to the north and away from the River Dee running through both Torphins and Lumphanan involving the laying of an additional two miles of track. A claim at the time was that this deviation from plan had actually saved money by economising on land purchase and on construction costs but this seems dubious since the gradients, in an era when long inclines were a serious problem for the steam trains, on both sides of the Torphins loop involved major groundworks. A more likely explanation, familiar to the residents of the Moray Coast town of Cullen where the Countess of Seafield's refusal to allow the trains to cross her estate left the townsfolk cowering beneath a series of vast railway viaducts, is that one Deeside landowner simply refused to release the land required by the railway engineers while another more enlightened laird welcomed the permanent way with open palms.

At the very least however, the railway route through Torphins avoided major disruption to the existing settlement and there were few issues such as those in the neighbouring settlement of Lumphanan where Kirktown of Lumphanan was not only left stranded a good half mile from the railway station but was, according to Deeside historian G.M. Fraser "cut off from the very church itself by the intervening railway line". The railway delivered prosperity to Torphins and even today a brief wander around the village reveals a number of solidly constructed granite railway buildings nowadays converted or extended for use as dwellings. A poignant reminder of the village's railway heritage is Platform 22 on Station Road. Multi-tasking as a licensed bistro, a gallery space for local artists and a popular cosy café, Platform 22 is situated on the site of the original railway station and although, according to joint owner and ceramicist Emma Pattullo, little apart from a few scattered stones from the original platform remain above ground, the café with its nostalgic blue and white railway signage is clearly a hub of village life. "Torphins Market is held in our forecourt each and every Wednesday" says Emma. "It's the only outdoor weekly produce market in Scotland to run throughout the entire year, winter and summer." Popular with locals, the venue also attracts tourists. "We had an exciting afternoon recently" recalled Emma. "At around 3 pm a chap walked in asking if we could cater for a small group to which we replied 'yes of course we can'. Great, he said 'I'll go get my bus!' By 4 pm all we had left was one portion of waffles!" Unsurprisingly, Emma has plans in place to extend the building and expand the business.

Twenty-first century Torphins - population 1483 at the 2011 census - boasts a good selection of local shops, some very fine architecture and an easy daily commute to the Oil Capital of Europe. A veritable hub for walkers, horse riders, off-road bikers and cyclists, the village's position in the heart of the Deeside countryside allows easy access to a wide variety of managed woodland paths, local Core Paths and estate tracks. The Deeside Way, part of the National Cycle Network, runs through the village following for the most part the original route of the Victorian rail line linking Duthie Park in Aberdeen with Ballater. The surrounding countryside hosts innovative farm diversification businesses such as Cairnton Farm Cottages. Cairnton consists of a suite of self-catering tourist accommodation set within the grounds of an Aberdeen Angus beef farm on the newly formed Aberdeen Angus Trail. Nearby, the Deeside Activity Park, described by joint-owner Ken Howie as "a farm diversion project that has gotten out of control!" offers kart racing, a paintball killing ground and 4x4 off road driving. Unconventionally perhaps, the park entrance is defended by a rusting British Army self-propelled gun.

There can't be many places in Scotland where folk can buy the Sunday papers, a National Lottery ticket, some cat food and a litre of milk from the local church and for many locals, attending the Grade B listed South Church on Craigour Road has become an accepted part of daily routine. Nowadays a Scotmid Co-operative convenience store the building was completed in 1905 by Aberdeen based architect George Watt, a Building Construction graduate of Gray's School of Art. The pinned-granite building started life as a United Free Church. Watt had been involved in a number of similar high profile commissions including Frank Matcham's 1897 renovation of the interior of Aberdeen's Tivoli Theatre, an extension to the Aberdeen Central Library on Rosemount Viaduct and the 1896 addition of a family wing at Crathes Castle. Nowadays the large former nave space in the South Church is used as the main shopping floor for a Cooperative Convenience Supermarket but despite the shelves full of bakery products, tea-bags and breakfast cereals, the interior of the building retains many key elements of the architect's original design concept. The village's other church, the Mid Deeside Parish Church on St Marnan Road, remains in ecclesiastical use and recently underwent a £770,000 upgrade. Famous both for its scissor truss roof and Boer War Commemoration Tablet, the original building was completed in 1875 to a design by John Russell Mackenzie the architect responsible for the 1862 construction of Inverurie Town Hall, Ballater Parish Church and the Aberdeen Steam Laundry.

With the seven-thousand acre Learney Estate on the doorstep, it's surprising

Learney Arms and Queen Victoria Jubilee Fountain

that the railway planners of the Victorian era opted to name the railway halt Torphins, even commentators of the time thought that 'Learney' would have been a more suitable choice. Nowadays offering a wide range of sporting and countryside activities including deer stalking, game shooting, photo-safari and team building events, Learney House, described as a baronial gem of a country house, lies just north of the village. The B listed mansion house, originally completed around 1747 was rebuilt and extended following a fire in the 1830s with reconstruction being carried out by Aberdeen architect John Smith better known perhaps as Tudor Johnny due to his predilection for Tudor Gothic styling.

Smith's architectural creations can be seen throughout the North East, most notably scattered around Buchan's Pitfour Estate where his legacy includes the stable block, the Observatory and several follies including the quite extraordinary Temple of Theseus. Used as a military recruiting centre and drill hall during the First War and sited on a plot gifted by the Learney Estate, the village's 1899 granite built Learney Hall plays host to a wide range of community events including fund raisers for the local Amateur Football Club, fashion shows, Breakneck Comedy Club and events connected to the annual Torphins Gala. A Gala highlight for 2016 was a talk by 1988 Calgary Winter Olympics ski-jump superstar Eddie the Eagle with tickets selling out months in advance. Opposite the hall sits the distinctive Star and Griffin building. Bearing the coat of arms of the Learney family the place was once a popular stopping off place for Deeside tourists. Known far and wide as the Sunshine Café the structure nowadays doubles as a family home and pre-school nursery.

Just over the road from the Star and Griffin is the Learney Arms Hotel. Once the railway hotel for travellers to the village, the building dates from the late Eighteenth century and in the winter of 1929 welcomed several unexpected guests. A trio of German hot air balloonists had been blown off course during the short trip from Leipzig to Hanover, a distance of some 134 miles. An epic thousand-mile voyage over France and then across the North Sea ensued. Finally, the exhausted balloonists crash landed at Claydykes Farm near Tornaveen and were duly transported by road to the Learney Arms for rest and recuperation prior to repatriation back home by rail via Aberdeen.

The Old Baker's Shop on Craigour Road, also known as Calder's Bakery, is nowadays home to the Bread of Life charity shop operated by volunteers from Mid Deeside Church but in the distant past the bakery spawned a shortbread empire. Run for many years by the Calder family the business was until quite recently operated by local bakers Robbie and Agnes Garden who fired up the ovens for one final time in the September of 2013 prior to retiring after a quarter of a century of 2 am starts. But it is the Torphins connection with Walker's Shortbread which draws tourists to the shop.

The Walkers' Torphins connection began in 1898 when company founder, Joseph Walker, borrowed fifty pounds to take on the lease of the Craigour Road premises. Alongside traditional bakery products, he began baking batches of shortbread with the intention of perfecting the finest shortbread in the entire world and soon locals and even shooting parties from many of Deeside's estates were beating a path to his shop door. As word spread and demand increased, Joseph's business outgrew the Torphins bakery and, in around 1910, he moved to the Speyside village of Aberlour where he expanded output and invested in a horse drawn bakery cart to deliver his produce around the surrounding villages. By the 1930s petrol powered delivery vehicles had replaced the horse drawn variety and by the 1960s, just a few years after Joseph Walker died, the company was operating a fleet of delivery vans and was supplying the newly emerging supermarkets. Expansion continued and nowadays Walkers produce 40,000 tons of shortbread each year using up a whopping fifty tons of flour, ten tons of sugar and twenty tons of butter daily in the process. In 2015, the Walkers brand reported a turnover of £140.8 million, forty-two percent of which was earned from worldwide exports, and the business was employing around 1,450 staff. Not bad for a micro-business which started off as a tiny operation in a wee bakery shop in Torphins.

The village cannot really lay much of a claim to Macbeth since his gruesome ending happened a few miles up the road at Lumphanan but in 1993, Torphins made the national headlines when three local young men reported an encounter with a large, dark and very hairy figure which ran alongside their car as they drove into Aberdeen for a night out. After running alongside the vehicle for nearly five minutes and at speeds of up to 50 mph, the hairy apparition suddenly vanished. Around the same time, a local woman living in a secluded cottage just outside the village reported seeing a dark hairy figure hiding in the forest just outside her front door. There has never really been a satisfactory explanation for the sightings, although some at the time wondered if Banquo's ghost had taken a wrong turning on his way to Lumphanan.

33
TURRIFF – LENDRUM TAE LEEKS

National Museums Scotland holds an oil on canvas portrait of Piper George Findlater VC (1872-1942) by artist Richard Weatherby. But unless you're a military history buff, you've maybe never heard of the man. A regimental bandsman serving with the Gordon Highlanders, George was born near Turriff in Aberdeenshire. One of eleven children of a local miller he came to fame in October 1897 when the British Army assaulted the Dargai Heights on the North West Frontier. It had something to do with controlling rebellious tribes in the Empire and made the headlines in the United Kingdom. Shot through both ankles during the initial charge, he continued to play the regimental march *The Cock o' the North* throughout the engagement hence the award of the Victoria Cross. An account of the time records that "He propped himself against a rock and continued playing lustily, in the hope that the inspiring strains would cheer his comrades to greater efforts."

George seemingly made a full recovery, which must be quite a rarity for a VC holder, and went on to re-enact his exploit on the stage. In fact, it seems that Piper Findlater made a decent living on the back of his celebrity and was eventually able to buy a farm over at Forglen just outside his native Turriff. Perhaps the final take on the heroic matter must come from Dundee's McGonagall. In his published account of the battle of Dargai Heights he fails to mention Findlater by name and writes awkwardly that:

"In that famous charge it was a most beautiful sight,
To see the regimental pipers playing with all their might;
But, alas! one of them was shot through both ankles, and fell to the ground,
But still he played away while bullets fell on every side around."

Historically a Royal Burgh, Turriff, population 4,454 at the 2011 census, sits on the lower beat of the River Deveron half way between Aberdeen and Elgin on the old inland route north. Described in James Macpherson's somewhat contentious 'translation' of *Ossian* as the dark rolling stream Duvrana, the Deveron boasts the fifth highest salmon and sea trout annual catches in the whole of Scotland and holds the record for the heaviest UK fly caught salmon. Landed at Lower Shaws, Mountblairy in October 1924 by Mrs Clementina Morison, the huge male fish weighed in at a massive sixty-one pounds and was sent to Aberdeen for a plaster cast to be made of the corpse before being smoked and consumed. Catches nowadays may be more modest but double figures of salmon are still landed each year leading to the Deveron being described in angling circles as Scotland's best kept angling secret. James Macpherson was obviously quite taken by the river and records that "Had I dwelt at Duvrana in the 66 bright beams of my fame … the virgins would bless my steps."

On a much more earthy plane, there's the story of Turra' Golf Club. The club moved to its current site at Rosehall in 1924. The original ten-hole course at Hutcheon Park suffered from lack of space to expand and never really recovered from being ploughed up for tatties during the Great War. Described as "A perfect walking course at just over 6000 yards" and with a par of seventy, the eighteen-hole course sits alongside the Deveron and boasts a par five number twelve hole which provides an ideal opportunity for what the club terms "long hitters to bring out the big guns." This maybe stems from the dark days of the 1940s. During WW2, Rosehall was home to the Ministry of Supply Flax Works which processed locally grown flax into the raw material for linen, medicines and even soap. Indeed, rumour has it that a portion of the factory output was destined to end up flying over Nazi occupied Europe in the form of the flax based fabric covering of the de Havilland Mosquito fighter bomber affectionately known as the Flax Mosquito. Known as madapolam, the fabric covering normally consisted of a cotton cloth more usually employed in the clothing industry or in embroidery. But, given wartime shortages, other fibrous crops were substituted out of necessity.

Although at its peak the factory employed over one-hundred folk the wartime project was not a great success in part because the local farmland features a heavy rich soil unsuited to the crop. Additionally, there was no local expertise available to manage the harvesting process, so it was necessary to draft in Belgium refugees who had the required knowledge and could run the operation. Sadly, the factory process was to have lasting effects on the health of many local workers - mainly women - who in later life were to attribute various cancers and respiratory diseases to their wartime work at Rosehall. A digital article on the Secret Scotland website describes conditions as poor due to a lack of filtration with workers recollecting that the atmosphere on the production line was so polluted that it was like working in a thick fog.

Flax production ceased in the 1940s and the Turriff of 2020 boasts a wide selection of local businesses ranging from those catering for the agricultural industry to a bustling array of high street shops and restaurants including that rarity nowadays, a local fishmonger offering a vast and varied range of fresh seafood. Locals often point out that the town is one of the very few North East communities which retains a strong and thriving town centre and both the residents and Aberdeenshire Council are keen to keep it that way. The Turriff Town Centre Steering Group has in recent years been instrumental in pushing forward various town centre projects including a revived version of the traditional farmer's market rebranded as 'Turra' Market'. Then there is the annual 'Turra' Show'.

Turra' Show President Bruce Ferguson and HRH Queen Elizabeth at the Haughs - 2014

In 2014 the Turra' Show celebrated its 150th anniversary at the Haughs showground and to mark the historic occasion HRH Queen Elizabeth II attended on day two to present the Champion of Champions award. Claimed to be the largest event of its kind in the whole of the North East of Scotland, farming folk from all over the UK descend on the town during the show weekend seeking livestock prizes, farming machinery and quite frankly lots of fun. Bargains are struck, tractors and combines are purchased and just occasionally, wedding matches are made just as they have been for the last one and a half centuries of the show's history. Kicking off with a pre-show ceilidh, the 2014 event hosted just over three hundred trade stands selling everything from a shovel to a sat/nav guided combine harvester. Alongside the literally hundreds of horse, cattle and sheep entries the Industrial Marquee at the Turra' Show is one of the largest in the country with over 1700 craft exhibits plus a horticultural section generally featuring giant neeps, fat leeks plus some humongous marrows.

However even today, the town's public persona is firmly fixated on the Turra' Coo episode and that infamous political slogan "Frae Lendrum to Leeks." In a 1969 interview with Observer journalist Kenneth Harris, the former King Edward VIII described Lloyd George in glowing terms. He was, said the ex-king "A wonderful man and full of colour … he taught me a very few words in Welsh which have stood me in good stead." Welsh-born politician Lloyd George was however not a popular figure amongst the farming and fisherfolk of rural Scotland. His 1909 Peoples Budget had far reaching effects throughout the UK. With welfare reforms, involving the imposition of compulsory National Insurance payments on employers, and land valuation taxes in prospect the bill led to a constitutional standoff when the House of Lords vetoed the proposals perhaps fearing the thin end of a socialist wedge.

Following much debate in Parliament, including statements by the Welshborn Chancellor such as "A fully equipped Duke costs as much to keep as two dreadnaught battleships" but "is much less easy to scrap," the Parliament Act of 1911 deprived the Lords of their power of veto.

A Dreadnought was a heavily armoured and hugely expensive piece of military kit and nowadays all bar one - the USS Texas - are either at the bottom of the sea or have been recycled to produce razor blades or perhaps even tanks. A few years later the German Kaiser, when faced with the dreadnought threat, was to deny the danger completely declaring loudly that "Dreadnoughts have no wheels". But the 1909 People's Budget threat was real and a beleaguered House of Lords soon found themselves outgunned on home soil.

When the National Health Insurance Act of 1911 came into force as a consequence of the 1909 budget folk in Turriff, and indeed in many towns and villages up and down Scotland, became incensed at what they perceived as nanny state interference in local affairs. Meetings were held during which paid hecklers allegedly shouted down government speakers sent to persuade them of the benefits of health insurance. Effigies of Lloyd George and a local Aberdeenshire MP were burned in the square at Inverurie and in Turriff feelings ran high amongst both farm workers and their masters. What occurred next is well known and still remembered in the town as if it had happened just yesterday. A local farmer, Robert Paterson of Lendrum, became the focus of sheriff officers when he refused to pay the National Insurance Contributions arrears due for his workforce. As a consequence, one of his milk cows was seized to be sold at auction to pay the accumulated arrears. After some often hilarious and widely reported events including the pelting of the local bobbies with eggs and worse, plus the painting of slogans such as "Frae Lendrum to

Coo Corner at Turra – A Braw Image o' the Coo staans proodly in the toon!

Leeks" on the poor coo's flanks in reference to the Chancellor's Welsh heritage, the animal was returned home to Lendrum Farm. She lived out the rest of her days blissfully unaware of her celebrity status.

Doric poet Bob Smith, better known as the 'Poetry Mannie', had a take on the episode in his classic poem *Braw Image o' the Coo*:

> A bronze statue o the Turra Coo
> Noo staans proodly in the toon
> Ti commemorate a gweed story
> A've kent since a wis a loon
>
> The fite coo fae Lendrum
> Wis the celebrity o it's day
> Fin fairmer Robert Paterson
> Thocht NI wisna fair play
>
> Sheriff Geordie Keith set oot
> Tae seize property as a fine
> Bit the locals widna help him
> An refused tae tae the line

The coo wis pit up fer auction
Fegs iss nearly caused a riot
Syne up steps Alexander Craig
As the bodie faa wid buy it

Noo iss is nae the eyn o the story
Fowk an injustice they hid seen
A fair pucklie did rally roon
Wi fairmer Craig a deal wis deen

The coo wis noo back at Lendrum
Tae see oot the rest o her days
Nae doot neen the wiser o
The stooshie she did raise

At a junction in the bonnie toon
Iss a sculture o the beast
Faa brocht a fair bit o fame
Tae Turra an the haill North East."

Turriff town has many other claims to historical fame however. The red Delgatie sandstone buildings sprout from land once occupied by the Beaker People and Roman Legions marched past in around AD 83 as evidenced by the Roman marching camp at Glenmailen near Ythanwells. A Roman era glass jug found on the site of the camp in 1857 is now in the permanent collection of the National Museum of Antiquities although there has been some doubt regarding its Roman heritage. A 1934 report on the object written by W.A. Thorpe, a curator at the Victoria and Albert Museum, concludes that "The Turriff jug is a gaffer's job and has nothing remotely Roman about it!"

In the mid-Seventeenth century, so called 'Troubles' between Royalists and Covenanters led to violence and Turriff found itself at the centre of the action. During a recruiting drive, opposing sides in the conflict found themselves face to face on the outskirts of the town. Dramatized in Nigel Tranter's historical novel *Montrose* both forces decided that discretion was the better part of valour and retired without a shot being fired. A few months later however, in May of 1639, the Royalists again mustered outside the town. Since the Covenanters were in possession of the town centre at the time, battle became inevitable. At daybreak on the fourteenth of May, Royalist forces swept through the streets and with "a great blowing of trumpets and firing of muskets", drove the defenders out in what would become known as 'The Trott o' Turriff'. In this, probably the very first engagement of the civil war in Scotland, there were just three fatalities. Two of the Covenanters were killed by musket fire while a Royalist soldier was seemingly shot by his own side in an early blue on blue incident.

When the railways arrived in 1857 in the form of the Inveramsay to Turriff rail extension, investors anticipated good profits but in truth the line never really became particularly busy. A combination of competition from the Banff, Portsoy and Strathisla line and a succession of poor harvests was blamed by the directors for the poor financial results. Mind you the situation was probably not helped by the action of the Turriff Post Office in sending the local posties up and down the line carrying the mailbags as hand held luggage thus paying only an ordinary passenger fare instead of the higher cargo rates. As one local wag commented at the time "Turra' folk hiv aye liked a guid bargain an fits wrang wi at?"

The town sits in the heart of castle country and is surrounded by ancient fortifications. The old castle at Turriff stood until the early part of the Seventeenth century. Located within an area bounded by Castlehill, Mill Road, Gall Street and Deveron Street it was known locally as the Tower of Torrey. Nowadays there are several surviving castles within a few miles of the town boundaries. Alongside Craigston, the ancestral home of the Urquhart family and Hatton - essentially a castellated Nineteenth century mansion house built on the site of the Castle of Balquholly - the quirkiest of the bunch is Delgatie. A four star visitor attraction lying two miles east of Turriff, and dating from about AD 1030, Delgatie Castle has been in the ownership of various strands of the Hay family for a large part of the last 650 years having been taken from Henry de Beaumont Earl of Buchan following Robert the Bruce's rout of the English army at Bannockburn. The Earl had supported the English side at Bannockburn and was subsequently stripped of his land and title by a vengeful Scottish Parliament.

The most recent of the Hay family to occupy the castle and estate was the rather eccentric Captain Jock Hay of Delgatie (1906-1997). Captain Hay took over the running of the property in the 1950s following an extensive military career. After soldiering in Asia where, prior to partition he commanded a fort near the Afghan border, he returned to Scotland to plan Home Guard preparations for a feared German invasion of Shetland. The Shetland defences came to nothing since the invasion never came but a 1997 Glasgow Herald obituary recalls a tale from his Afghan adventures:

"He noticed, after some weeks of desultory hostilities, that the fort he was shelling flew a flag which suggested that its commander was, like himself, a Mason of high degree. A runner was dispatched with a white flag and in due course the Afghan warlord came to dinner. He was indeed a Mason. Jock could not offer much in the way of good food but he had an inexhaustible supply of excellent whisky, much appreciated by his Moslem guest. The enemy reciprocated with a lavish dinner of roasted goat and, Jock hinted, with the favours of his harem. The two conspirators agreed as brother Masons, to stop endangering each other's chaps and for several months enjoyed convivial visits where they concocted fictitious reports of imaginary battles, duly dispatched to HQ in Kabul and Peshawar."

Delgatie Castle

After WW2 'The Captain' took over management of the family estate in Shetland before, along with his wife Everild, embarking on a quite remarkable restoration project at Delgatie. Today, Delgatie Castle is run as the Delgatie Castle Trust and trustee Joan Johnson has fond memories. Describing him as a towering six-foot seven man in tartan bonnet and kilt she recalled "You couldn't miss him, we often opened the newspaper or turned on the news to find that he was being featured attending some SNP conference or other. The press seemed to love him." She continued "When he bought Delgatie it was in a very run-down state. Owned by the Countess of Errol it had been a field hospital in WW2 and was in danger of having its roof removed to reduce taxation. The Captain was determined to buy and restore the building so he took out his cheque book and wrote the countess a cheque for everything he owned. He then returned home to his wife to tell that he loved her and had in consequence bought her a castle."

And in the best tradition of all good castles, Delgatie has a resident ghost in the form of a young redhead named Rohaise and boasts a tiny bedroom once occupied by Mary Queen of Scots. Seemingly she stayed three nights in Queen Mary's Bower, a room high up the tower, following the Battle of Corrichie in 1562. Corrichie was a victory for Mary although maybe not for her reputation since following the bloody fight she had the putrefying corpse of a rebel leader - the Earl of Huntly - put on trial in Edinburgh. Found guilty of high treason but already dead from a stroke, there was no other possible sentence than forfeiture of all of his lands and possessions and this was duly done. In 1566, when passions had cooled, the guilty corpse was returned to his family for burial at Elgin. As for Mary, she was beheaded in 1587 following trial and conviction for plotting against her cousin the Queen. Her last words were a Latinised version of "Into thy hands, O Lord I commend my spirit" After which the executioner severed her head and held it up for all to see.

Well, not quite; it took three blows before the Royal head was finally held up for all to see. Then the clumsy man dropped it onto the scaffold and was left holding her bloodied wig in his upraised hand. You might be forgiven for thinking that that might have been quite enough drama for one day, but there was even more to come. Mary had always had a thing about tiny dogs and it appears that terriers were her favourite breed although some accounts tell of spaniels. Accounts differ widely, but some say that as the executioner lifted up the queen's dress to remove her garters for sale as souvenirs he was startled when her tiny terrier dog Geddon emerged from under her petticoats and bit his hand. However, Mary's stay in Turriff was somewhat less problematic and following her Delgatie visit she was to live on for another twenty-five years.

Delgatie Castle is also home to a rather special doocot. Most Scottish 'Big Houses' at one time sported walled gardens, ice houses and maybe a doocot or two. The ice houses are often difficult to find nowadays and many have simply disappeared into the landscape. Walled gardens have fared slightly better although instead of fresh produce for the laird's table, many are now in neglect or have been sold off as plots for bungalows and the like. As for doocots, well they have maybe fared better. Domesday seemingly makes no mention of pigeon rearing so we can't blame the likes of the Romans for introducing pigeon pie to Britain. More likely it was down to the Normans. No matter, in

Scotland at least, large scale domestic pigeon rearing dates from the Twelfth century and the birds yielded not only a crop of eggs and meat, but also fertiliser and even albumen for the making of lime mortar for building purposes. Seemingly doves can produce up to sixteen young each year which makes them ideal for farming.

There are various styles of doocot. The one at Delgatie Castle boasts a total of seven-hundred and eight individual stone nesting boxes and is known as a beehive doocot. The design incorporates a system of internal protruding horizontal courses of stone intended to prevent rats from raiding the nesting boxes. Some estates boasted several doocots despite the widespread superstition that a surfeit might cause a death in the family. The Moray laird Sir Robert Gordon built four of them on his land at Gordonstoun, leading to speculation that he was intent on ridding himself of a particularly troublesome wife.

In the big scheme of things though, Turriff will always be associated with the tale of the 'Fite Coo frae Lendrum'. And just to emphasise that important wee bit of history, a life size bronze of the animal now stands at Coo Corner on the High Street.

Mind you, she has two memorials to her name. Just a few miles south at Lendrum, there is a second statue commemorating that hilarious episode of political agitation of almost a century ago. But as Doric poet Bob Smith pointed out, she was "Nae doot neen the wiser o' the stooshie she did raise!"

About the Author

Duncan Harley has written extensively about the history and the mythology of Scotland. Duncan lives in rural Aberdeenshire and is surrounded by a huge pile of other people's books. At weekends and holidays, he likes nothing better than to explore the history and the landscape of Scotland.

BIBLIOGRAPHY

Aberdeen Voice. *Various editions 2010 onwards* (Community owned digital newspaper – editor Fred Wilkinson)
Aitken, Margaret. *Six Buchan Villages* (Self-published circa 1975)
Aitken, Margaret. *Six Buchan Villages* (Scottish Cultural Press 2004)
Anderson, James. *The Black Book of Kincardineshire* (Johnston 1853)
Anson, Peter. *The Caravan Pilgrim* (Cranton 1938)
Bailies of Bennachie. *Bennachie Again* (William Culross and Son 1983)
Balfour, Bernard. *Secrets, Stories, Memories and Stones* (Cranstone 1993)Barclay, Gordon. *If Hitler Comes* (Padstow 2013)
Braemar Gathering Annual – Various (Dee Publishing)
Burnett, Allan. *Duff House at War* (Aberdeenshire Council, unknown date)
Campbell, Valerie. *Camp 165 Watten: Scotland's Most Secretive POW Camp* (Whittles Publishing 2007)
Chorlton, Martyn. *Scottish Airfields Vol.3* (Countryside 2010)
Christie, Elizabeth. *The Empty Shore* (Bruce 1974)
Christie, Elizabeth. *The Haven under the Hill – The Story of Stonehaven* (Bruce 1977)
Cunningham, Tom. *Your Fathers the Ghosts* (Black & White 2007)
Davidson, John. *Inverurie and the Earldom of the Garioch* (A. Brown & Co 1878)
Duff, David. *Queen Victoria's Highland Journals* (Lomond Books 1998)
Fenton, Alexander. *The Turra Coo* (Aberdeen University Press 1989)
Ferguson, David. *Shipwrecks of North East Scotland* (Aberdeen University Press 1991)
Gordon Forum for the Arts. *In Celebration of Inverurie* (Culross - no date)
Grampian Regional Council. *A Historical Walk Around Peterhead* (School Resources Department 1998)
Hamilton, Sheila. *What's in a name* (Aberdeen Journals Ltd 1986)
Harley, Duncan. *The A-Z of Curious Aberdeenshire* (The History Press 2017)
Isherwood and Welsh. *Deeside Donside and Angus* (Clan Books 2004)
Kilbride-Jones, FE. *An Account of the Excavation of the Stone Circles at Loanhead of Daviot* (H.M. Office of Works)
Leopard Magazine. *Various editions* (Aberdeen University/Judy Mackie editor)
Mackie, Alexander. *Aberdeenshire* (Cambridge University Press 1911)
Marren, Peter. *Grampian Battlefields* (Mercat Press 1990)
McConnachie, Alex Inkson. *Donside* (James G. Bisset 1900 edition)

McGinty, Stephen. *Fire in the Night*. (Macmillan 2008)
McKean, Charles. *Banff and Buchan - an Illustrated Guide* (Mainstream 1990)
Meldrum, Edward. *Aberdeen of Old* (Rainbow 1993)
Morgan, Diane. *Various including Footdee* (Highland Printers Inverness 1993)
Osborne, Mike. *Defending Britain* (The History Press 2011)
Osborne, Dod – *Master of the Girl Pat* (Country Life Press 1923)
Pittock, Murray. *A New History of Scotland* (Sutton Publishing 2002)
Porter and Williams. *Epidemic Diseases in Aberdeen and the History of the City Hospital* (Polestar 1971)
Robb, William. *Victorian Scenes* (Keith and District Heritage Group circa 1980)
Rowe, Anthony. *The Brown Caravan* (Cranton 1935)
Shepherd, Ian. *Exploring Scotland's Heritage* (HMSO 1986)
Shepherd, Mike. *Oil Strike North Sea* (Luath Press 2016)
Shepherd, Mike. *When Brave Men Shudder: The Scottish Origins of Dracula* (Wild Wolf Publishing 2018)
Smith, Robert. *Discovering Aberdeenshire* (John Donald Publishers 1998)
Smith, Robert. *Land of the Lost* (Birlinn1997)
Smith, Robert. *The Road to Maggieknockater* (Birlin 2004)
Stewart, Alan. *North East Scotland at War* (Self Published 2018)
Swan, Eddi. *His Majesty's Theatre – One Hundred Years of Glorious Damnation* (Black & White Publishing 2006)
Tacitus. *Agricola* (Various AD 83)
Taylor, Les. *Luftwaffe over Scotland* (Whittles 2013)
The Bailies of Bennachie. *The Book of Bennachie* (Culross & Son 1976)
The Buchan Heritage Society. *Heirship '94* (Buchan Heritage Society 1994)
Thomson, Arthur. *The North East* (Aberdeen University Press 1930)
Toulmin, David. *Straw into Gold* (Impulse Books Aberdeen 1973)
Toulmin, David. *The Tillycorthie Story* (University of Aberdeen 1986)
Vallance, Hugh. *The Great North of Scotland Railway* (David St John 1991)
Watt, Brian. *Old Stonehaven* (Stanlake Publishing 2000)
Watt, William. *A History of Aberdeen and Banff* (William Blackwood 1900)
Webster, Jack. *Jack Webster's Aberdeen* (Birlinn Books Ltd 2007)
Wood, Sydney. *The Shaping of Aberdeenshire* (SPA Books 1985)
Wyness, Fenton. *Royal Valley* (Reid 1968)

Printed in Great Britain
by Amazon